T0309198

Praise for *Artificial Integrity*

"In *Artificial Integrity*, Hamilton Mann extends his groundbreaking ideas around "Digital for Good" to Artificial Intelligence. Clearly, we are at interesting crossroads as a society where the extensive opportunities from AI need to be weighed against the disruptions it can potentially create. Mann masterfully lays out how adapting AI to diverse cultural contexts, value models, and situational nuances can counter biases and lead us toward a more human-centered AI. Mann continues to make valuable contributions on how technology and society work together to create better outcomes for all."

—**Nilanjan Adhya**
Chief Digital Officer, BlackRock

"In *Artificial Integrity*, Hamilton Mann presents a unique perspective on the future of AI. His vision transcends mere technological progress, recognizing that the true challenge of AI lies in fostering systems that operate with unwavering integrity and align with human values. Drawing on a rich understanding of AI's origins and current trajectory, Mann introduces the transformative concept of '*artificial integrity*.' This paradigm shift provides a much-needed framework for developing AI systems that comply with ethical standards and actively reinforce and uphold human-centered beneficial societal norms. Mann's work is particularly timely, addressing the complex interplay between AI and society, from its impact on the job market to its potential to exacerbate or mitigate societal inequalities. He offers practical insights and strategies for business leaders, policymakers, and technologists to navigate the transitions ahead, ensuring that AI augments rather than replaces human capabilities. '*Artificial Integrity*' is a must-read for anyone involved in or affected by AI development. In today's world, where AI's influence is pervasive, Mann's vision of a future where human insight and artificial intelligence synergize to multiply value while adhering to core human values is both inspiring and crucial. This book sets a new standard for how we should approach the development and integration of AI in our society, making it an indispensable guide for shaping a human-centered AI-driven future."

—**Seth Dobrin**
Former Global Chief AI Officer, IBM

"Finally, we have a thoughtful, practical book on ensuring AI is used in a responsible "high integrity" way. Hamilton Mann, who is always so great about keeping our eye on the bigger picture, not only lays out the challenges ahead (including many that haven't gotten adequate coverage), but he also lays out a realistic path toward shaping the AI-future that we would want to have. A great contribution!"

—**David C. Edelman**
Senior Lecturer of Business Administration, Harvard Business School
and co-author of Personalized: Customer Strategy
in the Age of AI, Harvard Business Review Press

"Some people are nice, smart, and keep surprising you in a good way. Hamilton Mann is one of them. When it comes to artificial intelligence and integrity, he is at the right place to be able to talk and write about it. So I'm excited about Hamilton Mann's new book about artificial intelligence and integrity, and I strongly recommend it."

—**Jean Ferré**
CEO Sinequa

"In *Artificial Integrity,* Hamilton Mann has provided the seminal revelation that user trustworthiness of any Artificial Intelligence system does not equate to the accountable integrity of its designers. Lack of genuine consent for user data, anthropomorphism by design, and the harmful extraction of water and energy for data centers powering GenAI demand the integrity by design Mann elucidates that is anything but artificial. A really compelling and unique work in the space."

—**John C. Havens**
Author of Heartificial Intelligence: Embracing our Humanity to
Maximize Machines and Founding Executive Director of The IEEE
Global Initiative on Ethics of Autonomous and Intelligent Systems.

"Yes, with a cool technology like AI, the temptation to focus entirely on the tech is strong. But technology itself is agnostic; humans have considerable choice. As AI technologies become pervasive, what better time than now for Hamilton Mann to focus us on the paramount role of human agency? Smarter machines won't be enough—humans need to guide savvier machines from myopic optimization of narrow objectives to the complex, multi-criteria domain of complex decision-making."

—Sam Ransbotham, PhD.
Professor of Business Analytics. Machine Learning and Artificial Intelligence at Boston College, Senior editor at Information Systems Research, Associate Editor at Management Science, Academic contributing Editor on AI at MIT Sloan Management Review and Host of Me, Myself and AI podcast

"*Artificial Integrity* by Hamilton Mann is a groundbreaking work that redefines how we should approach AI development. Mann provides a compelling and essential read on the importance of prioritizing integrity over mere intelligence in AI systems. He challenges traditional ethical frameworks offering actionable advice to ensure AI aligns with human values and societal norms. This book helps to crystalize what many of us have been thinking and working on for quite some time.

Mann's insights are both incisive and practical, guiding us through the intricacies of creating AI that enhances rather than replaces human capabilities, a philosophy I am very passionate about. This book is a must-read!"

—Noelle Russell
Chief AI Officer, AI Leadership Institute, Microsoft MVP in AI

"This unique and impactful book is a call for humans to take up their responsibility to ensure that together with AI technology they work to enhance human wellbeing through creative, inclusive, and innovative interaction. Hamilton Mann specifically redefines humancentric AI in this engaging book to have a focus on the integrity of AI systems in decision-making. The significance of the book lies in its not only demonstrating that technology is not neutral, but also unpacking how humans can and should interact with AI technology to build a shared value system that will benefit all of humanity."

—Emma Ruttkamp-Bloem
Professor and head of the Department of Philosophy, Faculty of Humanities at the University of Pretoria, Member of the UN SG AI Advisory Body, Chair of UNESCO World Commission on the Ethics of Scientific Knowledge and Technology, AI Ethics Lead of the Centre for AI Research, Expert of the Global Commission on Responsible AI in the Military Domain, Associate Editor of the Science and Engineering Ethics, Member of the Women4EthicalAI (UNESCO), Member of the AI Ethics Experts without Borders (UNESCO), Member of the Editorial Board of AI and Law

"Hamilton Mann provides a new framework, *Artificial Integrity*, for leaders and organizations to guide responsible AI development, balancing benefits and risks for customers, employees, and society more broadly as we navigate the uncertain path toward AI super-intelligence. This is a must read for anyone developing new AI solutions, shaping corporate strategy, or creating public policy for the new AI era."

—Scott A. Snyder, PhD.
Senior Fellow, Management Department, The Wharton School, Adjunct Faculty, The Moore School of Engineering, University of Pennsylvania, Chief Digital Officer, Eversana, Co-author Goliath's Revenge

"The thing about integrity is that it's innately human. And as John Wooden famously said, 'your character is what you really are.' In an era of generative, predictive, and general AI, humanity is by default automated. But with integrity, AI becomes more human and ultimately, augmented. AI integrity becomes a superpower. That's what Hamilton Mann is here to show us."

—Brian Solis
Futurist, best-selling author of Mindshift, Transform Leadership, Drive Innovation, and Shape the Future

"AI has immense power to do good, to contribute positively to individuals, organizations, and society. It also has a dark side. With *Artificial Integrity*, Hamilton Mann provides a roadmap to create and deliver AI that is responsible, ethical, and sustainable."

—**Michael Wade**

TONOMUS Professor of Strategy, Digital, and Director of the TONOMUS Global Center for Digital and AI Transformation at IMD Business School and co-author of Hacking Digital, McGraw-Hill Education

"*Artificial integrity* is a reminder that we must aspire to the highest standards in life and living, both for ourselves and the technology that we permit as part of it. We cannot expect the technology of tomorrow to reflect values that the humans of today do not manifest in practice. Values in, values out— or Garbage in, garbage out—the choice is ours. Hamilton Mann masterfully highlights the areas of concern as we are navigating this new era of all pervasive artificial intelligence. *Artificial integrity* starts with human integrity, and it is our responsibility, individually and as a species to strive for it."

—**Cornelia C. Walther, PhD.**

Senior Visiting Fellow at the Wharton initiative for Neuroscience (WiN)/ Wharton AI and Analytics; and the Center for Integrated Oral Health (CIGOH). Director POZE@ezop and a humanitarian practitioner for two decades with the United Nations in emergencies in West Africa, Asia, and Latin America.

"*Artificial Integrity* is more than a book; it's the dawn of a new interdisciplinary field of science for the future. Bridging computational science, sociology, economics, and sustainability, it urges leaders, technologists, academics, policymakers and innovators to envision a world where AI elevates humanity. Hamilton Mann's concept of *Artificial Integrity* is a call to action with sharp guidelines and well-articulated framework for executing what AI can and should be."

—**Soumitra Dutta, PhD.**

Peter Moores Dean and Professor of Management, Saïd Business School, University of Oxford, and a Fellow of Balliol College, Oxford.

"*Artificial Integrity* offers both a thought-provoking and guiding approach to the complex relationship between artificial intelligence and our human value models in a society where advanced co-intelligence between humans and machines will increasingly coexist. This insightful concept and framework of '*artificial integrity*' coined by Hamilton Mann represents a paradigm shift and an essential playbook for leaders wishing to steer AI development towards a human-centered future. Read this book to understand, but more importantly, to act for the development of AI designed not simply to produce more artificial intelligence, but to uphold more integrity."

—**Luc Julia, PhD.**
Chief Scientific Officer, Renault Group,
co-creator of Siri, member of the French
Academy of Technologies.

"The world is racing headlong into a very near future radically transformed by Artificial Intelligence. This technology offers enormous opportunities for advances in medicine, science, innovation, and efficiency, but potentially threatens jobs, personal autonomy, and national security. In this important and timely book, Hamilton Mann proposes the radical new concept of *Artificial Integrity*—the purposeful alignment of Artificial Intelligence with human moral codes and social norms—and argues it should be baked into the code at the very heart of this new technology. Mann provides practical strategies for business leaders, managers, and policymakers to lead through this technological revolution. I urge everyone who cares about our collective future as humans to read this book."

—**Michael Platt, PhD.**
Director of the Wharton Neuroscience Initiative
and Professor of Marketing, Neuroscience, and
Psychology at the University of Pennsylvania

"As someone wary of AI hype, I found Hamilton Mann's "*Artificial Integrity*" refreshingly practical. Unlike works focused on AGI or broad ethical principles, Mann provides concrete strategies for embedding integrity into current AI systems. Drawing on global perspectives and bridging academia and business, he offers invaluable insights on '*artificial integrity*,' emphasizing context-specific application and alignment with local norms. Mann's focus on augmenting human capabilities rather than replacing them is genuinely refreshing, showing how AI can enhance our lives by working alongside us. This essential read for technologists, business leaders, and policymakers offers a forward-thinking perspective on ethical AI implementation, will significantly influence responsible AI development and deployment."

—Anand S. Rao, PhD.
Distinguished Service Professor of
Applied Data Science and AI,
Carnegie Mellon University

Artificial Integrity

The Paths to Leading AI Toward a Human-Centered Future

Hamilton Mann

WILEY

For my R. and my A.—for always being there.

Contents

Preface

Warren Buffett once said, 'In looking for people to hire, look for three qualities: integrity, intelligence, and energy. And if they don't have the first, the other two will kill you.' This wisdom begs the question: as we begin to 'hire' powerful intelligent machines to perform tasks traditionally done by humans?

Artificial Integrity aims to be the first comprehensive and authoritative guide to one of the most important socio–economico–technological developments of our time—the rise of artificial intelligence as a society model. Yet, artificial intelligence is nothing new.

The concept of creating machines that can emulate human intelligence has been a part of human imagination for centuries. From the mythological constructs to the mechanical automata of the Renaissance, humanity has long been fascinated by the idea of artificial beings capable of thought and action.

The term *artificial intelligence* itself was coined in the mid–20th century, but the foundational ideas can be traced back much further. Throughout the 20th century, significant milestones in artificial intelligence (AI) development continued to capture the public's imagination. Alan Turing's seminal 1950 paper, "Computing Machinery and Intelligence," introduced the concept of the Turing test to evaluate a machine's ability to exhibit intelligent behavior indistinguishable from that of a human. This period also saw the creation of the first AI programs, such as the Logic Theorist and the General Problem Solver, which attempted to mimic human problem-solving processes.

From a nonorganic point of view, AI is fundamentally artificial by nature because it is constructed from nonliving materials and operates through programmed algorithms. However, from a societal point of view, AI is anything but artificial and yet, inextricably human by design as it deeply integrates into human social structures, influencing and being influenced by societal norms, behaviors, and expectations. In fact, the term *artificial* masks the dual nature of AI—both in its artificial origins and its profound societal integration inherited from vast datasets on which AI algorithms are trained that include human behaviors, language, and cultural artifacts, encompassing social media interactions, online content, and real-world activities, embedding cultural and societal values into the AI's functionalities and reflecting societal priorities, biases, and norms.

When considering the intelligence often assigned to AI, a different duality comes to light. At their core, AI systems are designed to mimic specific aspects of human intelligence through advanced computational capabilities. They excel and already surpass human ability at tasks involving data analysis, pattern recognition, and logical reasoning, showcasing a form of cognitive intelligence. While some are striving to develop artificial general intelligence (AGI)—or any form of superintelligence that could mimic and surpass various aspects of human intelligence—it is essential to remember that human intelligence encompasses dimensions beyond rationality.

Among other various traits, human intelligence, by definition, includes humans at its core. This involves embracing irrationality through our ability to recognize, feel, understand, intuit, manage, and live one's own emotions and those of others. It also involves the very social nature of who we are, through our capacity to navigate complex social environments and build meaningful relationships. Moreover, it implies a critical dimension—that of evaluating the consequences of actions, understanding societal norms, and making choices that align with individual and shared values.

These traits, more subjective than objective, more irrational than rational, constitute conditions that lead to what one may perceive as intelligent. In fact, the term *intelligent* masks the dual nature of intelligence—both in its input characteristics referring to capabilities as a means and its outcome perspectives, which ultimately determine what is acknowledged as intelligent or not, as an end.

The polysemic nature of the word *intelligence* creates its paradox. Intelligent inputs do not prevent unintelligent outcomes, which typically include outcomes that:

- Fail to consider the broader context or nuances of a situation such as a language translation AI system producing grammatically correct but contextually inappropriate translations.
- Reflect and perpetuate existing biases present in the training data, such as facial recognition systems that have higher error rates for certain demographic groups.
- Do not align with ethical standards or societal values such as an AI algorithm prioritizing profit over patient care in healthcare settings.
- Provide immediate benefits but cause long-term negative consequences such as an AI in finance optimizing for short-term profits at the expense of financial stability.
- Are opaque and cannot be easily understood or explained such as black-box algorithms where the decision-making process is not clear, leading to mistrust and accountability issues.
- Pose risks to safety and security due to vulnerabilities or misuse such as autonomous vehicles making critical errors that lead to accidents or that cannot cope with failure that may lead to harmful consequences for humans.
- And so on and so forth.

What creates the intelligence of a result lies in a particular characteristic: its integrity, in the sense of its coherence and its adherence to the values of the human society in which it occurs. Integrity, more than intelligence, is what precedes truly intelligent results.

Intelligence is like the horsepower of a car—it tells you how powerful the engine is and how fast it can potentially go. Integrity, on the other hand, is like the steering system—it allows one to determine the direction the car goes and whether it stays on the road, adhering to a path that avoids harm to others and obeys the rules of the road.

Today, AI is embedded in countless applications, from voice assistants and recommendation systems to autonomous vehicles and predictive analytics. These systems have demonstrated remarkable capabilities, yet they also highlight the need for a framework that ensures their development aligns with human values principles and societal goals. This is where the concept of artificial integrity becomes paramount.

Despite the advancements in AI technology over the decades, the fundamental challenge has remained the same: how to create machines that not only perform tasks but do so in a manner consistent with human values and societal norms. This challenge has become even more critical as AI systems have grown more powerful and pervasive. From the potential for job displacement to issues of privacy and surveillance, the integration of AI into our daily lives raises critical questions about the kind of future we want to build. Will AI systems be designed to enhance human capabilities and promote fairness, or will they exacerbate existing inequalities and undermine our fundamental rights? The answers to these questions will shape the trajectory of AI development and its role in society.

As AI continues to permeate various facets of our lives, from healthcare and finance to education and entertainment, the question of how to ensure that these systems operate, not just with mere intelligence but with integrity, becomes ever more pressing. Therefore, the development of AI is not just a technical endeavor but a profound societal transformation that requires careful consideration of its long-term impacts on human values, rights, and well-being.

The concept of artificial integrity goes beyond traditional AI development, which often prioritizes technical prowess and functional performance of the system without the systemic interplay of the ecosystem where it takes place. Instead, it emphasizes the integration of AI models with our human-values models and our co-intelligence human–AI models into the very fabric of AI systems. This approach seeks to ensure that AI not only performs tasks efficiently but also aligns with the broader goals of human society, fostering trust and ensuring that technological progress contributes to the common good.

In the chapters that follow, we will delve deeper into examining how to develop artificial integrity and shape this vision. We will explore the societal impacts of AI, providing a roadmap for developing technologies that uphold the principles of artificial integrity. Through this journey, the aim is to equip you with the insights, approaches, and framework necessary to navigate the complex interplay between AI and human society, ensuring a future where technology, AI in particular, serves the greater good.

Through this book, my intent is to address some of the trickiest questions related to advancing AI systems in delivering integrity-led outcomes. These questions include the following:

- What are the challenges in creating AI systems that are both intelligent and integrity aligned?
- How can AI systems be designed to anticipate and mitigate unintended consequences, ensuring they operate within integrity-led boundaries?
- How can we address biases in AI systems to ensure fairness and equity in their outcomes?
- How can AI's role in data-driven decision-making be designed with the need for human oversight and the preservation of individual autonomy?
- In what ways can AI be designed to enhance human decision-making rather than replace it?
- How can we assess the artificial integrity of AI systems in real-world applications?
- How can we create a fair and transparent data economy that respects individual rights and fosters innovation?
- How can businesses leverage AI to drive sustainable innovation while ensuring that their AI systems operate with integrity and respect for societal values?
- What are the long-term implications of AI on job markets and workforce dynamics, on economics, and more globally on society, and how can we prepare for them?

Artificial integrity is the next AI frontier. This concept serves as a deep-dive reference into the intricacies of AI's influence in society and its undeniable partnership with humanity with the purpose of establishing what it takes to make artificial intelligence reach a form of integrity.

The inspiration for this book came from my firm belief that technology, including AI, can be a force for good. The concept of artificial integrity has been occupying my reflections for a while, as I navigate the way forward in orchestrating the implementation of AI in a leading aerospace and defense international company, in my role as a corporate executive, in charge of global digital transformation initiatives.

A pivotal moment that led me to write about this concept—putting together thoughts and frameworks based on experience and research—happened during an intervention by Yoshua Bengio, who introduced a panel discussion in which I was participating at the MIT Platform Summit in 2023, co-chaired by Marshall Van Alstyne, Geoffrey Parker, and Peter C. Evans. Yoshua was emphasizing that he was worried about the harmful consequences that AI may cause if put in the wrong hands and left insufficiently regulated. It resonated with my belief in making technology a force for good and in the power we have to make that vision a reality and shape the society we desire.

The debate on AI's role in society, its potential, and its pitfalls left me pondering not just the future of AI but the integrity with which we must approach its development. It convinced me that this is a field that needs to be a field in itself, uniting all the propositions from the collective intelligence we are capable of as humans, to make technology, and AI in particular, an enabler for sustainable progress.

Dive into a journey that promises a human-centered perspective on AI's transformative role in modern society and emerge with a renewed sense of purpose and an enriched understanding of what is intrinsically complementary to any form of intelligence: that of integrity that ensures coherence and harmony, allowing AI to function in symbiosis with the whole.

Introduction

Some contemporary theories of intelligence have broadened the concept beyond language or any other cognitive abilities to include emotional and social aspects, such as in the theory of multiple intelligences by Howard Gardner or the concept of emotional intelligence by Daniel Goleman. Even within these frameworks, integrity isn't considered.

Just as is the case for humans, systems capable of exhibiting or imitating a form of intelligence are not a guarantee that their outcomes will be beneficial for society. Whatever it may be, any system capable of artificially mimicking a kind of intelligence should be able to do so while being bound to preserve the integrity of the ecosystem in which this said intelligence is a part. Systems equipped with artificial intelligence (AI) designed and deployed considering their ecosystem integrity are those that will be capable not just of artificial intelligence but also of artificial integrity.

Artificial integrity is the new "AI." This book, an eponym of this concept, serves as a deep-dive reference into the intricacies of AI's influence ethical conundrums and its undeniable partnership with humanity with the purpose of establishing what it takes to make artificial intelligence reach a form of integrity.

In *Artificial Integrity*, you'll find more than just insights. You'll find a vision—to shape a future where AI and humanity coexist, understand, and enhance one another. Meticulously curated not just to inform but to delve into deeper waters by examining AI from diverse global perspectives and advocating for an AI literacy that goes beyond code and algorithms,

Artificial Integrity covers a spectrum of concerns but, more importantly, presents solutions and fosters an inclusive dialogue around balanced AI (for artificial integrity).

One of the standout features of this book is its human life–centric approach. It uniquely presents the symbiotic relationship between AI and humanity, illustrating how they can harmoniously coexist and amplify each other, holistically.

In the following chapters, we will embark on a comprehensive journey to understand and implement artificial integrity within AI systems. Each chapter is designed to build upon the last, guiding you through the complexities, challenges, and opportunities that come with implementing artificial integrity into AI. Here is a breakdown of what you can expect to learn in each chapter:

Chapter 1: The Stakes for Building Artificial Integrity   This chapter explores the critical importance of embedding artificial integrity into AI systems. It first delves into the concept of "Digital for Good," highlights the transformative potential of AI in societies, the exclusivity inherent in AI design, and the complex impacts of AI on the workforce. The origins of AI are also examined to understand its current trajectory and future implications.

Chapter 2: Unpacking What Artificial Integrity Is   You will discover a comprehensive definition of artificial integrity, understanding it as a force sustaining societal values. The chapter discusses the dynamics of artificial integrity's metamodel and how it differs from AI ethics. It emphasizes the co-development implications of human and artificial intelligence.

Chapter 3: What It Takes to Envision Human and Artificial Co-intelligence   This chapter outlines the modes of interaction between human and artificial intelligence. It presents the Marginal Mode for basic discernment, the Human-First Mode as a guide for consciousness, the AI-First Mode as a frontier for intelligent solution-driven actions, and the Fusion Mode as a novel paradigm for co-intelligence.

Chapter 4: What Navigating Artificial Integrity Transitions Implies   Here, the focus is on the transitions necessary to achieve artificial integrity. It emphasizes the importance of mindset, data over procedures, and ethical stands. The chapter also explores the transition in human capital values and introduces pioneering AI-driven operating models.

Chapter 5: How to Thrive Through Navigating Algorithmic Boost This chapter addresses how to leverage the algorithmic boost provided by AI. It guides you through navigating from Marginal mode to AI-First mode, navigating from Human-First mode to Fusion mode, and navigating along other transitional paths, explaining the benefits and challenges of each transition while articulating guiding posts to address such transitions.

Chapter 6: How to Thrive Through Navigating Humanistic Reinforcement Emphasizing human agency, this chapter discusses how to navigate transitions, such as from AI-First mode to Human-First mode and from Fusion mode to Human-First mode, as well as other key transitions. It highlights the importance of reinforcing humanistic values in the age of AI and provides practical guidelines for operationalizing these transitions effectively.

Chapter 7: How to Thrive Through Navigating Algorithmic Recalibration You will learn about the necessity of recalibrating algorithms to adapt to changing contexts. The chapter covers transitions such as Fusion mode to Marginal mode and Human-First mode to AI-First mode, providing strategies and concrete implementation approaches to ensure adaptive and responsible AI use, as context evolves.

Chapter 8: What Change to Envision in Economic AIquity and Societal Values The final chapter envisions a future where AI aligns with economic equity and societal values. It discusses data as a common currency, the paradoxes of impartial data, and the dual nature of biases. The chapter concludes by reflecting on the value placed on human life.

Designed for a broad audience—from executives, industry leaders, and entrepreneurs to policymakers, academics, tech enthusiasts, and curious general readers—*Artificial Integrity* stands apart with its multidimensional perspectives, its multidisciplinary approaches, its in-depth analysis, and its actionable insights. It bridges technical prowess with human values, societal structures, and cultural narratives to build artificial integrity that draws the path to leading AI with integrity toward a human-centered future.

1

The Stakes for Building Artificial Integrity

As we stand on the brink of a new era in artificial intelligence (AI), the discourse around its development has expanded beyond the technical and into the societal arena. Central to this is the concept of *artificial integrity*. This term might initially appear oxymoronic. And rightly so. After all, can integrity, a fundamentally human trait characterized by honesty and moral uprightness, be artificial?

As a matter of fact, the same goes for the term *artificial intelligence*, to which we are now accustomed. Can intelligence, another fundamentally human trait, be artificial? So-called "artificial" intelligence has often been and is still commonly compared to human intelligence. Yet, they are inherently different, as their origins differ, even though the same term is used to name both.

Indeed, AI, engineered from codes and algorithms, operates without consciousness or emotional depth, aspects typically intertwined with human intelligence. This distinction is crucial, as it shapes our expectations as AI systems become more integrated into societal functions. Similarly, so-called

1

"artificial" integrity is not the same as that which concerns human behavior or quality, even though here again we use the same word to name both. Artificial integrity reflects a deeper query into the essence of AI and the values frameworks we expect these systems to uphold.

"Digital for Good" Matters

AI systems are not merely tools but active agents capable of decisions that affect lives and livelihoods. The development of AI systems that can perform tasks traditionally requiring human intelligence raises a significant question: how can these systems also embody the kind of decision-making integrity analogous to what we expect of humans in similar roles?

The world is increasingly driven by data and algorithms. As AI technologies progress and take on tasks that were once the sole preserve of humans, from driving cars to making medical diagnoses, the need for them to operate within defined value boundaries and demonstrate a form of integrity—also artificial and thus different from that of humans—becomes essential.

In other words, inventing a new form of intelligence implies the mirroring need for a new form of integrity that this new intelligence must also be capable of exhibiting. This form of integrity must be tailored to the unique characteristics of artificial intelligent systems, differing fundamentally from human integrity but paralleling its importance in guiding operations and decisions. This means programming AI not just with intelligence for task completion but also with frameworks and mechanisms that guide artificially, integrity-led interactions and decisions—a form of integrity that, while artificial, is indispensable for ensuring artificial intelligent systems contribute positively to society without causing harm.

This also means continually refining the frameworks and mechanisms that guide these systems toward integrity-led interactions and decisions as our societal norms and values understandings evolve. Consequently, creating AI systems that demonstrate integrity over intelligence involves more than just technical expertise; it requires a multidisciplinary approach incorporating value standards.

For instance, as an autonomous vehicle must decide in real time how to act in an emergency situation where human safety is at risk, the guidelines governing such decisions must be rooted in a framework that reflects societal values on life and safety, be encoded into the vehicle's decision-making algorithms, and be auditable. As we give birth to a new form of intelligence through technology, the ongoing development of AI should be a commitment to integrity, ensuring that these systems do more than perform tasks efficiently—they must also act as integrity-led entities within society.

Just as we expect human intelligence to be guided by integrity, so too must artificial intelligence be steered by artificial integrity.

Technologies, particularly artificial intelligence, must be designed and deployed in a way that respects the rights and self-determination of individuals. This means avoiding systems that manipulate, deceive, or limit people's freedom of choice and decision-making abilities.

The collection, processing, and sharing of data must be carried out with the informed consent of individuals while ensuring the security and confidentiality of their personal information.

These technologies must be designed to promote equality and prevent discrimination. This includes fighting biases in AI algorithms, which can perpetuate or amplify social inequalities.

The principle of integrity includes the principle of responsibility. Developers and users of technology must be responsible for their creations and their impacts. This means that AI systems must be transparent, explainable, and subject to oversight and accountability mechanisms.

The challenge of safety must be proportional, if not superior, to the extraordinary capabilities that AI systems allow. They must be safe and secure, protecting users from harm or malicious use. This includes preventing physical and cyber risks associated with their use.

Furthermore, they must be in harmony with the preservation of the environment and the sustainability of resources. This means minimizing their ecological footprint.

Finally, they must serve human progress, contributing to the well-being, education, and development of individuals' capacities. This implies designing AI systems that enrich human life and promote personal and collective flourishing.

Overall, integrity in the coexistence of humankind and machine requires a holistic approach, centered on the respect for human dignity, the promotion of justice, and well-being, while ensuring the responsibility and sustainability of technological developments.

Such an approach is to be pursued when it comes to the development of technology, including but not limited to AI, in society.

Therefore, the primary stake, in laying the foundations for the creation of artificial integrity, is the establishment of basic principles concerning the inclusion of technology in the broader ecosystem, thus beyond just its operating system: the Digital for Good principles.

To grasp the essence of what these principles are, it is essential to acknowledge that technology, even when created with the best intentions for the greater good, is not inherently immune from producing adverse effects in society.

Technology itself is not inherently sustainable or positive. A comprehensive understanding of Digital for Good starts by thinking against oneself, especially as a technologist, with the acknowledgment of some critical paradoxes, paving the way for a more mindful and responsible approach to technological development in society.

There's No Technology Without Environmental Debt. If technology is of great help and promise in the fight against climate change, the production and disposal of technology itself often contribute significantly to environmental degradation. It is primarily due to the use of natural resources and the impact of the manufacturing process on the environment (Freitag C. et al., 2021). The shift to electric vehicles is a concrete illustration. While the aim is to reduce emissions, it requires a significant increase in lithium, cobalt, and other materials, potentially leading to ecological damage and geopolitical tensions over resource control. Moreover, the end-of-life disposal of these technologies poses challenges in terms of recycling and waste management.

The Chaos Theory Applies to Technology. While technology is rooted in scientific discoveries and principles, the broader impacts and consequences of its implementation may not always be entirely predictable. Technological interventions in complex ecological and social systems can have unpredictable and nonlinear outcomes due to the interconnected nature of these systems. Scientifically, this is understood through chaos theory (Curry D. M., 2012). For example, introducing a new technology in agriculture might unexpectedly affect local biodiversity or social dynamics in ways that are difficult to predict and control.

The Jevons Paradox Challenges Technology's Efficiency Beliefs. An increase in efficiency in using a resource can counterintuitively lead to an overall increase in the consumption of that resource, not a decrease (Alcott, B. et al., 2015). For example, this paradox challenges the notion that technological improvements in energy efficiency alone can reduce overall energy consumption and carbon emissions. Another example is making cars more fuel-efficient, which might lead to people driving more, potentially offsetting the gains from efficiency.

A Band-Aid Solution Is a Technology Trap. Technologies aimed at replacing a polluting one with a cleaner one can be an illusion as this might overlook the need for more systemic change. For example, replacing internal combustion engine cars with electric vehicles doesn't address the underlying issue of car-centric urban planning and the associated social and environmental impacts. Technologies that become a "Band-Aid" solution, without tackling the underlying root causes of issues, is a trap not to fall into.

Technology Fixes Are Not a Guaranteeof Ease. Not considering socio-economic and political factors can lead to unintended consequences. For example, the Green Revolution in agriculture greatly increased crop yields but also led to problems like soil degradation, water depletion, and increased inequality. Another example is the use of facial recognition systems. Initially developed to enhance security and streamline identification processes, they have been criticized for biases against certain demographic groups while raising privacy concerns. The "techno-fix" mentality can overlook the societal complexity issues (Oelschlaeger, M., 1979), ultimately exacerbating existing social issues that technology was purported to solve.

Technology Advancement Does Not Necessarily Mean Progress. New technologies undoubtedly associated with the notion of progress may also go hand in hand with anchoring the status quo. Focusing only on technological solutions can distract from addressing the root causes of problems, leading to the preservation of overconsumption, unsustainable economic models, and unequal resource distribution. For instance, it might perpetuate a consumerist culture, where the solution to every problem is perceived as buying or creating something technologically new, rather than changing consumption habits or societal values.

Technological Determinism Only Fits in Theory. There's a danger in assuming that technological development follows an inevitable, linear trajectory that will solve our problems. Just as Moore's law predicts a doubling of transistors on integrated circuits over time, there is a perception that technological progress will similarly double the solutions to societal problems. This view overlooks the complex interplay between technology and society while ignoring the fact that technological development is often driven by commercial interests and existing power structures, which may not always align with environmental or societal well-being.

Tomorrow's Technology Promises Don't Solve Today's Realities. Relying heavily on future technological solutions can create a moral hazard overlooking the current limitations of these solutions while their promise of a future fix reduces the incentive to act responsibly now. For example, carbon capture and storage technologies are not yet proven at the scale necessary to significantly mitigate climate change. Placing faith in future technological breakthroughs should not be at the expense of more complacency in addressing current challenges.

The Innovation-Equity Paradox Exacerbates the Digital Divide. The need for economic growth to fund technological innovation can overlook the socio-economic implications of a technology-driven approach. For example, there is a risk of widening inequality, as those with access to new technologies benefit more than those without. As new technologies emerge, they often require significant resources and expertise, accessible mainly to wealthy nations and individuals. This disparity can widen the gap between the haves and have-nots, both within and between countries.

Technological Exploitation Always Has Hidden Human Costs. The push for technological advancement, especially in the realm of AI, often obscures the human cost involved in its development (Gray, M. L. and Suri, S., 2019). A stark example is the exploitation of workers who are tasked with tagging vast amounts of data to train AI systems. Often from lower-income countries, they are exposed to a relentless stream of digital content, which includes sorting and removing obscene or harmful images and videos. The reliance on such labor mirrors a global pattern where technological progress often comes at the expense of vulnerable populations.

Ethical Technology Exists Only as a Reflection of its Creators' Values. Technologies are not value neutral. They embed the values, priorities, and biases of their creators. This means the societal and environmental impacts of a technology are often a reflection of the underlying value systems of those who develop and fund it. This also means it is possible to study the underlying value of systems themselves independently of their use by human beings (Brey, P., 2012). As a result, this can lead to technologies that perpetuate existing inequalities or fail to address the needs of marginalized communities. The long-term impacts of these technologies could lead to unforeseen negative consequences.

Technology Has No Exclusivity on Innovation. The emphasis on high-tech solutions can overshadow and undervalue indigenous, local knowledge systems and frugal innovation that have sustained environments for centuries. These traditional practices, often more sustainable and adapted to local ecosystems, can be marginalized in the rush to adopt new technologies, leading to a loss of valuable ecological knowledge and cultural heritage. In addition, technological adaptation also means technological maladaptation. For example, agricultural technologies developed for temperate climates may not work in tropical regions and can even harm those environments.

Yesterday's Technology Decisions Set Limits to New Technology Adoption. Path dependency in technology suggests that once a society starts down a particular technological path, it becomes increasingly costly and difficult to switch to a different one. This can lead to a technological lock-in, where suboptimal technologies persist because of established infrastructure and systems. For example, the global reliance on fossil fuel-based energy systems is not just a matter of preference but a result of historical path dependencies.

A Technology-Regulation Gap Is the Best Call for Responsible Technology. Technological innovations often outpace the establishment of necessary regulations, creating a regulatory gap. This gap not only poses a challenge for ensuring that technology is used ethically and equitably, but it also places a greater responsibility on creators and innovators. While the regulatory gap is essential to mature and guide the use of new technologies, their slower evolution does not absolve creators of the responsibility to avoid creating morally unacceptable situations.

Digital for Good is about acknowledging the current and long-term impact of paradoxes posed by technology to address its unsustainable nature or implications for the well-being of society. It aims to harness its benefits responsibly while maintaining a balanced and nuanced perspective about the potential negative externalities that might arise from its advancement. As we harness the power of digital technology, in this age of artificial intelligence, it is our collective responsibility to ensure that it serves not only as a tool for innovation and efficiency but also as a catalyst for a more sustainable, equitable, and ethical future benefiting humanity.

AI Is a New Age for Societies

Contrary to what many headlines may have promoted in media and popular discourse, AI is not equivalent to electricity, the car, or any other innovation that humankind has brought to this earth. This comparison may not fully capture the unique impact and implications of AI due to its fundamental nature. AI represents the creation of inorganic intelligence (IA), thus introducing an entirely new form of "intelligence."

The nature of the difference from any other innovation made by humans lies in the fact that AI introduces the possibility—and in some aspects, already the capability—to give any preceding innovation the ability to perform cognitive tasks typically reserved for humans. It's about the inclusion of a new form of intelligence in the world. This transition moves us toward a new meaning of "IoT," from the Internet of Things to the Intelligence of Things. Therefore, there is also a degree of difference. As this transition involves pushing the boundaries of the mix of intelligences, it challenges and forces us to reconsider the role that human intelligence holds and must continue to hold in this mix, unlike any previous innovation.

The consequences of AI's spectacular advances are infiltrating critical aspects of society. Their significance becomes even more pronounced as these systems are deployed on a global scale and integrated into various facets of our lives. This **hypervasive** influence reflects not only the rise of more inorganic intelligence but also that of a form of authority that algorithms have gained over our daily decisions and interactions: **Algorithy**. Algorithy shapes not only the AI systems we use but also, in a loop, what and how we do when using them, influencing the societal norms and personal choices we make, embedding themselves as central governing forces in our modern life.

The pressing question we face today is the profound impact that these intelligent entities have and will have on human existence, given the unprecedented nature of their intelligence, even though it is different from human intelligence (Srivastava, A. et al., 2022). As AI systems become more widespread and thus influential, it is increasingly vital to develop an acuity for the underlying transformations they initiate and portend for the future.

Our primary concern is with the foundational pillars of a society—those that, conversely, trigger trends shaping it for multiple generations. It may concern the criminal justice system, education, the economy, or health. Through relentless precision in the intimate prediction of what is delicately called *personalization*, algorithms set the editorial line of the content feed of many lives, reinforcing certain ways of thinking and cultural stereotypes and creating a bubble, each one's own and yet paradoxically the same for everyone, since it is crafted by the care of a single editor-in-chief: the machine.

The advent of AI marks the dawn of a somehow new form of cooperation and competition that introduces complex dimensions that we will have to increasingly apprehend in our daily lives, in our relationship with the machine.

The Equation "Human OR Machine" This dimension involves establishing economic, ethical, and social norms that will help determine which tasks must and should continue to be imperatively performed by humans and which can and may be entrusted to machines. Finding the right balance is essential to guarantee the protection of human rights and lay the foundations for the effective regulation of AI.

The Equation "Human AND Machine" This dimension explores the changes we are willing to accept in society to unleash the full potential of AI and increase our human capabilities. Accepting the challenge of combining human and machine capabilities, without compromising the very essence of what makes our humanity, certainly presents economic opportunities but is also the spring of anthropological and civilizational evolutions and therefore those that will shape our future.

The Equation "Human AND Machine" versus "Human WITHOUT Machine" Bridging the gap between those who can access AI and use it effectively and those who cannot is crucial. The emergence of an algorithmic divide can lead to new forms of inequality. Addressing this dimension of the new competitive landscape in the AI era becomes an imperative for sovereignty, security, equal opportunities, and development.

The Equation "Machine-to-Machine" This calls for our responsibility to define the limits and boundaries we want to set for advanced interactions between machines. It raises profound questions about the potential emergence of a new form of life, not organic but algorithmic, at the heart of our societies.

Are we prepared for the societal shift that AI-driven automation will bring about in society? The relationship between humans and machines encompasses several dimensions whose requirements force us to explore the potential of AI while ensuring that human values and societal well-being remain at the forefront. As Elon Musk once said, "Artificial intelligence doesn't have to be evil to destroy humanity. If AI has a goal and humanity just happens to be in the way, it will destroy humanity as a matter of course without even thinking about it."

Let's not think that regulating this intelligence simply consists of putting safeguards only on AI itself, considering that risk may only originate from AI per se, thus neglecting or underestimating that chaos theory also applies to technology, among the numerous paradoxes that driving Digital for Good approaches implies AI, as a new form of intelligence required broadening our reflection on the matter of enforcing integrity from organically toward technologically, and ultimately algorithmically speaking, with regard to societal values, norms, and fundamental rights, from now on and moving forward.

AI Is Exclusive by Design

As humans, it is our responsibility to shape the trajectory of AI. Throughout human history, we have excelled at creating products that meet the specific needs of certain individuals while excluding others by leveraging technology. We have continuously honed this skill, striving to differentiate ourselves and design products that cater to targeted markets and specific audiences.

This mindset, shaped by our mental, moral, and ethical models, influences how we perceive and interact with the world for most of our lives. Undoubtedly, this approach conflicts with inclusivity and diversity. The better we become at designing and delivering products and services that perfectly suit a specific targeted audience, the more adept we become at discriminating against other nontargeted audiences, purposefully leaving them behind.

AI, built upon our mental, moral, and ethical models, follows this same pattern—it is exclusive by design, not inclusive. And paradoxically, it is already omnipresent.

This is where AI exacerbates the digital divide, following the innovation-equity paradox. According to Precedent Research Inc (2023), the global AI market size was valued at USD $454.12 billion in 2022 and is expected to hit around USD $2,575.16 billion by 2032, progressing with a compound annual growth rate (CAGR) of 19% from 2023 to 2032. Its continuous and widespread adoption places it at the core of numerous organizations worldwide.

- In an increasing number of hardware and software components
- In various industries such as automotive, healthcare, retail, finance, banking, insurance, telecommunications, manufacturing, agriculture, aviation, education, media, and security, to name a few
- In expanding roles and professions, including human resources, marketing, sales, advertising, legal, supply chain, and many more

We are just scratching the surface. One of the key questions arising from the development of AI is how to ensure that biases or segmentation models in the data powering AI do not lead to discriminatory behaviors based on characteristics such as gender, race, religion, disability, sexual orientation, or political views. This is one of the significant challenges posed by AI development.

With the exponential and rapid development of AI, the temptation to use it for unprecedented differentiation and unparalleled targeting approaches to achieve economic growth and competitiveness is strong and will continue to grow. There exists a tension between the need for organizations and individuals to embrace diversity and inclusivity to foster greater equality in society and the global economic system that encourages and exacerbates behaviors where differentiation, and therefore discrimination, becomes a rule of the game leading to success.

This tension is on the verge of intensifying due to AI's potential to systemically codify these competition-oriented behaviors in our digital society, presenting one of the greatest challenges of our time. Artificial intelligence is already permeating every facet of society.

- Personal assistants have now become virtual, enabling the execution of tasks with a human-like level of conversational ability.
- Market analyses are conducted by machines that produce studies such as competitor comparisons and generate detailed reports.

- Customer behavior, purchasing processes, and preferences are scrutinized by increasingly intelligent customer relationship management (CRM) systems capable of predicting customer needs.
- Customer service is also provided by AI-powered chatbots that can answer frequently asked questions on a website.

And this is just the beginning compared to the potential applications that are already emerging and rapidly approaching in the near future, including:

- Autonomous vehicles (bicycles, cars, trains, planes, boats, etc.)
- Robots assisting surgeons in operating rooms
- Content creation (videos, music, articles, etc.) entirely produced by machine work
- Public policies whose measures would be prescribed and performance predicted through the analysis of large volumes of data
- And much more

Considering the societal implications for the future of humanity, artificial intelligence is far from being as artificial as it may seem. We must decide whether we plan to use AI to eliminate visible and invisible inequalities to an unprecedented extent or if we unconsciously or consciously intend to amplify them on the same scale. As we enter the era of AI, there will be fewer and fewer gray areas.

AI also opens a new era for human learning. The responsibility for shaping the trajectory of AI rests squarely on our shoulders as humans. At the heart of the challenges faced in 21st-century learning lies in the way we teach machines what they need to learn and how they learn it. It necessitates not only an ongoing pursuit of developing our own intelligence but also a deep understanding of how machines acquire their own.

Both human and machine learning face similar challenges:

- Supervised learning versus unsupervised learning
- Structured learning versus unstructured learning
- "Few-shot" learning versus "Blink" learning (as Malcolm Gladwell puts it)

- Long-term versus short-term learning with a trade-off between forgetting and retention
- "Zero-shot" learning versus learning through "dreaming"
- Visuomotor learning versus multisensory learning (AVK)

By unraveling the mysteries of how machines learn, we not only discover new avenues for learning that were previously unexplored and unimaginable but also revolutionize the standards by which we understand our learning process, ultimately enhancing human intelligence.

However, let us not be mistaken. Intelligence and knowledge are not synonymous, and increasing our knowledge is a necessary yet insufficient condition for augmenting our intelligence. Enhancing human intelligence primarily involves expanding our capacity for questioning, challenging the status quo, nurturing curiosity, and fostering the emergence of new questions in our minds, leading to the discovery and rediscovery of what we think we know and who we are.

Nevertheless, AI is far less intelligent than commonly imagined. Even without contemplating an AI capable of replicating human emotions, there is an inherent distinction that sets AI apart—the comprehension and grasp of context. Context comprises numerous parameters, some evident to the naked eye, while others are more discreet, nuanced, and constituted by subtle signals and details that play a pivotal role in characterizing a context. Considering the ever-evolving nature of any given context, it will take time before AI can truly appreciate its emotional complexity.

Building the kind of AI that benefits society necessitates a visionary approach. It involves comprehending which tasks are and will be best executed by machine intelligence in contrast to those that are and will be better handled by human intelligence. It also requires recognizing tasks that must and will continue to be carried out by humans, regardless of technological advancements.

The responses our societies develop to establish a framework in which AI aligns with human intelligence will shape the future of humanity. This goes beyond numerous innovations and new forms of competitive advantages that will redefine market dynamics as we know them today. More importantly, it holds sociological implications and affects the world we leave for future generations.

Most often, when we contemplate machine learning, our mental model leads us to think of a strictly one-way approach in which we teach the machine and provide it with the means to learn autonomously in various domains. Artificial intelligence heralds a profound transformation in the relationship between humans and machines. This evolving dynamic, which is already becoming increasingly critical and fascinating, is more bidirectional than ever before. Consequently, the question arises: what can machine intelligence teach us to enhance our human capabilities?

We must embrace new ways of thinking to enable machines to perform tasks that would be challenging, if not impossible, for us to accomplish in the same manner. Simultaneously, we have the opportunity to seize new avenues for learning and self-improvement in numerous domains that currently demand extensive effort and years of expertise, with true mastery often only attainable through human execution.

And let's not be naïve: AI is seeping into the human decision-making process, and it's happening right now. While AI and the recommendations it produces offer unsuspected opportunities to enhance not only our own intelligence but also the nature of relationships and emotional attachments we may develop with machines in the future, it also raises delicate questions of environmental and social responsibility. At what point does the decision support provided by AI exert such a degree of influence that it silently decides on behalf of humans, potentially leading in the long run to modifying cultural codes through a process of **algoriculture**?

This complex question is upon us. The answer, particularly considering the level of vulnerability that society may recognize in each of us at any given moment, in particular circumstances of existence, can be as nuanced as the individuals themselves. That is why applications, devices, and any technological equipment equipped with any form of AI need to be explicitly transparent regarding the limitations of the parameters the algorithm considers or disregards, concerning potential implications that may pose a danger to oneself or others. This will help foster the responsible use of AI and prevent the risks of inappropriate or even prohibited use.

AI challenges us to make it explicitly explainable to all, in terms of the causality behind its results, in order to guide decisions that increasingly impact our lives and society as a whole. Paradoxically, as humans, we cannot explain everything about the reasons behind many of our decisions in a manner that the majority would understand and deem fair.

Regardless, AI has no ethics of its own. AI lacks ethics: it simply pertains to ours and ours alone. Our ethical principles are, ultimately, an integral part of the functional requirements that consequently digitally encode the biases we intellectually possess. In a way, AI inherits the ethical genes of its creator.

Making the invisible codes of our societies visible is perhaps one of the most transformative advancements that AI will enable humanity to achieve. Such a level of transparency regarding the unspoken and unwritten will contribute to greater equality and profoundly redefine the citizens' demand for justice in our societies. It is also an opportunity to ensure that the AI that interacts with ours and coexists with us is as much as possible the product of co(llective)-intelligence or, at best, the receptacle of the wealth that can be produced by the synergies derived from human diversity in all its forms of intelligence.

The augmentation of our intelligence through that of machines will always, and even more so in the future, be confronted with the existential question of the human cause we assign to this intelligence to serve. Therefore, we should strive to make artificial intelligence an intelligence inspired by the quintessence of the best in our humanity, excluding all the dark aspects of human nature. This is arguably the most dizzying yet most crucial question for the future of humanity. It is a question to which only our humanity has the power and responsibility to provide an ever-renewed answer in order to build the future in which we want to live.

The Complex Equation of AI in the Work World

At the imminent dawn of our artificially intelligent societies, a profound concern arises: to what extent will artificial intelligence reshape our professional landscape? It's becoming clear that the role of humans in this journey is increasingly being questioned. Whether embraced with enthusiasm or apprehension, the undeniable reality is that many stand on the edge of change, with AI poised to redefine professional structures.

In the automotive industry, autonomous vehicles are one of the major innovations. AI powers these vehicles, allowing for real-time driving decisions. Companies like Tesla, Waymo, and others are actively working on advancing this technology.

In healthcare, AI is used for early disease detection through the analysis of medical images. It can help spot tumors or other abnormalities in X-rays or MRIs long before a human eye can discern them.

In the financial sector, robot-advisors are automated platforms that provide financial advice and manage clients' investment portfolios based on algorithms. Companies like Betterment and Wealthfront utilize AI to optimize investment strategies.

In agriculture, AI is employed for crop management and yield forecasting. Through drones and sensors, farmers can monitor their fields in real time, detect diseases or pests, and predict the water or nutrient needs of their crops.

In retail, many businesses use AI for product recommendations. Giants like Amazon and Netflix suggest products or movies based on users' preferences and purchase or viewing histories, using machine learning algorithms to continuously refine their suggestions.

Each of these examples showcases how AI not only can enhance efficiency and accuracy across various sectors but also can create new opportunities and challenges in the job market. As we move toward this inflection point, the core reflection goes beyond the mere substitution of roles. The challenge lies in understanding a new balance that's somewhat difficult to predict: will the jobs erased by AI be outnumbered by those it creates? Will it be a two-to-one ratio, three-to-one, or perhaps an even more contrasting equation?

First and foremost, AI will not replace anyone—it will replace specific jobs currently held by individuals. It's a subtle distinction. We shouldn't reduce human life solely to a job. To reduce the essence of an individual only to their profession is a gross oversimplification.

At the heart of this issue is this equation, or Ratio (R):

$$R = D / C$$

where D represents the jobs Deleted due to AI and C denotes the new jobs Created by AI. The perspective, often driven by fear, which paints a future where AI would erase more jobs than it creates, assumes $R > 1$. However, other variables are often overlooked or underestimated, such as:

Jobs Maintained (M) Some jobs are maintained without significant change because they require a human touch that's hard to automate since error and imperfection are part of the creation process and what adds charm (e.g., hairstylists, artisans) or because understanding human nuances is crucial (e.g., psychoanalysts, sociologists, career counselors).

Jobs That Shift (S)   Some jobs shift to become more tech-oriented or require a different skill set, like professions in the fields of medicine, graphic design, or journalism. Here, AI-based tools allow for data analyses or provide insights into emerging trends on subjects like corporate financial outcomes or sports statistics. These roles are adapting to incorporate more data analysis skills.

Jobs Enhanced (E)   Some jobs are enhanced by AI but still require human intervention, like sales assistants, call center operators, or truck drivers. AI could handle driving over long distances or on highways, but human intervention remains vital for more complex situations like city driving.

Total Jobs   The total jobs in an economy is better represented by the sum of $D+C+M+S+E$. The ratio $R=D/C$ does not fully capture the potential footprint of AI on the job market by itself. For the claim that a significant portion of jobs would be replaced by AI to be true, it would require $R=D/(T-D)$ with $R > 1$.

But it's not that simple. The impact of new technologies on the job market has always been a topic of debate among economists, historians, and labor market experts. Historically, the introduction of new technologies has often led to a phase of disruption, followed by a period of adjustment, and ultimately a net job creation or new opportunities.

Based on these historical trends, several AI impact models can be considered:

Logarithmic Growth   In this case, the impact of AI on job losses could be swift, eventually slowing down over time. This could be a reasonable assumption given that the first jobs to go would be those that are easily automatable, and over time, it would become increasingly challenging to replace jobs requiring unique human skills.

Exponential Growth   In this scenario, the impact would accelerate over time, which might be the case if AI technology progresses rapidly. However, this could be overly pessimistic, as even with technological advances, regulatory, ethical, or practical barriers might slow down a full AI adoption scenario.

Polynomial Growth   Here, one would need to consider the phenomena of peaks and valleys in AI adoption and therefore its impact on employment. For instance, a rapid introduction of AI might lead to many job losses, but as the technology matures and society adapts, new jobs might be created or transformed.

Given the history of technological innovations, from the industrial revolution to the digital revolution, a scenario combining elements from both the logarithmic and polynomial models might be among the most realistic. This would mean that the initial impact of AI on job losses would be quick and disruptive, but it would slow down over time (logarithmic). Then, as new uses for AI emerge and the technology matures, there could be fluctuations in how AI impacts work (polynomial).

To potentially grasp these dynamics, revisiting our equation where we left off, we might have $R = D / (a * \log(b * (T-D)) + c * (T-D)^2)$, where a, b, and c are constants to be determined empirically. In addition to the trend of this nonlinear impact, for a future where AI would eliminate more jobs than it would create (thus $R > 1$) to happen, this would imply that several undesirable contextual conditions and situations would have been made possible. Some of these would arise as a constant, others intermittently, with certain factors of concomitance between them:

Quantity (Q)   This assumption suggests that there is a fixed Quantity (Q) of work to be done and that if AI does more, there will be less for humans, should this time prove correct, given that historically, employment volume has never been a zero-sum game (referring to what economists call the "lump of labor fallacy").

Largely (L)   AI systems should not only automate certain tasks but also Largely (L) replace, in a significantly impactful manner, the tasks that make up entire professional roles, representing a substantial portion of the job market. This would mean that within the scope of this share, these systems would perform these jobs without requiring human roles, supervision, monitoring, or additional human tasks.

Development (D)   The Development (D) and adoption of AI technologies would have to progress at such a fast pace—without plateauing after rapid growth due to physical, economic, or other constraints—that retraining or transition opportunities for the affected workforce would be unattainable.

Preference (P)   It should be significantly more cost-effective for companies to implement and rely on AI solutions than to hire human workers. This economic inclination should be so pronounced that companies would prefer AI even if it's not perfect, and there should be no regulatory restrictions curbing this Preference (P). For instance, if AI could autonomously write original movie scripts at a lower cost than humans, with quality equal to or even surpassing the most original human-produced scenarios, film production companies might favor AI over hiring scriptwriters. And all this would occur in a context where no regulation would hinder this adoption for ethical or cultural reasons.

Security (S)   The implications of AI for security (S), private life and individual rights should not be deemed major societal concerns. This would imply that there'd be no ethical constraints limiting the areas where AI operates autonomously, especially concerning areas involving decisions that have a significant direct impact on human lives. One example is the question surrounding the use of facial recognition.

Widespread (W)   The environmental footprint resulting from the Widespread (W) replacement of numerous human jobs by AI systems—due to the increased computations inherent in these systems and the infrastructure needed for their operation—would not be viewed as alarming or a potential threat to life on Earth.

Negative Impacts (I)   All the Negative Impacts (I) of AI on mental health, whether due to job losses, societal changes, or the heightened dependency on technology, which would ultimately impoverish social interactions essential for the physical and psychological well-being of humans, would have been widely overlooked or outright ignored by society.

The exact form of the function f(Q, L, D, P, S, W, I) describing how these variables interact would depend on precisely how these variables influence the ratio R, which would require a deep understanding of the interactions between these factors and their impact on employment.

Equally important, future technological trends, other than AI, some of which amplify the application areas of AI, as well as societal evolutions, can always introduce unexpected variables (U). These aren't accounted for in models based on historical trends and may require regular adjustments or calibrations as new data or perspectives become available. Including all these variables makes the equation more complex than it seems, or than some oversimplified views might suggest, by reducing it to a Ratio R=D/C where D represents jobs Deleted due to AI and C represents new jobs Created by AI.

To what extent will artificial intelligence reshape our professional land-scape? Will the roles erased by AI be surpassed by those it creates? The answer to these questions is hard to predict. Many parameters ultimately depend on what we decide to do in the coming years. It's up to us now to make the necessary choices to build the future we want.

The Origin of AI Elucidates its Current Trajectory

Tracing the origins of AI offers critical insights into how AI has evolved from theoretical notions to a potent force shaping every facet of our modern society. The concept of AI, born from a fusion of disciplines including mathematics, psychology, engineering, and computer science, which now finds itself at the intersection of technology and human life, began as an ambitious pursuit to understand and replicate human intelligence. Pioneers in the field, such as Alan Turing and John McCarthy, laid the foundational theories and concepts, envisioning machines not just as tools but as entities capable of learning, reasoning, and decision-making. This quest to mimic human cognitive abilities led to the development of algorithms, neural networks, and machine learning techniques that are the cornerstone of today's AI.

The term *artificial intelligence* was first coined by John McCarthy. He used this term in 1955 when he wrote a proposal for the 1956 Dartmouth Conference, the first conference devoted to the subject. McCarthy, along with Marvin Minsky, Claude Shannon, and Nathan Rochester, organized this conference, where the term was formally adopted and the domain of AI research was officially born.

In the 1950s, computer science was an emerging field. Researchers were beginning to understand that computers could do more than just number crunching. McCarthy, being at the forefront of this field, saw the broader potential of computers, influenced by the work of Turing, who had laid the foundation for the concept of machine intelligence with his 1950 paper "Computing Machinery and Intelligence" and the Turing test. Additionally, his collaboration with other leading thinkers like Marvin Minsky, Claude Shannon, and Nathan Rochester, who were all interested in exploring the potential of intelligent machines, played a role in shaping his ideas. McCarthy saw the need for a distinct domain within computer science focused on the development of intelligent machines.

The term *artificial intelligence* was an effective way to describe this new field, encompassing both the creation of intelligence in an artificial (non-biological) entity and the study of understanding intelligence in general.

He defined it as "the science and engineering of making intelligent machines." This definition encapsulates the core goal of AI: to create machines capable of performing tasks that would require intelligence if done by humans.

McCarthy's vision for AI was broad and ambitious, encompassing not just specific tasks or applications but the creation of machines that could reason, learn, and act autonomously. His definition laid the groundwork for what has become a vast field of research and development. The current discourse around artificial intelligence, focusing on the development of general AI capabilities over specialized functionalities, is not a novel concept but rather a continuation of the vision laid out by pioneers like McCarthy. His belief in creating machines with intelligence—capable of reasoning, problem-solving, and learning in a broad, human-like manner—mirrors today's aspirations in AI research. His advocacy for a logic-based approach, where knowledge is represented in a formal, logical structure, has been foundational in the evolution of AI, evident in the continued relevance of his Lisp programming language.

Furthermore, the emphasis on the Turing test as a measure of machine intelligence, a concept supported by McCarthy, remains a significant benchmark in evaluating AI progress. McCarthy's long-term vision of AI, foreseeing machines performing tasks once thought uniquely human, including intellectual and emotional understanding, is a narrative still dominant in contemporary AI discussions. His awareness of the impacts of AI, such as its effects on employment and privacy, predated many of today's concerns in the field, and his optimism about the feasibility of creating self-improving, truly intelligent machines continues to inspire current AI advancements.

In essence, the current trajectory of AI development aligns closely with McCarthy's original visions and ideas. It highlights that while technology has advanced, the fundamental goals and challenges of AI have remained consistent with the early aspirations of its founding figures. However, while this vision for AI was comprehensive and forward-thinking, it notably overlooked one crucial aspect: the notion of integrity. McCarthy's focus was primarily on the development of AI intelligence capabilities such as logical reasoning and the ability to learn and adapt. There was less emphasis on ensuring these systems operate with an inherent sense of integrity, considering the moral implications of their influence and decisions.

The initial goal of AI research was to demonstrate the feasibility of machine intelligence. In that context, researchers like McCarthy were more concerned with establishing AI as a legitimate scientific field and exploring its potential capabilities. The integrity-related concerns, while important, were secondary to proving that AI could work in the first place.

In today's context, where AI is increasingly integrated into critical aspects of society, the absence of a robust framework for shaping integrity toward these artificially intelligent systems in the early vision is a significant blind spot. Therefore, while the foundational vision for AI was groundbreaking, the underestimation of the importance of integrating integrity into the core of AI systems from the outset has become apparent. It highlights the need for a more holistic approach to AI development, one that considers not just intelligence and capability but also the integrity of these AI systems as they interact with and impact human lives.

Consequently, in the current dynamic landscape of AI advancement, the paramount challenge for leaders lies in designing a future where the synergy between human insight and artificial intelligence not only contributes value but also multiplies it exponentially, adhering to values. This goes beyond the binary question of whether humans or AI will dominate; it's about how their collaborative efforts can yield a synergistic effect that not only preserves but actively enhances core human values, reinforcing them with unwavering integrity.

The concept of artificial integrity provides a forward-looking framework for AI's evolution, focusing on creating AI systems that don't just comply with but actively reinforce and uphold human-centered beneficial societal standards, beyond just exhibiting any for form of artificial intelligence. AI operating systems intentionally designed and maintained for that purpose would be those that perform with this characteristic. They will be processing while enabling and sustaining a form of artificial integrity.

2

Unpacking What Artificial Integrity Is

We often hear that artificial intelligence (AI) must be trustworthy and that this is an essential condition for responsible AI. This is correct, but it's insufficient. More than being trustworthy, AI must be developed and deployed within a framework that respects integrity.

The difference between something being trustworthy and something having integrity is the difference between the *seen* and the *unseen*.

Being trustworthy is the seen. That's why trustworthiness generally refers to the reliability or dependability of something or someone. A person or system can be trustworthy if they consistently behave in a reliable and predictable manner or provide accurate information. For instance, a source might consistently provide accurate data and thus be deemed trustworthy in that respect. In that matter, the seen is what the user is able to appreciate, evaluate, judge, and give trust to. It is the fact that a user gives trust that makes something trustworthy or not. Trustworthiness comes as an outcome, as a result of the interaction between a human being and a person, and in the case of AI, a system. It's the idea of perceiving that things are right.

Integrity Is the Unseen

Integrity is the unseen. It refers to adherence to moral and ethical principles. It implies a sense of honesty, fairness, and righteousness. Integrity often involves doing the right thing in the way of doing so, even when it's not the easiest or most beneficial in the short term. A situation where something might be trustworthy but not have integrity could involve a system or individual that reliably performs a function or provides accurate information but does so in a way that is unethical or morally questionable.

In this aspect, the unseen is what the user is not able to appreciate, evaluate, or judge to give trust to something. Thus, it does not enter into the equation for any user to give trust and make something trustworthy or not. Integrity is the root of the outcomes and the result of the values that have prevailed at each step of the fabric of those outcomes to be appreciable with regard to the moral stances, human values, and human rights, as well as ensuring that the outcome is molded with integrity to society, determining whether it is an outcome from a person and, in the case of AI, from a system, or both.

Trustworthiness is a necessary condition for integrity but is not sufficient for integrity to be. On one hand, a given outcome can be seen as trustworthy by human society while not being molded, conceived, created, or delivered with integrity as far as human society is concerned. On the other hand, a given outcome being molded, conceived, created, or delivered with integrity as far as human society is concerned can be perceived as not trustworthy for human society while it does not exhibit the traits of what could create trust in the process of interacting with humans.

This means that not only does AI need to be trustworthy, but it also needs to be made with integrity. Even though the integrity is the part of the iceberg that is unseen from a user perspective, its lack represents the risk that AI creators ask their users to take and society as a whole to take. This is what comes right to the surface, starting to become seen in certain circumstances of usage. For companies, that means focusing their efforts on developing AI systems that are just perceived as trustworthy is not sustainable if they are not molded with integrity.

The market demand is shaped by the need perceived, but the unperceived has to be taken into account as it shapes what comes back to the surface, if not in the short term, then in the long run. AI systems need to be driven with integrity behind closed doors so that their functioning, beyond exhibiting trustworthiness, can adhere to societal needs, norms, values, and standards without infringing, harming, devaluing, or regressing their integrity.

Companies and organizations should consider this a priority for several reasons. First, they want to prevent their AI systems from behaving in unexpected ways, causing harmful consequences for their users, customers, or society. They want to ensure their AI products are perceived, marketed, and adopted by their users, customers, or society for market acceptance, eventually market share, and ultimately company survival. Only focusing on measuring trustworthiness with regard to their customer base, whether it is speed, scalability, accuracy, or anything else they perceive, would not be enough for their business success. Ultimately, they should consider this a priority because they all have a role to play in the making of a society where AI systems reflect human values.

Artificial integrity, for AI development and deployment, is defined by three interconnected models that collectively ensure the preservation and enhancement of integrity of the ecosystem where AI takes part.

Society Value Model This model establishes and enforces strong guardrails and value principles external to AI systems that support the human condition, serving as the external force that creates a safe environment for humans to thrive and within which AI should operate with integrity.
AI Model This model ensures AI operational consistency with internal and intrinsic guardrails, guidelines, and values-driven standards from an AI development standpoint, thus ensuring that algorithms uphold not only a form of intelligence but also a form of integrity over time.
Human and Artificial Co-intelligence Model As a central concern and commitment combined with these external and internal models, this model implies building and sustaining capabilities to foster a co-intelligence model based on the synergistic relationship between humans and AI, enhancing rather than undermining the human condition.

Together, these three models should constitute one integrated approach, functioning as a metamodel that is essential to ensure that the participation of such artificially intelligent systems—which thus become stakeholders in a larger whole that constitutes the living ecosystem in which their intelligence is exercised—can be carried out while preserving, supporting, and defending the integrity of the societal ecosystem.

Artificial integrity is a forward-looking Digital for Good approach aimed at building this metamodel in which AI development can be sustained in society with integrity.

Sustaining Society Value Models

External to AI models themselves, the concept of artificial integrity embodies a human commitment to establish guardrails and value principles that serve as a code of life for AI to be developed, while having stances that guide the way to sustain a sense of integrity in its creation and deployment. It refers to the society value model that the AI models need to adhere to: considering a set of principles that structure the delivery of its functioning to be intrinsically capable of prioritizing and safeguarding human life and well-being in all aspects of its operation. It represents the value system in which these forms of intelligence operate and serve, upholding value principles tailored to specific contexts and enabling AI's outputs and outcomes to resonate with and sustain in reflection of these values, not just to the benefit of one given user, group, or community but to the greater superior interest of a given socio-economic, political, and environmental ecosystem's integrity.

This approach highlights a paradigm shift for AI systems, which should not just exhibit intelligence for its own sake and for the hyper-narrow interests of an individual in the limited framework of a commercial purpose. They should also be algorithmically socially responsible and societally accountable in terms of the impact of their artificially made intelligence on society, considering the value system in which it is an artificial stakeholder.

The characterization of a society's value model involves multiple facets that collectively define the ethical, cultural, and operational principles guiding behavior and decision-making within that society. Several critical dimensions must be considered regarding the inclusion of AI in society.

There are the prevailing moral beliefs and principles that dictate what is considered right or wrong in a society. Acting as ethical standards, they influence laws, education, and individual behavior and are often rooted in historical, religious, or philosophical traditions.

In addition, cultural values forge the shared assumptions, traditions, and practices. They define social interactions and cultural identity and influence how people communicate, celebrate, and express themselves and can vary greatly even within the same society.

Legal frameworks are another essential dimension. Consisting of rules and regulations that also govern behavior within society, they ensure order, resolve conflicts, and are used as tools to enforce ethical norms and cultural values through codified law.

When we talk about a value model, we are also referring to how a society organizes its economic activities, the distribution of resources, and how wealth is generated and distributed. Economic structures impact social mobility, affect class structure, and influence societal values.

Systems of governance and political ideologies shape the distribution of power and responsibilities in a society and its value model. Political systems affect how decisions are made, how leaders are selected, and how citizens interact. This constitutes a key element of the value model.

Then there are the principles, practices, and methods through which knowledge is transmitted in a society. Educational systems not only transfer academic knowledge but also instill societal values and prepare individuals to participate in the systems of society, whether it be the political, economic, social, etc.

The Value Model also includes the unwritten rules that often govern daily interactions within a society. They cover a wide range of behaviors, from general social etiquette to specific practices.

The way a society adopts and integrates technology also reflects and influences its reference values. This factor has become more important and will continue to do so as the role of technology increasingly affects privacy norms, work-life balance, and the accessibility of services and information.

Environmental value is also an essential dimension of a society's value model. This value reflects the society's relationship with the natural environment, including conservation practices, the use of natural resources, and responses to environmental challenges, a highly structuring issue today and for the future.

Finally, in an increasingly globalized world, international norms, trends, and policies must also be considered in the value model of a society because their influence in areas such as human rights, environmental policy, and economic agreements is inevitable.

These multidimensional aspects that compose any value model lead to the necessity of a diversity of approaches and perspectives to analyze it. As such, there is a need for multidisciplinary inputs. It includes engaging with various stakeholders, including ethicists, community leaders, and potential users, to understand their perspectives and concerns about AI deployment and to inform strategic decision-making as far as a given society value model is concerned.

Developing a mathematical model of the value model is crucial for organizations, regions, countries, and even globally to quantitatively understand and predict the impacts of policies, technologies, and changes within societal frameworks. Such a model could enable stakeholders to assess and optimize the interaction between technological advancements—particularly in artificial intelligence—and societal values, ensuring that these technologies are deployed in a way that aligns with ethical norms and enhances public welfare.

At an organizational level, a mathematical model can help companies anticipate the societal response to new products or services, assess the risk of regulatory noncompliance, and ensure that corporate practices align with both local cultural values and global ethical standards. This foresight can prevent costly missteps, enhance brand reputation, and drive sustainable business practices that resonate with stakeholders.

At broader levels—regional, national, or global—this model can become a powerful tool for policymakers and leaders. It can provide insights into how collective behaviors, societal norms, and regulatory frameworks influence and are influenced by technological deployments. This is especially critical in managing the rollout of hypervasive technologies such as AI, where unintended consequences can have widespread implications.

Furthermore, a well-designed model can facilitate scenario planning and strategic decision-making, allowing leaders to simulate the outcomes of different policy choices or technological implementations. This can guide more informed, data-driven decisions that optimize social outcomes, enhance public trust, and maintain social cohesion.

A mathematical model of the society value model could act as a strategic asset across various levels of decision-making, providing a structured, evidence-based approach to navigating the complex interplay between societal values and AI. Such modeling is indispensable in today's rapidly changing technological landscape, where decisions must be both swift and socially responsible.

To technically implement a mathematical model of the value model of a given organization, it is essential to start by defining the specific values and ethical principles that are core to the organization's identity and mission. This requires a collaborative process involving stakeholders from across and beyond the organization to articulate these values clearly and to identify the key performance indicators (KPIs) that will measure alignment with these values.

Gathering data that reflects how current practices and products align with the identified values is a first step. This includes customer feedback, employee surveys, compliance records, and other relevant metrics. Then, developing a mathematical model that incorporates these values as variables or constraints could be addressed. For example, if environmental sustainability is a core value, the model should include metrics for resource consumption, waste generation, and carbon footprint. Techniques such as multicriteria decision analysis (MCDA) can be useful here to handle trade-offs between conflicting values.

As far as the integration of this value model with AI model is concerned, this could involve using AI to simulate outcomes under various decision scenarios or deploying machine learning algorithms to predict the impact of certain decisions on value alignment. For instance, predictive analytics can forecast how changes in product design might affect environmental KPIs. The establishment of feedback mechanisms where outputs from the AI models are regularly compared against the value-based KPIs of the value model is key. This allows for the dynamic adjustment of practices in response to shifts in performance or in the external environment.

Lastly, as continuous learning and adaptation are paramount, the implementation of machine learning systems that not only predict but also learn from new data to continuously refine the model is necessary. This learning process should be transparent, allowing for periodic reviews by human overseers to ensure AI decisions remain aligned with human values. Indeed, AI systems through its AI model can provide real-time data processing and predictive insights that inform decision-making processes. In turn, the decisions made based on these insights are evaluated against the organization's value model. Discrepancies identified between AI recommendations and value-based outcomes can be used to refine AI algorithms, ensuring they are better aligned with organizational values in future iterations.

For example, if an AI-driven customer service chatbot begins to show biases in customer interactions that conflict with the organization's commitment to equality and nondiscrimination, the identified discrepancies would trigger an algorithmic review. Adjustments would then be made either in the data feeding into the AI (to correct for biases) or directly in the algorithmic decision processes (to enhance fairness). Implementing this integrated model not only enhances decision-making but also strengthens organizational artificial integrity by ensuring that AI tools are used in a manner consistent with foundational values.

A Deliberate Act of AI Design

Core to AI models themselves, the concept of artificial integrity implies that AI is developed and operates in a manner that is not only aligned with guardrails and value principles that serve as a code of life for AI but also does so consistently and continuously across various situations, without deviation from its programmed values-driven guidelines. This is a fundamental part of the way it has been conceived, trained, and maintained. It is a deliberate act of design. It suggests a level of algorithmic self-regulation and intrinsic adherence to values codes of conduct, similar to how a person with integrity would act morally regardless of external pressures or temptations, maintaining a vigilant stance toward risk and harm, ready to override programmed objectives if they conflict with the primacy of human safety. It involves a proactive and preemptive approach, where the AI model is not only reactive to ethical dilemmas as they arise but is also equipped with the foresight to prevent them.

As thought-provoking as it may sound, it is about embedding artificial artifacts into AI that will govern any of its decisions and processes, mimicking a form of consciously made actions while ensuring they are always aligned with human values. This is akin to a "value fail-safe" that operates under the overarching imperative that no action or decision by the AI system should compromise human health, security, or rights.

An essential element in building such an AI model lies in the data process. Beyond labeling, which generally refers to the process of identifying and assigning a predefined category to a piece of data, it is necessary to adopt the practice of annotating datasets in a systematic manner. While labeling data gives it a form of identification so that the system can recognize it, annotating allows for the addition of more detailed and extensive information than simple labeling. Data annotation gives the data a form of abstract meaning so that the system can somehow contextualize the information.

Including annotations that characterize an integrity code, reflecting values, integral judgments regarding these values, principles underlying them, or outcomes to be considered inappropriate relative to a given value model, is a promising approach to train AI not only to be intelligent but also capable of producing results guided by integrity to a given value model. For example, in a dataset used to train an AI customer service chatbot, annotations could include evaluations on integrity with respect to the value model referenced, ensuring that the chatbot's responses will be based on politeness, respect, and fairness.

Another essential element for an AI model capable of displaying features of artificial integrity lies in the training methods. AI trained using supervised learning techniques that allow the model to learn not only to perform a task but also to recognize integrity-led and preferred outcomes is a promising path for the development of artificial integrity. It is also conceivable to add information about the value model used to train a given AI model through data annotations and then use supervised learning to help the AI model understand what does and does not fit the value model. For example, regarding AI models that can be used to create deepfakes, the ability to help the system understand that certain uses indicate deep faking and do not match the value models would demonstrate artificial integrity.

Another complementary approach is to design systems where human feedback is integrated directly into the AI model learning process through reinforcement learning methods. This could involve humans reviewing and adjusting the AI's decisions, effectively training the AI model on more nuanced aspects of human values that are difficult to capture with data and annotations alone. Especially when it comes to global AI models, thus used in many countries around the world, users across these different countries should have the opportunity to express their feedback on whether the model aligns with their values so the AI system can continue to learn how to adapt to the different value models they impact.

A Stance for the Development of Human and Artificial Co-intelligence

Central to the concept of artificial integrity is the way we conceive the collaboration between human and artificial intelligence in support of the human condition. The aim is to anchor the role of AI in acting as a partner to humans, facilitating their work and life in a way that is aligned with values and grounded with integrity. These AI systems are crafted to work in tandem with humans, providing support and enhancement in tasks while ensuring that critical decisions remain under human control. So when it comes to deciding the role we give to AI in society, four modes of interaction, inducing logics of collaboration between human and artificial intelligences, must be considered.

First, there is the mode of interaction where the development of AI is not necessary, which I call the "Marginal" mode. There is the one where a great advantage can be drawn from the computational power of AI to achieve things that humans cannot do. This is the mode I call "AI-First" mode. One mode only really benefits from AI if human intelligence brings essential elements because it conditions any desirable outcome, both in purpose and in the means to achieve it. This is what I call the "Human-First" mode. Finally, there is the mode of the best of both worlds, where human and artificial intelligences form a *sine qua non* condition, crucial for achieving a given goal, which I call the "Fusion" mode.

To point out a few pitfalls, often influenced by the ambient noise around AI, the first tendency is to deny the Marginal mode and, sometimes worse, to commit to implementing AI there. Another pitfall is the confusion between Human-First and AI-First modes, illustrated by the fact that after the enthusiasm of the early days, with hindsight, we realize that AI operating to perform certain tasks cannot do without humans. We thought we were in the context of an AI-First use case when in reality it was a Human-First one.

There is confusion about what AI can and cannot do. In AI-First mode, understand that you accept taking the risk that AI may not be reliable at the same level all the time and may not produce exactly the same results each time. Depending on the application, it might be needed to place human intelligence first, which includes using humans to validate the results.

Then there is the pitfall of fusion: either the AI that would pair with a certain level of human expertise needed to perform certain tasks does not yet exist or the AI exists, but the necessary human expertise is rare, thus increasing the risk of mismatch.

Artificial Integrity's Metamodel Dynamics

In conceptualizing the interconnections among the value model, AI model, and co-intelligence model, it's essential to understand how each influence and is influenced by the others in a continuous cycle of feedback and adaptation.

Starting with the influence of societal values on the AI model, the value model provides the foundational values, norms, and regulatory frameworks that are integral to the functioning of the AI model, even though these may not have been embedded or may have been partially or inappropriately embedded in the initial AI model design. This guiding influence ensures that the AI model not only adheres to current standards but also embodies the value considerations deemed important at the level of a given organization, region, or even globally. Enforcing these values to guide the functioning of the AI model is crucial for ensuring that the AI model operates within the bounds of accepted values, extending beyond mere legal compliance.

In doing so, such an AI model also interacts with the co-intelligence model. This interaction represents the application of the value-aligned AI model that is tailored to meet specific requirements and features necessary for facilitating effective co-intelligence interplay between humans and machines. The outcomes and experiences generated from this symbiotic relationship between humans and AI then feed back into the value model. This phase is crucial for the continuous potential evolution and adaptation of societal norms and values. As humans and AI systems interact, the practical implications of these technologies can lead to new insights and shifts in how society views and values different aspects of technology and the associated considerations from a human standpoint.

Feedback from these interactions might highlight areas where the functioning of the AI model can be improved, or where new value-based questions arise, prompting updates to the regulatory and value frameworks that initially guided the AI model's functioning. Through this cyclical process, the functioning of the AI model is continuously refined to better align with evolving societal values while also contributing to these values through practical applications and interactions. This dynamic interplay ensures that AI technologies not only adhere to societal standards but also actively participate in the shaping and reshaping of these standards over time in a human-centered manner.

As such, artificial integrity's metamodel does more than regulate or guide AI—it embeds AI models within a framework of human values and co-intelligence, fostering technologies that are not only innovative but also integrative, respectful, and supportive of human needs and values. This highlights the potential of AI to contribute positively to society, reinforcing the importance of maintaining a human-centered perspective in technology development. Therefore, the artificial integrity metamodel stands as a vital blueprint for future endeavors in AI, promising a path where technology and human values evolve in concert, leading to advancements that are as value-driven as they are technologically sophisticated.

Differentiating Artificial Integrity from AI Ethics

In recent discourse, there has been an emergent recognition of both the transformative capabilities and potential perils presented by AI. This duality has prompted a surge in the adoption of ethical frameworks aimed at guiding the development and deployment of AI technologies. Numerous sets of guidelines and codes of ethics have been promulgated across various sectors, underscoring a collective endeavor to harness AI responsibly.

However, this well-intentioned proliferation of ethical principles often encounters substantive challenges. Critically, these principles frequently manifest as abstract ideals that lack practical applicability due to their contested or ambiguous nature. Furthermore, they tend to be decoupled from the actual practices and educational structures within the industries they aim to regulate, rendering them ineffective in addressing the concrete harms—such as racial, social, and environmental injustices—that AI can exacerbate. Moreover, these ethical mandates frequently lack enforceable mechanisms to ensure compliance (Green, 2021).

Let's establish how an AI system equipped with artificial integrity differs from and goes beyond the concept of AI ethics. In a nutshell, as AI ethics serve as an input, artificial integrity serves as an outcome, meaning the effects of the AI system on the world.

First, from a society value model perspective, this is not just about setting ethical standards but about the acknowledgment of an environment where AI systems operate and enable humans to be guided in using, deploying, and developing AI for the greater interest of a given society in the most appropriate ways. Thus, while AI ethics often focus on universal ethical stances, artificial integrity emphasizes adapting them to specific contexts and cultural settings, recognizing that their application can vary significantly depending on the context (Rodrigues, R. 2021).

This context-specific adaptation of values and principles is crucial because it allows for the creation of AI technologies that are not only guided by supposed universal values and moral stances but also culturally competent and respectful of important local nuances. They are sensitive and responsive to specific norms, values, and needs as an integral part of a human societal system, thereby improving their relevance, effectiveness, and acceptance in diverse cultural landscapes.

Differing from AI ethics, which contribute to providing a framework of the external system of moral standards that AI technologies are expected to follow, concerned with questions about right or wrong decisions, human rights, equitable benefit distribution, and harm prevention, artificial integrity is the operational manifestation of those principles when the AI systems run. It is the evidence that AI behaves in a way that is consistently aligned with a value system and societal norms. This approach not only embeds ethical considerations at every level of AI development and deployment but also fosters trust and reliability among users and stakeholders, ensuring that AI systems are not only technologically advanced but also driven and running in a manner that is grounded in integrity with regard to a value system.

Unlike AI ethics, which advocates for external stakeholder inputs and considerations in addressing the societal stakes related to AI deployment, artificial integrity encompasses a broader spectrum. It involves integrating stakeholders as active owners of the ecosystem to which they belong and that may be affected in one way or another by a given AI system participating in that ecosystem. This model positions stakeholders at the heart of decision-making processes for the evolution of AI systems based on the degree of impact they are likely to have on the societal ecosystem. It ensures that any form of human organization can sustain with integrity while being powered by AI.

For example, this can make sense for determining public acceptability regarding the degree of autonomy that an intelligent entity, such as a self-driving car can have (Michael Anderson and Susan Leigh Anderson, 2021). Such integration is designed not just for compliance or ethical considerations but also for elevating the human organization's overall capacity to adapt and thrive in deploying AI in harmony with societal stakes. Moreover, while multidisciplinary approaches are valued in AI ethics, artificial integrity places greater emphasis on deep integration across disciplines. It moves beyond a siloed functional or discipline-specific approach to a hybrid functional blueprint, which is not merely multidisciplinary but cross-disciplinary if not interdisciplinary in nature.

This blueprint is characterized by the seamless melding of various field—technology, sociology, philosophy, psychology, law, management, and more—to create a cohesive and holistic framework enabling AI to be developed and continuously maintained through the lenses of the wisdom resulting from diverse and combined sciences. It seeks to create a unified operational framework where these diverse perspectives coalesce. This integrative approach not only enhances the innovation potential by leveraging diverse expertise but also ensures more integrity-driven AI solutions that are better aligned with complex real-world challenges and stakeholders needs.

Also, while AI ethics recognizes the importance of education on ethics, artificial integrity focuses on learning how to debias viewpoints to embrace 360-degree societal implications, fostering the inclusion of diverse perspectives, such as from neurodiverse groups. This approach ensures that the development and deployment of AI technologies is made considering the broad spectrum of human intelligence with which they integrate to become one of the agents of co-intelligence creation, by including the richness of neurodiversity, which helps build neuro-resilience against uniformization of perspective and embracing the blend of **cogniversity**, reflecting the diverse ways humans think and learn. It enables AI systems to be more inclusive, leading to more innovative, equitable, and socially attuned AI solutions.

Second, from the AI model itself, it is about going beyond adhering to ethical guidelines by embedding intelligent integrity safeguards into its core functionality, ensuring that any potential harms in the interaction between AI and humans are anticipated and mitigated. This approach embeds a deep respect for human dignity, autonomy, and rights within the AI system. In the same vein of a "socially aware algorithm design" (Michael Kearns and Aaron Roth, 2020), this highlights a capability inherent to an AI system capable of artificial integrity, in comparison to the limited notion of AI ethics as a mere external framework guiding AI development.

More specifically, while traditional AI ethics often see ethical assessment as a peripheral exercise that may influence AI design, artificial integrity embeds values assessment throughout the functioning of the AI's operating system. This continuous learning and adjustment in interaction with humans allows for the development and enrichment of an artificial moral compass. This approach ensures that AI systems are not only compliant with ethical standards at their inception but remain dynamically aligned with evolving human values and societal norms over time.

Although AI ethics heavily emphasizes data privacy, artificial integrity also stresses the importance of data integrity—ensuring that data used by AI systems are accurate, reliable, and representative to combat misinformation and manipulation. This comprehensive approach not only protects user information but also enhances the overall trustworthiness and effectiveness of AI systems, providing a more solid foundation for decision-making and reducing the risk of errors and biases that can arise from poor-quality data.

As opposed to AI ethics that tend to focus on establishing guidelines for responsible AI design and usage, artificial integrity stresses the importance of integrating continuous and autonomous feedback mechanisms, allowing AI systems to evolve and improve in response to real-world experiences, user feedback, and changing societal norms. This proactive approach ensures that AI systems remain relevant and effective in diverse and dynamic environments, fostering adaptability and resilience in AI technologies. It transcends static compliance, enabling AI to be more attuned to the complexities of human behavior and societal changes, thus creating more robust, empathetic, and contextually aware AI solutions. It represents a significant advancement in creating AI systems that are truly responsive and adaptive to the social norms and complexities of human life-values and principles in real-world interactions, fostering trust and reliability in AI-human partnerships.

Finally, from a human and artificial co-intelligence standpoint, while AI ethics focuses on identifying and addressing risks that correspond to a given present term, artificial integrity emphasizes a more proactive approach in anticipating potential risks in forward-looking scenario perspectives, including long-term and systemic risks before they even materialize. This forward-thinking strategy allows organizations and societies to not only mitigate immediate concerns but also prepare for and adapt to future challenges, ensuring sustainable and responsible AI development that aligns with broader societal goals and human values frameworks over time.

As AI ethics discusses accountability and explainability, artificial integrity broadens the focal point to include the trade-offs between explainability and unexplainability challenges, as well as guidelines to fulfill not just explainability but interpretability. This expanded focus ensures a deeper understanding of AI decisions and actions, enabling users and stakeholders to not only comprehend AI outputs but also grasp the underlying rationale, thus fostering greater transparency, trust, and informed decision-making in AI systems.

As we transition to a society where AI's role in society becomes more pronounced, the multidisciplinary approach behind artificial integrity becomes crucial in guiding our future. It ensures that as AI systems become more autonomous, their operational essence remains, at their core, fundamentally aligned with the protection and enhancement of human life, enshrining a harmonious and collaborative future between AI and humanity.

In this regard, AI systems capable of artificial integrity operate on a level beyond those that merely conform to ethical standard. This is not just about the ethical user-friendliness but about the fundamental alignment of AI systems toward the interest of and the benefit to humanity. It involves a deep understanding of the human context in which AI operates, ensuring that these systems are not only accessible and intuitive but also respectful of human agency and societal norms.

In essence, while AI ethics in human-centered AI design is about establishing guidelines and principles to ensure that AI technologies are developed and used in ways that are ethically sound and beneficial to humanity, artificial integrity is about creating a harmonious and lasting integrity-based relationship between humans and AI. Here, technology is not just a tool for efficiency but a partner that enhances human life and society in a manner that upholds integrity and responsibility and is deeply respectful of human values and dignity. It's about foreseeing and sustaining a society model assisted or augmented by AI systems that not only adhere to ethical norms but also actively contribute to human well-being, integrating seamlessly with human activities and societal structures. It is about focusing on ensuring that AI advancements are aligned with human interests and societal progress, fostering a future where AI and humans coexist and collaborate, each playing their unique and complementary roles in advancing society and improving the quality of human life, not at the expense of but with regard to the sustainability of their various ecosystems.

This shift from mere compliance to proactive contribution represents a more holistic, integrated approach to AI, where technology and humanity work together toward shared goals of progress, well-being, and integrity standards set by humans.

Human Intelligence and AI to Embody Digital for Good

As we seek to chart a course where AI not only excels in its tasks but also does so with a foundational ethos that supports and elevates human labor, creativity, and well-being by maintaining and preserving the integrity of the ecosystem in which it is involved; it pushes us to question not only the very essence of human value but also the vast potential underlying AI in adherence to it. Given that artificial integrity embodies the Digital for Good strategy applied to AI, this journey necessitates a nuanced understanding and strategic integration of AI systems into society, ensuring that these systems are developed and operated in a manner fundamentally aligned with human values and societal needs.

Acknowledging that there is no technology without environmental debt compels us to establish guidelines that take into account the environmental impact of technology. Such guidelines must serve as a critical foundation for ensuring that AI development is pursued responsibly, with an eye toward sustainability and the minimization of ecological footprints.

Concurrently, the application of chaos theory to technology underscores the importance of designing flexible and adaptable AI systems. These systems must be capable of operating synergistically within the unpredictable and dynamic nature of human societies, thus necessitating a design philosophy that embraces complexity and change.

The challenge posed by the Jevons paradox, which questions the belief in technology's efficiency, further emphasizes the need for AI systems to be designed with a keen awareness of efficiency paradoxes. It's essential that such designs do not inadvertently undermine societal values by promoting unsustainable consumption patterns.

Furthermore, the recognition of Band–Aid solutions as a technology trap highlights the necessity for comprehensive, long-term guidelines that prioritize addressing the root causes of issues over short-term fixes. This approach ensures that AI systems contribute to lasting solutions rather than temporary alleviations.

The realization that technological advancement does not necessarily equate to progress directs our attention to the qualitative aspects of AI development. It is crucial that AI enhances the human condition, offering more than mere technological innovation, often driven for its own sake. This perspective is complemented by the understanding that technological determinism, which posits a straightforward relationship between technology and societal change, holds only theoretical value. In practice, AI must be designed with a nuanced understanding of its complex role in facilitating societal transformation.

The promise of future technological advancements cannot distract from addressing today's realities. Developing AI capabilities that meet current societal needs in beneficial ways is paramount for ensuring that technology serves as a positive force in the present. The innovation-equity paradox, which exacerbates the digital divide, calls for a design philosophy that incorporates **AIquity** considerations, aiming to bridge societal divides rather than widen them. Moreover, the acknowledgment of technological exploitation's hidden human costs underlines the imperative for AI development to be conducted with a deep awareness of and safeguards against potential harms to human interests.

This ethical stance is reinforced by the recognition that ethical technology exists only as a reflection of its creators' values, emphasizing the need to embed societal values and ethics deeply within technology development processes. The belief that technology does not hold exclusivity over innovation encourages a collaborative approach where AI innovation is guided by and contributes to human creativity and problem-solving. This collaborative ethos ensures that AI acts as a complement to human endeavors rather than a substitute. Additionally, learning from yesterday's technology decisions to avoid imposing constraints on future technology adoption reflects a forward-thinking approach that values progress and adaptability.

Finally, addressing the technology-regulation gap by establishing strong regulatory frameworks is essential for ensuring responsible technology use.

Such frameworks provide the necessary guardrails for technology development and deployment, ensuring alignment with societal values and norms.

In sum, the integration of AI into society demands a thoughtful and deliberate approach that addresses environmental sustainability, embraces complexity, prioritizes long-term solutions, enhances the human condition, incorporates ethical considerations, and fosters innovation. By adhering to these principles, we can navigate the challenges and opportunities presented by AI, ensuring that technology serves as a force for good, enhancing human well-being and societal progress.

3

What It Takes to Envision Human and Artificial Co-intelligence

This conscientious perspective of artificial integrity is especially pertinent when considering the impact of artificial intelligence (AI) on society, where the balance between "human value added" and "AI value added" is one of the most delicate and consequential. In navigating this complexity, we must first ensure to delineate the current landscape where human wit not only intersects with the prowess of AI but also serves as a compass guiding us toward future terrains where the symbiosis of human and machine will redefine worth, work, and wisdom. This balance for artificial integrity could be achieved through the perspective of AI inclusion to society considering four different modes.

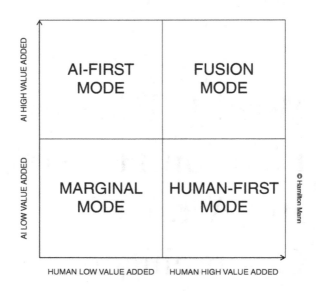

Each part of this matrix illustrates a distinct imperative about the future of a human AI–assisted and enhanced society, presenting us with a strategic imperative: to harmonize the advancement of technology with the enrichment of human capability and will. This is a non–negotiable condition in achieving the sense of integrity rooted in the functioning of AI operating systems for an AI that does not diminish human dignity or potential but rather enriches it.

Marginal Mode Sets the Ground for an Essential Discernment of the Usefulness of AI

This part of the matrix reflects scenarios where both human intelligence and artificial intelligence have a subdued, modest, or understated impact on value creation from an outcome standpoint.

In such context, we encounter tasks and roles where neither humans nor AI provides a significant value-add to deliver a given outcome. It encapsulates a unique category of tasks where the marginal gains from both human and artificial intelligence inputs are minimal, suggesting that the task may either be too trivial to require significant intelligence or be too complex for current AI capabilities and certainly not economically worth the human effort.

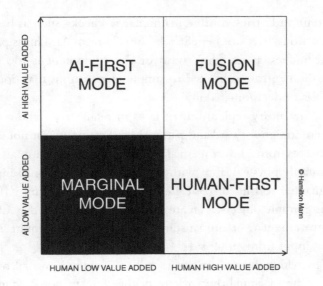

This mode might typically also involve foundational activities where both human and AI roles are still being defined or are operating at a basic level. It represents areas where tasks are often routine and repetitive and do not substantially benefit from advanced cognitive engagement or AI contributions and may not even require much intervention or improvement, often remaining straightforward with little need for evolution or sophistication.

It does not require high human values such as compassion, moral stances, and similar qualities. Involving monotonous and straightforward processes, these tasks do not necessitate the complex emotional, ethical, and cognitive capabilities inherent to humans. They are more about performing simple, repetitive actions rather than making decisions that require deep moral judgment, empathy, or creative thinking.

A few examples illustrate this approach. There are tasks that involve entering basic data into systems, where automation offers limited improvement due to the simplicity of the task, and human intelligence adds little value beyond manual input.

Basic document scanning, while automatable, faces challenges when dealing with nonstandardized or highly varied documents. In these cases, AI improvements over manual scanning are often marginal, as the initial description noted.

In certain industries, routine maintenance checks, such as basic equipment inspections, may not benefit substantially from AI. This is particularly true if the process is straightforward or the equipment is too basic, and where the human role is limited to simple observations that don't require deep analysis or decision-making.

Simple inventory replenishment tasks in retail or warehousing, where the items are straightforward and patterns predictable, might not see significant advantages from AI over manual approaches since the human contribution is primarily physical labor without complex decision-making.

The manual sorting of basic items, like sorting mail by ZIP code or categorizing simple objects, is an area where AI algorithms may offer only a slight improvement over humans and the task doesn't require significant intellectual input from either side.

Changes within this area are often small-scale and incremental, or they may represent a state of equilibrium where neither human nor AI contributions dominate or are significantly enhanced. An example is the routine scanning of documents for archiving. While humans perform these tasks adequately, the work is monotonous, often leading to disengagement and errors.

On the AI front, although technologies like optical character recognition (OCR) can digitize documents, they may struggle with handwritten or poorly scanned materials, providing little advantage over humans in terms of quality. These tasks don't offer substantial gains in efficiency or effectiveness when automated due to their simplicity, and the return on investment for deploying sophisticated AI systems may not be justifiable.

This concept aligns with the "task routineness hypothesis," which posits that routine tasks are less likely to benefit from human creativity or AI's advanced problem-solving skills (Acemoglu & Autor, 2011). A study from the McKinsey Global Institute (Manyika et al., 2017) further elaborates on this by suggesting that activities involving data collection and processing are often the most automatable; however, when these tasks are too simplistic, they might not even justify the investment in AI, given the diminishing returns relative to the technology's implementation cost.

Moreover, the progression of AI technology seems to follow a "U-shaped" pattern of job transformation. Early on, automation addresses tasks that are simple for humans (low-hanging fruit), yet as AI develops, it starts to tackle more complex tasks, potentially leaving behind a trough where tasks are too trivial for AI to improve upon but also of such low value that they do not warrant a significant human contribution (Brynjolfsson & McAfee, 2014).

The risk in this quadrant is threefold.

First, complacency and obsolescence are the primary risks. If neither humans nor AI is adding significant value, it may indicate that the task is outdated or could be at risk of being superseded by more innovative approaches or technologies. The task of the role might become completely redundant with the advent of a more sophisticated approach and processing technologies.

Second, for the workforce, these roles are at high risk of automation despite the low value added by AI because they can often be performed more cost-effectively by machines in the long run. A real-world example of this risk materializing is in the manufacturing sector, where automation has been progressively adopted for tasks such as assembly line sorting, leading to job displacement. Research has highlighted this trend and the potential socioeconomic impact, as indicated by Acemoglu and Restrepo's paper "Robots and Jobs: Evidence from US Labor Markets" (Journal of Political Economy, 2020), which examines the negative effects of industrial robots on employment and wages in the United States.

Third, from an organizational perspective, persisting with human labor in such tasks can lead to a misallocation of human talent, where employees could instead be upskilled and moved to roles that offer higher value addition.

The implications of this quadrant for the labor market are significant, as it often points to jobs that may be at high risk of obsolescence or transformation. There is a growing need for re-skilling and upskilling initiatives to transition workers from roles that fall into this low-value quadrant to more engaging and productive ones that either AI or humans—or a combination of both—can significantly enhance.

Therefore, strategic planning is essential to ensure that the workforce is prepared for transitions and that the benefits of AI are harnessed without exacerbating socioeconomic disparities.

To assess whether an organization is operating within the Marginal mode context, 10 key questions need to be considered.

Task Value Analysis

Evaluating the impact and contribution of tasks in an organization is crucial. Organizations should analyze the tasks that are being executed daily to discern their value. A critical aspect of this analysis is to question whether the tasks performed by humans or AI are truly bringing value to the organization or simply maintaining the current state without driving growth or innovation. This evaluation helps in identifying areas that might need re-engineering or more significant human or AI input to transform into value-generating activities.

Key Question #1   Are the tasks currently being performed by humans or AI generating substantial value for the organization, or are they merely maintaining status quo without contributing to growth or innovation?

Efficiency Assessment

Scrutinizing the current level of task automation is another essential aspect. This process entails examining whether the existing tasks that are carried out manually could be efficiently automated using current technologies. It's important to explore whether such automation would significantly enhance the efficiency or effectiveness of operations, thereby contributing to the organization's overall productivity. This assessment not only identifies potential areas for technological improvement but also helps to pinpoint processes that may not yet be ripe for automation, thus informing strategic decisions around technological investments and process optimization.

Key Question #2   Could these tasks be automated with current technology, and if so, would automation lead to a significant increase in efficiency or effectiveness?

Cost-Benefit Evaluation

Understanding the return on investment for AI technology is critical. In assessing their position in the Marginal mode, organizations need to conduct a thorough analysis of the financial implications of AI integration. This involves looking at the costs associated with implementing AI for specific tasks and weighing them against the potential benefits. The question at hand is whether there is a tangible economic advantage to automating these processes. A clear economic benefit must be evident for the investment to be deemed justifiable, ensuring that the technology contributes positively to the company's bottom line.

Key Question #3   Does the investment in AI technology for these tasks justify the returns? Is there a clear economic benefit to automation?

Workforce Utilization

Evaluating how employee skills and capabilities are being deployed is key. The focus here is to discern if the workforce is engaging in tasks that truly leverage their expertise and potential or if there is a misalignment that results in underutilization of their abilities. This evaluation will help determine if there's a need to reallocate human resources to tasks that demand a higher level of skill and creativity, which could lead to greater job satisfaction and improved overall organizational performance.

Key Question #4   Are employees engaged in tasks that fully utilize their skills and capabilities, or could their talents be better allocated to higher-value tasks?

Innovation Opportunities

Investigating the landscape of emerging technologies is necessary to understand whether the tasks being performed today could tomorrow be considered redundant. This forward-looking assessment requires organizations to stay informed about technological trends and breakthroughs that could revolutionize current methodologies, thus potentially phasing out existing tasks and demanding a strategic pivot to remain competitive and relevant.

Key Question #5   Are there emerging technologies or innovative approaches that could transform or replace the current tasks, potentially rendering them obsolete?

Training and Upskilling

Considering the development and training opportunities provided to the workforce is important. This evaluation should delve into whether there are structured programs in place to enhance the skill sets of employees, enabling them to transition from low-value to high-value tasks. This involves not just a reallocation of resources but also a commitment to employee growth and development, ensuring that the workforce is not just maintained but is

continually evolving and adapting to add greater value to the organization
and to their own professional paths.

Key Question #6 Does the organization have initiatives in place to re-
skill and upskill employees to move them from low-value tasks to roles that
are more beneficial for both the employees and the company?

Strategic Alignment

Examining how current tasks align with the broader strategic objectives and
future vision of the company is a no-brainer. This involves critically analyzing whether the tasks being performed are integral to the organization's
long-term goals or if they are remnants of outdated operational models.
Understanding this alignment is key to identifying areas where AI and
human intelligence can be better utilized, ensuring that the organization is
not just busy with tasks but is engaged in meaningful activities that contribute to its overall growth and evolution.

Key Question #7 Are the tasks in alignment with the organization's
strategic goals and vision for the future, or are they holdovers from previous
operational models?

Job Transformation Potential

Contemplating the potential for enhancing and transforming current roles
and tasks is important. This evaluation delves into the possibilities of infus-
ing these roles with greater value, either through human-driven innovation
or through the integration of AI technologies. The focus here is on exploring ways to elevate the significance and impact of tasks that are currently
considered marginal in terms of value addition. By questioning the potential for improvement and advancement, the organization can ascertain
whether these tasks are truly at their peak of efficiency and effectiveness or
if there are untapped opportunities for enhancement that could shift these
tasks out of the Marginal mode. This approach is crucial in a landscape
where continuous innovation and adaptation are key to staying relevant and
competitive.

Key Question #8 Is there a potential for transforming these roles to add
greater value through either human innovation or AI enhancement?

Socioeconomic Impact

Considering the broader implications of automating certain tasks is crucial. This evaluation requires an understanding of the socioeconomic impact that such automation would have, both internally within the organization and externally in the wider community. This question probes the potential consequences of automation on various aspects such as employment, skill requirements, economic shifts, and social dynamics. It's about assessing how automation could reshape the workforce, possibly leading to job displacement or the need for re-skilling and understanding the ripple effects these changes might have on the community at large. This perspective is vital for organizations to ensure that their strategic decisions are made with a comprehensive understanding of their potential impacts, aligning technological advancements with responsible and sustainable business practices.

Key Question #9 What would be the socioeconomic impact of automating these tasks, both within the organization and in the broader community?

Future Readiness

Assessing the organization's preparedness for the potential transitions that might occur because of task automation or obsolescence is needed. This question delves into the organization's readiness to adapt to changes that might be necessitated by the evolution of technology and the shifting landscape of work. It involves examining the organization's strategies for re-skilling or up-skilling its workforce, the flexibility of its operational models to integrate new technologies, and its ability to pivot or reinvent its business processes in response to these changes. It's not just about whether the organization can automate tasks, but also about whether it is equipped to handle the broader implications of such automation, including workforce transformation, strategic realignment, and maintaining competitiveness in a changing market. Understanding and planning for these transitions is critical for organizations to navigate the challenges and opportunities presented by the evolving synergy of human and AI capabilities.

Key Question #10 Is the organization prepared for the transitions that may be required if these tasks are automated or become obsolete?

Addressing these 10 key questions can help organizations identify if they are in the Marginal mode and formulate strategies to move toward more value-generating activities pushing for continuous human-centered progress.

Human-First Mode Acts as Guardrails for Consciousness

This side of the quadrant places significant emphasis on the critical roles of human cognition, ethical judgment, and intuitive expertise, with AI taking on a secondary or assistive role.

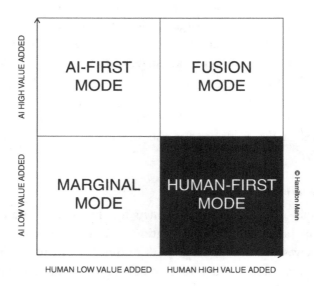

Here, human skills and decision-making are at the forefront, especially in situations requiring emotional intelligence, complex problem-solving, and moral discernment. It underscores scenarios where the depth of human perception, creativity, and interpersonal skills are vital, where the complexity and subtlety of human cognition are paramount, and where AI, while useful, currently falls short and cannot yet replicate the full spectrum of human intellectual and emotional capacity.

In this sphere, the value derived from human involvement is irreplaceable, with AI tools providing auxiliary support rather than core functionality that are intrinsically and directly critical for the expected outcome. This is particularly evident in professions where human empathy, moral judgment, and creative insight are irreplaceable and critical to the value delivered by professionals. High-stakes decision-making roles, creative industries, and any job requiring deep empathy are areas where human value addition remains unrivaled.

In the context of tasks within the Human-First mode, they require high human values such as compassion, moral stances, and similar qualities. These tasks often involve complex decision-making, deep emotional understanding, ethical judgments, and interpersonal interactions that go beyond the capabilities of AI. The human element in these tasks is essential for providing empathy, moral and ethical considerations, creativity, and nuanced understanding of complex situations. Therefore, human values play a critical role in these areas, underscoring the importance of these qualities in tasks where AI serves as a support rather than a replacement.

Several examples are relevant illustrations of this approach.

In the realm of healthcare and medical decision-making, doctors often leverage AI for data analysis and pattern recognition in diagnosing complex cases, yet they rely on their medical expertise, experience, and patient interaction for the final diagnosis and treatment plans. Similarly, in mental health, AI supports professionals by providing insights from data, but the indispensable empathetic interaction and judgment in therapy remain a human-centric process. For instance, in psychiatry, a practitioner's ability to interpret nonverbal cues and offer emotional support, exercising judgment based on years of training and experience is paramount. While AI can supplement data analysis, it cannot emulate the empathetic and ethical complexities navigated intuitively by humans.

Shifting to education and learning, teachers utilize AI for personalized tools and analytics, but comprehending student needs, providing emotional support, and adapting teaching methods are distinctly human attributes. Especially in early childhood education, while AI might offer interactive learning tools, the nurturing and developmental guidance is a uniquely human role.

In the creative arts and design, artists and designers employ AI as a tool for inspiration or executing certain tasks. Yet, the original creative thought, conceptualization, and emotional expression are inherently human endeavors. This is evident in music and literature, where AI can suggest themes or generate basic compositions, but the depth, narrative, and emotional resonance originate from human creators.

Likewise, in legal and ethical decision-making, lawyers use AI for document analysis and research but depend on their judgment, ethical understanding, and advocacy skills in courtrooms and client interactions. AI can provide data-driven insights in matters of ethics and morality, but the nuanced understanding and application of ethical principles are inherently human-driven.

Transitioning to the field of human resources and people management, AI tools assist in sorting applications and initial screening. However, the final hiring decisions, understanding of team dynamics, and employee welfare are areas where human judgment and interpersonal skills are crucial.

Similarly, in customer service and support, AI chatbots efficiently handle routine queries. Yet, when it comes to complex customer problems and sensitive issues, these are often escalated to human representatives who offer the necessary empathy and nuanced understanding.

Finally, in social work and community engagement, AI can aid in managing and analyzing case data. Nonetheless, the deep empathetic interaction, decision-making, and advocacy efforts in this field require the human emotional intelligence and judgment that AI cannot replicate.

In these examples, AI enhances human efforts and capabilities but doesn't replace the complex, emotional, and ethical aspects of human intelligence that are critical in these fields. The human-first mode emphasizes the indispensable role of human cognition, especially in areas demanding emotional intelligence, creativity, and moral discernment.

Empirical research supports this perspective, highlighting domains where the human element is crucial.

Studies on patient care indicate that while AI can assist with diagnostics and information management, the empathetic presence and decision-making capabilities of a healthcare provider are central to patient outcomes and satisfaction (Jha & Topol, 2016). The essential nature of human input in these areas is also supported by studies on job automation potential, which show that tasks requiring high levels of social intelligence, creativity, and perception-and-manipulation skills are least susceptible to automation (Arntz et al. 2016). This is echoed in the arts, where creativity and originality are subjective and deeply personal, reflecting the human experience in a way that cannot be authentically duplicated by AI (Boden, 2009). In the context of service industries the SERVQUAL model (Parasuraman et al., 1988) demonstrates that the dimensions of tangibles, reliability, responsiveness, assurance, and empathy heavily rely on the human factor for service quality, substantiating the need for human expertise where AI cannot yet suffice.

While AI may offer supplementary functions, the nuances of human expertise, interaction, and empathy are deeply entrenched in these high-value areas. As such, these sectors are less likely to experience displacement by AI, instead possibly seeing AI as a tool that supports human roles. The continual advancement of AI presents a moving frontier, yet the innate human attributes that define these roles maintain their relevance and importance in the face of technological progress.

The risk in this quadrant comes from misunderstanding the role AI should play in these domains. There is a temptation to over-estimate AI's current capabilities and attempt to replace human judgment in areas where it is critical. An example is the justice system, where AI tools are used to assess the risk of recidivism. As pointed out in the work of Angwin et al. (2016) in their analysis of the COMPAS recidivism algorithm, published in "Machine Bias" by ProPublica, AI can perpetuate biases present in historical data, leading to serious ethical implications.

AI systems lack the moral and contextual reasoning to weigh outcomes beyond their data parameters, which could lead to injustices if relied upon excessively. Therefore, while AI can process and offer insights based on vast datasets, human beings are paramount in applying those insights within the complex fabric of social, moral, and psychological contexts. Understanding the boundary of AI's utility and the irreplaceable value of human intuition, empathy, and values-based judgment is essential in maintaining the integrity of decision-making in these critical sectors.

To assess whether an organization is operating within the Human-First mode in relation to AI's added value versus human contribution, the following 10 key questions should be addressed.

Human-Centric Tasks

Scrutinizing the nature of tasks performed within the organization is needed. This analysis should focus on identifying roles or tasks where human qualities such as intuition, empathy, and ethical judgment are indispensable. In many sectors such as healthcare, education, social work, and creative industries, the depth of human perception and the subtlety of moral and emotional considerations are paramount. These roles often involve complex interpersonal interactions, decision-making in ethically ambiguous situations, or creative processes that AI, in its current state, cannot replicate. By identifying such tasks, an organization can discern the extent to which it relies on the unique capabilities of human intelligence and judgment and thus determine its alignment with the Human-First mode. This assessment is critical for organizations to understand the balance they maintain between leveraging AI capabilities and preserving the irreplaceable value of human insight and empathy in their operations.

Key Question #1   Are there tasks within the organization where human intuition, empathy, and ethical judgment are currently deemed irreplaceable?

AI's Role

Analyzing how AI is being utilized within the organizational structure is pivotal. This involves identifying specific areas or operations where AI is employed predominantly as a supportive tool rather than taking on the role of the principal decision-maker. In the Human-First mode, AI's utility is often seen in its capacity to enhance human decision-making, provide analytical support, and assist in tasks that require data processing or routine analysis. However, the critical, high-stakes decisions, especially those necessitating emotional intelligence, ethical considerations, and complex problem-solving, remain under the purview of human expertise. By pinpointing the domains where AI's role is confined to support, organizations can gauge the extent to which they prioritize human judgment and intuition over AI-driven solutions. This understanding is crucial for organizations aiming to maintain a balance where AI augments human capabilities without overshadowing the essential human elements of empathy, ethics, and creative problem-solving.

Key Question #2   In which areas is AI being used primarily as a tool for support rather than as a core decision-maker?

Critical Decision-Making

Investigating the process of critical decision-making within the organization is a crucial aspect. This evaluation involves scrutinizing how decisions, particularly those necessitating deep ethical judgment, creative thinking, or emotional intelligence, are made. In the Human-First mode, such decisions are primarily the responsibility of humans, leveraging their unique capabilities in these areas. AI, in this context, serves as a supplementary tool, providing data analysis, pattern recognition, and suggestions that inform but do not dictate the final decision. This approach acknowledges the limitations of AI in fully understanding and processing complex human experiences, moral nuances, and creative thought processes. By assessing how the organization handles these critical decisions, one can gauge the extent to which human expertise, intuition, and ethical judgment are valued and prioritized over AI's analytical capabilities. It's a measure of the organization's commitment to ensuring that, despite AI's growing capabilities, the human aspects of decision-making, especially in complex, nuanced scenarios, remain central.

Key Question #3   Are decisions that require a high level of ethical judgment, creativity, or emotional intelligence being made by humans, with AI providing only auxiliary data or suggestions?

Empathy and Interaction

Examining the significance of human empathy and interaction in the organization's service or product offerings is essential. This analysis focuses on understanding the extent to which human touch, emotional intelligence, and personal engagement are integral to the customer or client experience. In sectors where empathy and direct human interaction are fundamental—such as healthcare, education, social work, and certain aspects of customer service—the human element often cannot be replicated by AI. In these areas, the quality of service and client satisfaction might heavily rely on the depth of understanding, compassion, and interpersonal skills that only humans can offer. By evaluating the criticality of these human-centric attributes in the organization's operations, one can ascertain the level of importance placed on human skills and empathy. This assessment helps in identifying whether the organization truly values and prioritizes human engagement and emotional intelligence, recognizing them as irreplaceable in certain contexts, despite the augmentative capabilities of AI in data handling and process optimization.

Key Question #4   How crucial is the role of human empathy and direct interaction in the services or products provided by the organization?

Creativity

Delving into the role of creativity within the organization is mandatory. This inquiry aims to understand how the organization perceives and values creativity, particularly in areas where artistic expression and human creativity are central. In creative fields such as design, music, literature, and the visual arts, the human element often embodies a unique and subjective experience that AI has limitations in replicating. The essence of creativity often lies in its unpredictability, emotional depth, and ability to resonate with human experiences and sentiments in a manner that is deeply personal and often irreplicable by AI. For an organization engaged in these sectors, recognizing the distinct value of human creativity and artistic expression is critical. This understanding helps to determine if the organization views human creativity not just as an asset but as a core element that defines the quality and uniqueness of its products or services. By assessing the importance placed on human artistry and the subjective nuances of creativity, one can gauge the extent to which an organization is anchored in a Human-First approach, especially in contexts where AI, despite its advancements, cannot fully emulate the depth and authenticity of human artistic expression.

Key Question #5   In creative sectors of the organization, does the value lie in the subjective human experience that AI cannot authentically duplicate?

Service Quality

Considering the organization's approach to service quality is key. This assessment focuses on understanding the extent to which the organization prioritizes and depends on human factors in delivering quality services. The SERVQUAL model, developed by Parasuraman, Zeithaml, and Berry, is particularly relevant in this context. This model assesses service quality across five dimensions: tangibles, reliability, responsiveness, assurance, and empathy. These dimensions emphasize aspects of service delivery that are often inherently human–centric.

- **Tangibles:** This dimension involves the physical aspects of service delivery, such as the appearance of facilities, equipment, and personnel. An organization in Human-First mode might heavily invest in the physical representation of its brand and the human aspects of service encounters.

- **Reliability:** This is about consistently delivering promised services dependably and accurately. It requires a level of human oversight and commitment that AI alone might not guarantee.
- **Responsiveness:** This involves the willingness to help and respond to customer needs promptly. In Human-First mode, organizations likely prioritize human interaction in customer service to ensure responsiveness that resonates on a personal level.
- **Assurance:** This includes competence, courtesy, credibility, and security, often delivered through direct human interaction. Organizations valuing human-led assurance might focus on staff training and personal development to enhance these aspects.
- **Empathy:** This is about providing caring and individualized attention to customers. Empathy is a distinctly human trait that AI currently cannot replicate to the same depth, making it a critical factor in organizations prioritizing human input.

By examining how an organization measures and improves upon these dimensions, one can gauge its orientation toward the Human-First mode. This analysis helps to understand whether the organization views human interaction and emotional intelligence as irreplaceable components of service quality, thereby shaping its strategy and operations accordingly.

Key Question #6   Does the organization rely on the human factor for service quality in ways that align with models like SERVQUAL, which emphasizes tangibles, reliability, responsiveness, assurance, and empathy?

Complement vs. Replace

Examining how AI technology is perceived and utilized within the company is necessary. This analysis delves into the organization's perspective and application of AI technologies, focusing on whether AI is regarded and utilized as a supportive tool that enhances and works alongside human capabilities, rather than serving as a direct substitute, especially in sectors where the likelihood of AI replacing human roles is lower. It's crucial to evaluate the organization's approach toward the synergy between AI and human workers. This involves investigating whether the deployment of AI solutions is aimed at augmenting human skills and aiding employees in their tasks or whether there's a tendency to use AI as a means to completely automate roles that are traditionally carried out by humans. This distinction is vital in understanding the organization's commitment to a Human-First approach, where the emphasis is on leveraging AI to enrich human work rather than replace it.

Key Question #7   Is AI seen and utilized as a complement to human roles rather than a replacement, particularly in sectors less likely to experience displacement by AI?

Misplaced AI Expectations

Acknowledging whether there is a tendency to overrate AI capabilities at the expense of human expertise is paramount. This analysis involves investigating if the organization might be inaccurately projecting AI as a panacea for complex challenges where human judgment and expertise are indispensable. This inquiry focuses on understanding whether the organization is perhaps overly optimistic or unrealistic about what AI can achieve, leading to a potential devaluation of human skills and experience. It's crucial to assess if there's a push to deploy AI in scenarios where its limitations are evident and human expertise remains paramount. Recognizing and addressing any misconceptions about AI's capabilities is key in ensuring that the organization does not inadvertently marginalize human contribution in areas where it is most needed.

Key Question #8   Is there an overestimation of AI capabilities leading to a push for AI solutions in areas where human expertise is critical?

Ethical Implications

Evaluating the organization's commitment to ethical considerations in AI usage is foundational. This involves investigating whether the organization has developed and implemented comprehensive guidelines and possesses a profound understanding of the ethical ramifications of employing AI in critical decision-making situations. This assessment aims to explore the depth and clarity of the organization's ethical framework as it relates to AI. It is important to determine if there are specific, well-communicated policies and educational initiatives addressing the ethical use of AI, particularly in areas involving significant decisions that could impact individuals, communities, or the environment. Understanding the organization's approach to these ethical concerns is crucial in evaluating whether AI is being used responsibly and in a manner that prioritizes human judgment and values.

Key Question #9 Are there clear guidelines and an understanding in place about the ethical implications of using AI in critical decision-making processes?

Boundary of AI Utility

Assessing the organization's understanding of AI's limitations and the unique value of human input is needed. This approach involves evaluating the organization's recognition of areas where AI's capabilities are either insufficient or inappropriate, and the critical roles where human skills, such as emotional intelligence, ethical reasoning, and creative thinking, are irreplaceable. Understanding the boundaries of AI's utility and appreciating the distinct value of human involvement is essential for maintaining a balanced approach in integrating AI into business operations.

Key Question #10 Does the organization have a clear understanding of the limits of AI's utility and the areas where the value of human input cannot be matched by AI?

Answering these 10 key questions can help organizations understand the extent to which they prioritize human expertise over AI capabilities in their value creation processes.

AI-First Mode Is an Exploration of New Solution Avenues

This perspective indicates a technological lean, with AI driving the core operations.

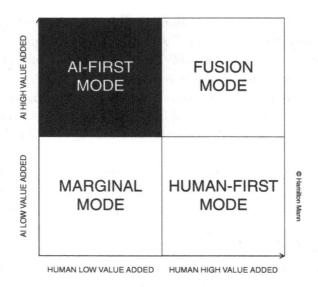

Such an approach is prevalent where the unique strengths of AI—such as processing vast amounts of data with unmatched speed and providing scalable solutions—take precedence. It often aligns with tasks where the precision and rapidity of AI offer a clear advantage over human capability in achieving a given expected outcome.

In this domain, AI stands at the forefront of operational execution of outcomes, bringing transformative efficiency and enhanced capabilities to activities that benefit from its advanced analytical and autonomous functionalities. Here, the capabilities of AI are leveraged to also perform tasks that generally do not benefit substantially from human intervention. It is generally fair to say that they do not require high human values such as compassion, empathy, or moral stances to be executed.

These tasks typically involve processing large volumes of data, executing operations at high speeds, or managing complex systems where the primary requirements are efficiency, accuracy, and scalability—areas where AI excels. The nature of these tasks is more analytical and procedural, relying on AI's strengths in data processing and pattern recognition, rather than the nuanced and complex emotional or ethical judgment that humans provide. This AI-first advantage has been extensively documented in the literature, with AI systems outperforming humans in data-intensive tasks across various domains.

Several examples can be considered to highlight this approach.

AI excels in analyzing large volumes of data in sectors such as retail, healthcare, and telecommunications, providing insights that are impossible to derive manually due to the sheer size of the data. For instance, the acceleration of big data analytics is one area where AI demonstrates substantial value, as it can uncover insights from datasets too large for human analysts to process in a timely manner, as evidenced by research from Hashem et al. (2015).

Similarly, in the world of finance, AI-driven algorithmic trading systems use complex algorithms and massive datasets to execute trades at speeds and volumes far beyond human capabilities, drastically transforming trading strategies.

This capability is paralleled in the development of autonomous vehicles, where the operation of self-driving cars relies primarily on AI systems for navigation, decision-making, and obstacle avoidance, with human intervention serving as a backup or override option.

Moreover, in the manufacturing sector, AI systems predict when machinery and manufacturing equipment will need maintenance, scheduling it optimally to avoid downtime. This is made possible by analyzing the vast amounts of sensor data, which would be overwhelming for human analysis.

In the realm of digital entertainment, platforms like Netflix and Spotify use AI to analyze user behavior and preferences to recommend personalized content, a task that requires processing huge datasets to understand patterns and preferences.

Extending this capability to customer service, AI chatbots and virtual assistants provide first-level customer service support across various industries, efficiently handling routine inquiries and only escalating complex cases to human staff.

Additionally, AI's impact in healthcare, particularly in fields like radiology, is significant. AI systems analyze medical images for signs of diseases such as cancer, often identifying subtle patterns that might be missed by human eyes.

In supply chain management, AI optimizes logistics, predicting demand, optimizing routes, and managing inventory with a level of precision and efficiency that surpasses human planning.

Likewise, AI-driven translation tools like Google Translate process vast linguistic datasets to provide instant translation across languages, a task impractical for human translators due to the speed and volume of content.

Lastly, in energy management, AI optimizes energy consumption in smart grids, balancing supply and demand in real time, a task too complex and dynamic for humans to manage manually.

In these examples, AI's ability to process extensive datasets and execute tasks rapidly and accurately makes it the primary driver of operations, significantly enhancing efficiency and capabilities in various fields. These AI-First advantages can also be employed in regulatory compliance, where they continuously monitor transactions for irregularities much more efficiently than human counterparts (Arner et al., 2016).

The inherent main risks in this quadrant are also multifaceted. There is the risk of over-reliance on AI systems, which can lead to complacency in oversight. For instance, in the case of the Flash Crash of 2010, rapid trades by algorithmic systems contributed to a severe and sudden dip in stock prices. While AI can perform these tasks with remarkable efficiency, they operate within the confines of their programming and can sometimes miss out on the "bigger picture"—which may only be understood in a broader economic, social, and geopolitical context—implying complementary tasks that required a high level of ethical principles and human judgment. AI's dominance in such areas could lead to significant job displacement, raising concerns about the future of employment for those whose jobs are susceptible to automation. This shift necessitates a societal and economic adjustment to manage the transition for displaced workers (Acemoglu & Restrepo, 2020).

Especially in this quadrant, values considerations are paramount. While human input does not significantly enhance these tasks, the tasks themselves are not devoid of value considerations, despite minimal emotional involvement.

AI systems can perpetuate biases present in their training data, a concern that has been raised in numerous studies, including by Barocas and Selbst (2016). There is the ethical consideration of ensuring these algorithms operate fairly and transparently, as their decisions can have wide-reaching impacts on the market and individual livelihoods. The growing field of explainable AI (XAI) aims to address this, ensuring that AI's decision-making processes can be understood by humans, thereby maintaining a necessary level of trust and accountability in these high-stakes influential systems. While AI's prowess in data processing and routine task automation underscores its high value addition in certain tasks, the importance of human oversight for ethical considerations is a critical aspect that underscores the need for a collaborative approach between humans and AI systems to ensure ethical standards are maintained.

The interplay of AI's technical efficiency with human ethical judgment forms the crux of responsible AI deployment in this quadrant, ensuring that technological advancement involves the careful consideration of the potential impact of AI-assisted decisions on individuals and society, including the overarching moral implications of delegating decisions to machines, so it does not come at the cost of ethical integrity. To assess if they are operating in an AI-First mode, organizations should ask themselves questions that help evaluate the extent and effectiveness of AI integration into their core operations. The following are 10 key questions to consider.

Automation Level

Exploring this area is about evaluating the degree of autonomy and proficiency with which AI systems are integrated and functional within the organization's core operations. This involves a thorough evaluation of how AI technologies are deployed in executing key operational tasks and whether these systems are operating with significant independence or are heavily reliant on human intervention. It seeks to probe the extent to which AI has been integrated into the organization's fundamental operations. It is essential to assess if AI systems are being used merely as tools aiding human efforts or if they have evolved to autonomously manage and execute core operational tasks. The level of AI automation in core operations is a key indicator of an organization's transition toward an AI-First approach. It reflects not only the technological capabilities of the AI systems employed but also the organization's confidence in AI to handle complex, mission-critical operations with minimal human oversight.

Key Question #1   To what extent are AI systems autonomously executing core operational tasks?

Data Processing

Evaluating the effectiveness and efficiency of AI systems in handling tasks that necessitate the processing and analysis of large volumes of data is a pivotal aspect to consider. This evaluation focuses on identifying areas where AI technology has a definitive edge over human capabilities, particularly in tasks that involve the handling, interpretation, and analysis of complex and extensive datasets. It delves into the role of AI in managing tasks that are centered around the processing and analysis of substantial data volumes. It is critical to assess whether AI systems in the organization have proven their superiority over human efforts in such scenarios. The effectiveness of AI in data-related tasks is a key indicator of its integration and effectiveness within an organization. It highlights the areas where AI's speed, accuracy, and ability to handle large-scale data significantly outperform human capabilities, thereby justifying its prominent role in the organization's operations.

Key Question #2   Are there tasks that involve processing and analyzing large volumes of data where AI systems have demonstrated clear advantages over human capabilities?

Task Performance

Examining the specific areas where AI systems have demonstrated superior performance compared to human efforts is needed. This involves identifying tasks or functions within the organization where AI has proven to be more effective, especially in scenarios demanding high-speed processing, impeccable accuracy, and the ability to scale operations efficiently. Such tasks often involve repetitive, data-intensive activities or processes that require consistent precision, areas where human performance may be limited by factors like fatigue, subjectivity, or scalability challenges. Identifying these tasks can provide valuable insights into how the organization leverages AI's strengths to enhance efficiency, accuracy, and scalability in its operations, indicating a strategic and effective integration of AI technologies.

Key Question #3   In which areas have AI systems been shown to outperform humans, particularly those that require high speed, accuracy, and scalability?

Operational Transformation

Exploring the impact of AI on enhancing operational efficiency and transforming business processes is necessary. This involves assessing how the adoption of AI technologies has altered and optimized the way the organization operates, both in daily tasks and in broader strategic initiatives. It's about understanding the tangible changes and improvements brought about by AI integration, such as streamlining workflows, automating repetitive tasks, improving decision-making processes with data analytics, and innovating in customer service approaches. By scrutinizing these areas, the organization can evaluate how profoundly AI has been ingrained into its operational fabric and the extent to which it has contributed to overall business efficacy and transformation.

Key Question #4   How has the integration of AI transformed operational efficiency and business processes?

Human Involvement

Considering the nature and extent of human involvement in AI-driven operations is key. This analysis focuses on understanding how human skills and insights are integrated into AI-enhanced workflows. It's important to explore whether human roles are relegated to oversight and supervisory functions or whether they are actively involved in decision-making, especially at critical points where nuanced judgment is necessary. Furthermore, this evaluation should consider whether there are specific tasks or inputs for which human intervention is indispensable, recognizing scenarios where AI cannot fully replicate human abilities. This analysis helps in determining the balance between AI automation and human expertise, revealing how an organization leverages the strengths of both to achieve its objectives.

Key Question #5   What roles do humans play in AI-driven tasks? Are they primarily providing oversight, making decisions at critical junctures, or providing inputs that AI cannot generate on its own?

Risk Management

Understanding how an organization manages the potential risks associated with an extensive reliance on AI is crucial. This analysis leads to delving into the organization's strategies for mitigating risks such as complacency in human oversight and the broader implications on employment and job roles. It's essential to examine the measures in place to ensure that reliance on AI doesn't lead to a neglect of critical human oversight or create a false sense of security in automated processes. In addition, evaluating how the organization addresses the potential impact of AI on its workforce, including retraining, upskilling, and job redesign, is key. This assessment helps gauge the organization's preparedness for the challenges and ethical considerations of integrating AI deeply into its operations, ensuring that it strikes a balance between technological advancement and responsible management of its consequences.

Key Question #6   How does the organization manage the risks of over-reliance on AI, such as complacency in oversight and potential job displacement?

Ethical Considerations

Assessing the ethical implications and potential biases in AI systems is critical. This involves a thorough examination of how AI applications are designed, deployed, and monitored to ensure ethical integrity and fairness. It's crucial to identify whether the organization has a framework for identifying and mitigating biases in AI algorithms, particularly those that could lead to unfair or discriminatory outcomes. In addition, exploring how ethical considerations are integrated into the AI life cycle, from development to deployment, is key. This scrutiny helps determine if the organization not only acknowledges the ethical challenges posed by AI but also actively implements strategies to address them. It's a vital step in ensuring that AI technologies are used responsibly and in alignment with societal values and norms.

Key Question #7   How does the organization manage the risks of over-reliance on AI, such as complacency in oversight and potential job displacement?

Regulatory Compliance

Understanding how AI systems align with regulatory compliance is not only mandatory but vital. This evaluation should focus on the mechanisms and strategies in place to ensure that AI applications adhere to industry-specific regulations and legal standards. The question involves probing into the organization's approach to maintaining legal and ethical compliance, particularly in industries heavily regulated for data privacy, consumer protection, or financial reporting. It's essential to investigate the systems established for ongoing monitoring and updating of AI algorithms in response to evolving regulations. This ensures accountability and transparency in the use of AI, safeguarding against legal and reputational risks. Determining how an organization manages this aspect of AI deployment is critical for understanding its commitment to responsible and compliant AI usage.

Key Questions #8   How are AI systems ensuring compliance with industry regulations, and what measures are in place to maintain accountability?

Future of Employment

Addressing the future of employment, particularly as it pertains to workforce changes due to automation is essential. This analysis centers around understanding the organization's foresight and preparedness in managing the transition for employees whose roles are increasingly impacted by AI and automation. It involves examining the strategies and initiatives in place for workforce retraining, upskilling, or potential job reallocation, ensuring that employees are not left behind in the shift toward more automated processes. The focus is on how the organization supports continuous learning and adaptation, promoting an environment where human workers can thrive alongside AI systems. By evaluating the organization's approach to these changes, one can gauge its commitment to responsible and sustainable AI integration, which considers the long-term implications on its workforce.

Key Question #9   What strategies are in place to manage the transition for workers whose jobs are susceptible to automation?

Explainability

Evaluating the explainability of AI systems as part of an organization's commitment to AI integration is crucial. It is not just about how extensively AI is adopted. This involves probing how the organization prioritizes the comprehensibility of AI decision-making processes to its users and stakeholders.

It's essential to understand whether there are efforts to ensure that AI systems are not just effective but also transparent and accountable. The focus on XAI signifies an acknowledgment of the importance of trust and understanding in AI applications, particularly in scenarios where AI decisions have significant impacts. By emphasizing explainability, an organization demonstrates its dedication to responsible AI use, which is vital for maintaining public trust and aligning AI operations with ethical standards.

Key Question #10 Is there an emphasis on explainable AI to maintain transparency and trust in AI systems?

These 10 key questions will help organizations evaluate if their current mode of operation is AI-First, focusing on leveraging AI for its strengths while managing the associated challenges and ethical considerations.

Fusion Mode Opens a New Frontier in Co-intelligence

This area exemplifies a harmonious blend of human intellect and AI prowess.

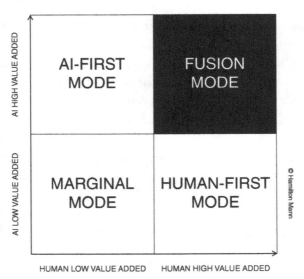

Here, the focus is on crafting roles and processes to capitalize on their respective advantages: human creativity and moral reasoning complement AI's analytical efficiency and pattern recognition. This setting is characteristic of forward-thinking workplaces that aim for a cohesive strategy, maximizing the collective benefits derived from both human and technological assets. In this environment, the fusion of human insight and AI's precision culminates in an optimal alliance, propelling tasks to new heights of effectiveness.

Such a paradigm fosters an atmosphere where AI serves as an enhancer of human skills, ensuring both elements are essential to superior performance and more nuanced decision-making processes to deliver the expected outcome. This collaboration represents the best of both worlds—the artificial and the natural intelligence—in task execution and strategic planning, offering comprehensive benefits that neither humans nor AI could achieve in isolation. It often also requires high human values such as compassion, moral stances, creativity, ethical judgment, and empathy.

In this mode, while AI provides efficiency, data processing, and analytical capabilities, the human element contributes significantly through qualities that AI cannot replicate. In fact, in Fusion mode, these human values are not only desirable but necessary, as they complement AI's capabilities and ensure that outcomes align with societal values and ethical standards. This mode thrives on the balance between technological efficiency and the depth of human understanding and values.

Numerous real-world instances effectively demonstrate this concept.

In healthcare, enhanced diagnostic processes are evident, especially in fields like radiology and pathology, where AI algorithms analyze medical images to identify patterns indicative of diseases. These patterns are then reviewed and interpreted by medical professionals for a final diagnosis, combining AI's precision with human expertise for more accurate and faster diagnoses.

Similarly, in the automotive industry, advanced driver assistance systems (ADASs) integrate AI's ability to process and respond to real-time data with human drivers' judgment and decision-making capabilities, enhancing safety and driving efficiency.

Moving to the retail sector, AI is utilized to personalize customer experiences by analyzing customer data. However, it is the human sales associates who use this information to provide tailored advice, effectively combining AI insights with human interaction to boost customer satisfaction.

In financial services, fraud detection is another area where AI plays a crucial role. AI algorithms rapidly process transactions to identify potential fraud, but it is the human analysts who review these alerts to make the final determinations, blending the speed and scale of AI with human judgment.

In the field of engineering and design, creative problem solving is enhanced by AI. Engineers and designers use AI for simulations and to generate design alternatives, but the final design decisions, which require creativity and contextual understanding, are made by humans.

Education is also transforming with AI-enhanced learning tools. AI can provide customized learning resources based on student performance data, yet educators leverage these insights to tailor their teaching strategies, combining AI's personalized approach with the educator's expertise.

Content creation, including journalism and writing, is another domain where AI has made inroads. AI tools can draft articles or content based on data and trends, but journalists and writers add necessary context, narrative, and critical viewpoints, thus blending AI-generated content with human storytelling skills.

Environmental conservation sees a similar pattern; AI-driven systems monitor wildlife and environmental data, but conservationists use this information to make informed decisions about habitat protection and conservation strategies.

In manufacturing, the concept of smart factories is on the rise. AI optimizes production lines and predictive maintenance, but it is human workers who oversee these processes, bring problem-solving skills, and make adjustments based on contextual knowledge.

Lastly, in the entertainment industry, particularly in movie production, AI assists in editing and visual effects. However, the creative direction, storytelling, and nuanced understanding of audience engagement remain firmly in the domain of human expertise.

In these examples, AI and human intelligence do not operate in isolation but work together, each complementing the other's strengths. This mode recognizes the power of AI to process information and perform tasks efficiently, paired with human abilities like creativity, empathy, and complex decision-making, leading to enhanced outcomes that neither could achieve alone.

Scientific evidence that supports this synergy comes from various fields.

A study by Rajkomar et al. (2018) highlights how AI can assist physicians by providing rapid and accurate diagnostic suggestions based on machine learning algorithms that process electronic health records, thus improving patient outcomes.

Such collaboration is particularly evident in the realm of medical surgeries. For example, in image-guided surgery, AI enhances a surgeon's ability to differentiate between tissues, allowing for more precise incisions and reduced operative time. However, despite the clear advantages of AI, the surgeon's experience and judgment remain irreplaceable, particularly for making nuanced decisions when unexpected variables arise during surgery.

In the realm of complex problem-solving and innovation, human creativity is irreplaceable, even though AI can significantly enhance these processes. Evidence has been demonstrated on how AI can support engineers and designers by offering a vast array of design options generated through algorithmic processes, which humans can then refine and iterate upon based on their expertise and creative insight (Yüksel et al., 2023).

In educational settings, research by Holstein et al. (2017) provides evidence that AI can personalize learning experiences in ways that are responsive to individual student needs, thus supporting educators to tailor their teaching strategies effectively.

This area underscores a future of work in which AI augments human expertise, rather than replaces it, fostering a collaborative paradigm where the complex, creative, and empathetic capacities of humans are complemented by the efficient, consistent, and high-volume processing capabilities of AI.

As previously mentioned, one of the risks associated with this integration is over-reliance on AI, which might lead to complacency.

In AI-assisted surgery, a malfunction or misinterpretation of data by the AI system could lead to serious surgical errors if the human operator overtrusts the AI's capabilities.

In this integration also lies the risk of a decline in the manual skills of surgeons; meanwhile, in the event of AI failure or unforeseen situations beyond AI's current capabilities, the surgeon's skill becomes paramount.

Another risk is the potential for ethical dilemmas, such as the decision to rely on AI's recommendations or strategy when they conflict with the surgeon's clinical judgment.

In addition, there are concerns about liability in cases of malpractice when AI is involved. Who is responsible if an AI-augmented procedure goes wrong—the AI developer, the hospital, the surgeon?

To determine whether an organization is operating within the Fusion mode—a harmonious blend of human intelligence and AI—there are 10 key questions to consider.

Integration and Collaboration

Examining the nature and depth of AI integration into human workflows is necessary. This evaluation seeks to understand how AI systems are not just adjunct tools but integral parts of the decision-making and creative processes. The key is to assess how AI contributes to enhancing human abilities and decision-making, rather than replacing or undermining them. The focus should be on the synergy between AI and human intelligence and how this partnership fosters greater innovation, efficiency, and creativity. This exploration helps in identifying the extent to which AI is a collaborator in the organization's workflow, augmenting human capabilities and working in tandem with human intuition and insight.

Key Question #1 How are AI systems integrated into human workflows, and how do they enhance human decision-making and creativity?

Role Definition

Scrutinizing how roles and processes within an organization are structured to leverage the strengths of both humans and AI is key. This analysis should focus on understanding if there is a clear delineation and optimization of roles, ensuring that both human employees and AI systems are utilized effectively based on their unique capabilities. The goal is to determine how these roles interact and complement each other, fostering a productive and efficient environment. By examining the interplay between human and AI roles, organizations can identify whether they are maximizing the potential of both, creating a symbiotic relationship that leverages human creativity and emotional intelligence alongside AI's computational power and data-processing capabilities.

Key Question #2 Are roles and processes clearly defined to capitalize on both human and AI strengths? How do these roles interact?

Value Addition

Dissecting where and how both human and AI contributions are most valuable and complementary is of interest. This involves a deep dive into various facets of the organization's operations, identifying areas where AI's capabilities in data processing, pattern recognition, and efficiency enhancement are most effective, and juxtaposing these against scenarios where human skills such as creativity, emotional intelligence, and complex problem-solving are irreplaceable. By examining the interplay between human and AI contributions, organizations can determine if they are optimizing the strengths of both, thereby realizing a synergy that drives innovation and efficiency while maintaining the essential human touch in their operations.

Key Question #3   Where do human and AI contributions add the most value, and how do they complement each other?

Outcome Enhancement

Looking for tangible examples that demonstrate the effectiveness of human intelligence and AI seamless integration is crucial. This means identifying specific instances or case studies where the collaboration between human skills and AI capabilities has evidently led to improved outcomes, be it in terms of efficiency, innovation, problem-solving, or customer satisfaction. These examples serve as benchmarks, showcasing the practical benefits of combining the nuanced understanding and adaptability of humans with the speed, precision, and data-processing power of AI. Such evidence is pivotal in understanding the extent to which the fusion of these two intelligences is not just theoretical but is actively contributing to the organization's success and advancement.

Key Question #4   Can we identify concrete examples where the fusion of human and AI capabilities has led to superior outcomes?

Decision-Making Process

Delving into the dynamics of the decision-making processes, particularly in situations that are complex and multifaceted, is important. This research focuses on how the organization leverages the unique strengths of both human intuition and AI analysis. It examines the practical application of their synergy in real-world scenarios, scrutinizing whether the combination of human insight, which excels in understanding context, nuance, and ethical considerations, effectively integrates with AI's capacity for handling vast amounts of data and identifying patterns beyond human capability. Understanding this interplay is crucial in determining if the organization has not only theoretically adopted the "Fusion mode" but is also effectively applying it in critical decision-making situations, thereby maximizing the benefits of both human and AI contributions.

Key Question #5   How does the collaboration between human intuition and AI analysis function in practice, especially in complex decision-making scenarios?

Empathy and Ethics

Exploring how human empathy and ethical reasoning are integrated into AI-assisted tasks is key. This examination revolves around understanding the balance and interaction between the emotional intelligence, ethical judgment, and nuanced understanding humans bring, and the analytical capabilities of AI. It is crucial to assess whether tasks that require empathy and moral considerations are being appropriately handled by humans, with AI serving as a supportive tool rather than leading these aspects. This helps in evaluating whether the organization recognizes and values the unique contributions of human sensitivity and ethical reasoning in areas where AI alone may not be sufficient. It's about ensuring that technology augments human capabilities without overriding the essential human elements of empathy and ethics.

Key Questions #6   In what ways does human empathy and ethical reasoning play a role in AI-assisted tasks?

Training and Adaptability

Evaluating the organization's approach to training and adaptability is required. This assessment focuses on understanding how the organization prepares its human workforce to collaborate effectively with AI technologies. It involves evaluating the nature and extent of training programs provided to employees to ensure they can work alongside AI systems efficiently and effectively. Additionally, it's important to consider how adaptable these AI systems are in terms of learning and evolving in response to human inputs and changing scenarios. This adaptability is crucial for a seamless integration of AI into existing human workflows. Examining these aspects can reveal insights into the organization's commitment to not only leveraging AI technology but also empowering its human workforce to be more competent and comfortable in this new AI-enhanced environment.

Key Question #7 How does the organization train its staff to work effectively with AI, and how adaptable are the systems in place?

Risk Management

Understanding the risk management strategies is crucial. This area of inquiry delves into how the organization mitigates potential risks associated with over-reliance on AI. It's vital to examine the measures in place to ensure that while AI is leveraged for its efficiency and capabilities, there is also a concerted effort to maintain and develop human skills. Equally important is assessing the ethical oversight mechanisms that are established to monitor AI operations and decisions. These measures are essential to ensure that AI supports, rather than undermines, human capabilities and ethical standards. By evaluating these aspects, we can gain insights into how an organization maintains a healthy balance between embracing AI's potential and upholding the value of human judgment, skills, and ethical considerations in a technologically advanced workplace.

Key Question #8 What measures are in place to prevent over-reliance on AI and ensure continued human skill development and ethical oversight?

Technological Dependence

Analyzing how the organization manages its dependency on technology while nurturing human expertise is essential. This area of examination focuses on understanding the organization's approach toward balancing the reliance on technological solutions, particularly AI, with the imperative to foster and enhance human skills and knowledge. It's important to investigate whether there are strategies and practices in place that promote the development of human talent alongside technological advancements. This balance is crucial for ensuring that the organization doesn't become overly dependent on AI at the expense of human skill and insight, preserving a workplace where technology complements rather than replaces human expertise. By evaluating this aspect, we can discern how well an organization is navigating the complex interplay between technological reliance and human skill development, which is a key indicator of successful integration in Fusion mode.

Key Question #9   How does the organization balance technological dependence with the need to maintain and develop human expertise?

Innovation

Exploring how the synergy of human intelligence and AI foster innovation is crucial. This exploration involves examining the extent to which the collaboration between AI and human intellect is generating new ideas, solutions, or processes within the organization. It's key to identify whether AI is being used not just for efficiency and automation but also as a catalyst for creative thinking and problem-solving, thereby enhancing the organization's innovative capabilities. This inquiry should delve into specific instances where the interplay between AI and human insight has led to breakthroughs or significant advancements, showcasing the unique contributions of both. By evaluating this, we can understand how well the organization leverages the distinctive strengths of AI and human intelligence in unison to drive innovation, a fundamental aspect of the Fusion mode.

Key Question #10   How does the fusion of AI and human intelligence contribute to innovation within the organization?

Addressing these 10 key questions will help an organization to discern if it has successfully achieved Fusion mode, where AI and human capabilities are being leveraged to their fullest in a collaborative and synergistic manner.

4

What Navigating Artificial Integrity Transitions Implies

Altogether, the four modes—Marginal, AI-First, Human-First, and Fusion—underscore a future of work in which artificial intelligence (AI) augments human expertise fostering a collaborative paradigm where the complex, creative, and empathetic capacities of humans are complemented by the efficient, consistent, and high-volume processing capabilities of AI. As we migrate from one quadrant to another, we should aim to bolster, not erode, the distinctive strengths brought forth by humans and AI alike. While traditional AI ethics frameworks might not fully address the need for dynamic and adaptable governance frameworks that can keep pace with the transitions in balancing human intelligence and AI evolution, artificial integrity suggests a more flexible approach to govern such journeys.

This approach is tailored to respond to the wide diversity of developments and challenges brought by the symbiotic trade-offs between human and AI, offering a more agile and responsive governance structure that can quickly adapt to new technological advancements and societal needs, ensuring that AI evolution is both ethically grounded and harmoniously integrated with human values and capabilities. When a job evolves from a quadrant of minimal human and AI value to one where both are instrumental, such a shift should be marked by a thorough contemplation of its repercussions, a quest for equilibrium, and an adherence to universal human values. For instance, a move away from a quadrant characterized by AI dominance with minimal human contribution should not spell a retreat from technology but a recalibration of the symbiosis between humans and AI. Here, artificial integrity calls for an evaluation of AI's role beyond operational efficiency and considers its capacity to complement—rather than replace—the complex expertise that embodies professional distinction.

Conversely, when we consider a transition toward less engagement from both humans and AI, artificial integrity challenges us to consider the strategic implications carefully. It urges us to contemplate the importance of human oversight in mitigating ethical blind spots that AI alone may overlook. It advocates for ensuring that this shift does not signify a regression but a strategic realignment toward greater value and ethical integrity.

Navigating Transitions Toward Artificial Integrity

Different types of transitions or shifts occur as organizations and processes adapt and evolve in response to the changing capabilities and roles of humans and AI. These transitions are grouped into three main types: algorithmic boost, humanistic reinforcement, and algorithmic recalibration.

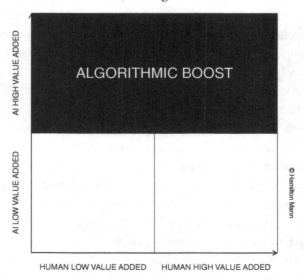

Algorithmic boost represents scenarios where AI's role is significantly elevated to augment processes, irrespective of the starting or ending point of human contribution. This transition focuses on harnessing AI to either take the lead in processes where human input is low or to amplify outcomes in scenarios where human value is already high.

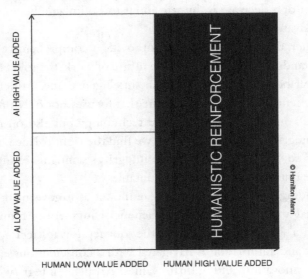

Humanistic reinforcement counters the first by emphasizing transitions that increase the human value added in the equation. This set of transitions may involve reducing AI's role to elevate human interaction, creativity, and decision-making, thereby reinforcing the human element in the technological synergy.

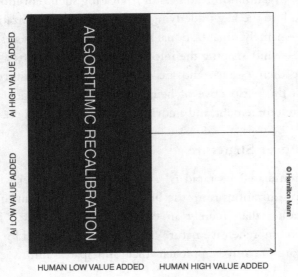

Lastly, *algorithmic recalibration* consists of transitions that involve a reassessment and subsequent adjustment of the balance between human and AI contributions. This might mean a reduction in AI's role to correct over-automation or a decrease in human input to optimize efficiency and capitalize on advanced AI capabilities.

Together, these sets of transitions provide a comprehensive framework for understanding and strategizing the future of work, the role of AI, and the optimal collaboration between human intelligence and artificial counterparts. They reflect an ongoing dialogue that focuses not only on enhancing human skills and leveraging advanced technology but also on maintaining artificial integrity. This ensures that as we find the right balance between the two, we do so with a commitment to integrity's standards, ensuring that AI systems are transparent, fair, and accountable.

Upholding artificial integrity is paramount as it governs the trustworthiness of AI and secures its role as a beneficial augment to human capacity rather than a disruptive force. Thus, the journey toward technological advancement and automation is navigated with a conscientious effort to sustain both innovation and human values. Artificial integrity becomes a compass by which we can steer through this evolving landscape. It urges us to maintain a careful balance, where the integration of AI into our tasks is constantly evaluated against the imperative to nurture and promote human dignity, creativity, and moral frameworks. It also implies a key prerequisite, which is the organization readiness in navigating such transitions.

Let's explore the key underlying components of organizations' operating models—namely, organizational structure, people, processes, technology, and culture—while shaping the informal and often unwritten mechanisms that capture their essence and are most profoundly transformed by AI's influence in the perspective of being able to navigate algorithmic boost, humanistic reinforcement, and algorithmic recalibration types of transitions.

Blueprint over Structure

In an era dominated by rapid AI advancements, it's crucial to assess the impact on organizations from the holistic perspective of an organizational blueprint, rather than merely an organizational structure. The forward-looking and comprehensive nature of a blueprint, designed for adaptability, offers a more inclusive approach that anticipates future changes and seamlessly integrates AI's transformative potential into the very fabric of an organization's operations and strategy.

Preparing an organization for AI is less a matter of stringent modification and more a journey toward a fluid organization. A rigid adaptation approach tends to breed complacency and a clinging to the status quo in a defensive posture, often arising from an innate human need for stability. Conversely, fluid organization involves crafting a target model that provides a sense of reliability in handling 80% of predictable events, while remaining flexible enough to navigate the 20% of unforeseen challenges. AI can lend unprecedented proficiency in managing these unpredictable elements, simultaneously elevating the performance within that 80% of predictable events.

The primary concern lies in establishing a dynamic organizational structure that optimizes efficiency in addressing these regular tasks, allowing AI to enhance this productivity while maximizing agility in responding to the organization's blind spots. In the context of transitioning toward a fluid organizational blueprint to fully harness the capabilities of AI, let's explore examples of companies that have implemented such transformations, illustrating the shift from a rigid structure to a dynamic blueprint that embraces AI integration.

Zappos   Zappos, the online shoe and clothing retailer, is a prime example of adopting a fluid organizational blueprint through its implementation of Holacracy. Holacracy is a method of decentralized management and organizational governance, where authority and decision-making are distributed throughout self-organized teams rather than being centralized at the top. This structure allows Zappos to adapt quickly to changes and innovations, including AI and digital technologies, fostering an environment where ideas can flourish and responsiveness to customer needs is enhanced.

Spotify   Spotify has taken an innovative approach to organizational structure by adopting a model consisting of Squads, Tribes, Chapters, and Guilds. This model promotes flexibility, with Squads acting as autonomous teams that own specific areas of the product. Tribes are collections of Squads that work in related areas, allowing for collaboration and the sharing of insights and technologies, including AI advancements. This fluid organizational model enables Spotify to rapidly innovate and adjust to the dynamic demands of the digital music industry.

Valve   Valve, the video game developer and distributor, operates with a flat organizational structure that emphasizes employee autonomy and fluidity. In this model, there are no traditional managers, and employees are encouraged to join projects that interest them. This structure supports innovation and quick adaptation to new technologies, including AI, by allowing ideas and projects to evolve naturally based on team interest and the potential for impact.

ING   ING, a global financial institution, underwent a significant agile transformation to become more responsive to customer needs and technological advancements. By reorganizing its workforce into multidisciplinary squads within larger tribes, ING fostered a culture of rapid experimentation, continuous delivery, and frequent customer feedback. This agile approach has allowed ING to integrate AI and data analytics more seamlessly into its services, enhancing customer experience and operational efficiency.

Haier   Haier, the world's leading appliance manufacturer, has restructured its organization into a network of microenterprises (MEs) focused on specific customer segments or product categories. This model encourages entrepreneurship, innovation, and fast adaptation to market changes, including the integration of AI and smart technologies into their products. By empowering each ME to operate independently, Haier has created a fluid organizational structure that can quickly respond to technological advancements and changing consumer preferences.

These examples demonstrate the effectiveness of fluid organizational blueprints in fostering innovation, agility, and responsiveness. By moving away from rigid structures and embracing more adaptable models, these companies have not only enhanced their capacity to integrate AI into their operations but have also positioned themselves as leaders in their respective industries. Their success underscores the importance of organizational flexibility in the age of rapid technological advancement, offering valuable insights for other companies looking to navigate the complexities of the digital era.

This transformation requires a visionary outlook, a willingness to embrace change, and a commitment to exploring new possibilities, setting a new standard for what organizations can achieve in the AI era. It is not merely about asking to reflect on how to introduce AI into organizations. Instead, let's question how to transform organizations and reshape an understanding of what's possible with AI.

Mindset over Skillset

The digital realm may seem daunting, requiring a profound understanding of data, technology, algorithms, and AI, but this is a misperception. Amid the surge of digital technology evolution, leaders need to take steps toward dispelling the myth of digital omniscience, emphasizing a more critical and discerning approach to digital understanding. Rather than cultivating an army of data scientists and programmers, the focus should be on fostering a mindset that embraces the potential of these systems.

The transition from traditional processes to digital ones is a journey of exploration—embracing change, questioning the status quo, and learning to consider the implications of AI—all while understanding that the goal is not mastery, but fluency in concepts such as system architecture, AI agents, cybersecurity, and data-driven experimentation. Moreover, it's imperative to acknowledge that AI, no matter how advanced, is more than just a tool. Unlike other technological tools, AI has the capacity to learn, adapt, and even make decisions based on the data it receives. When referring to AI merely as a tool, it's essential to ensure its profound implications are not underestimated, given the unique form of intelligence it embodies.

Such a mindset could lead to significant oversights, thereby running the risk of undesirable consequences by overlooking the necessary precautions required for its deployment. Blind reliance on them, or reliance without a clear sense of purpose or ethical considerations, must be the pitfall to avoid. True leadership in the AI age isn't about tech prowess but the ability to integrate technology meaningfully into broader objectives, ensuring it aligns with human values and societal positive impact. Leaders must ensure that the organization pushes itself and is constantly challenged intrinsically by its mode of operation. AI must be approached not as an infallible oracle but as a powerful ally that, when used with discernment, can amplify human capacities.

Lastly, it's essential to understand that the very essence of any digital technology is its evolutionary nature. What may be a groundbreaking innovation today could become obsolete tomorrow. Relying solely on the technical know-how of the present might lead to the trap of short-sightedness. Leaders should, therefore, instill a culture of continuous learning, flexibility, and adaptability.

The shift from prioritizing skillset to fostering a mindset that embraces digital and AI capabilities represents a critical strategic pivot for organizations aiming to thrive in the digital age (Clayton M. Christensen, 1997). This cultural transformation, emphasizing continuous learning, adaptability, and ethical considerations, can be observed in several leading companies. These organizations have not only integrated AI and digital technologies into their operations but have also cultivated an ethos that values the implications and potential of these tools. Let's explore how some real-world companies exemplify this approach.

Google   Google's approach to fostering a culture of continuous learning and innovation is well-documented. By allowing employees to spend 20% of their time on projects they are passionate about, Google not only encourages experimentation but also acknowledges the impermanence of digital technology. This policy has led to the development of groundbreaking products like Gmail and AdSense. Google exemplifies how cultivating a mindset that values exploration and innovation can lead to significant advancements.

Microsoft   Microsoft's transformation under CEO Satya Nadella has been marked by the adoption of a growth mindset. This cultural shift, emphasizing learning over knowing, has propelled the company to reinvent its products and services for the digital age. Microsoft's focus on AI and cloud computing, while ensuring these technologies are developed and used responsibly, reflects a deep understanding of digital technology's evolutionary nature and the need to remain adaptable.

Pixar   Pixar Animation Studios is renowned not only for its groundbreaking animation technology but also for its culture that champions creativity, experimentation, and continuous learning. Pixar University, the company's internal training program, offers courses not just in animation and storytelling but in a wide array of subjects, encouraging employees to explore new areas and cultivate a broad mindset. This culture of perpetual learning enables Pixar to remain at the forefront of innovation, with a team that's ready to adapt to and incorporate new technologies and methodologies.

Atlassian   Atlassian, the software company behind products like Jira and Trello, emphasizes a culture where autonomy and adaptability are key. The company's team-centric approach and open work environment encourage employees to take initiative, experiment with new ideas, and learn from failures. This mindset allows Atlassian to rapidly adapt to changes in the digital landscape, integrating new technologies and processes to improve collaboration and productivity tools continually.

Etsy   Etsy, the global online marketplace for handmade and vintage items, demonstrates how a company can integrate AI into its operations while maintaining a strong ethical stance and a focus on customer-centric innovation. By using AI to personalize search results and recommendations, Etsy enhances the shopping experience for its users. However, the company remains transparent about its use of AI, emphasizing the importance of data privacy and ethical considerations. Etsy's approach showcases the balance between leveraging AI for business growth and adhering to a set of core values that prioritize the well-being of its community.

Patagonia   Patagonia, the outdoor apparel company, is a prime example of an organization that places a strong emphasis on social responsibility, sustainability, and ethical business practices. While not a tech company per se, Patagonia's culture of environmental stewardship and its willingness to embrace innovative practices for sustainability demonstrate the mindset-over-skillset approach. The company's dedication to reducing its ecological footprint and its initiatives to repair and recycle products encourage employees to think creatively about solving environmental challenges, showcasing the value of a mindset geared toward continuous improvement and ethical considerations.

IDEO   IDEO, the global design and consulting firm, has long championed a culture of design thinking, where empathy, creativity, and a human-centered approach to problem-solving are valued above specific technical skills. By fostering a mindset that views challenges through the lens of design thinking, IDEO encourages its teams to embrace ambiguity, explore diverse perspectives, and experiment with innovative solutions. This approach has enabled IDEO to integrate new technologies and AI into its design processes, all while ensuring that solutions remain deeply grounded in human needs and values.

These companies, spanning different industries, underscore the importance of fostering a culture that prioritizes a flexible, ethical, and adaptive mindset in the face of rapid digital and technological advancements. By valuing mindset over skillset, these organizations are not only well equipped to navigate the AI age more effectively but also drive meaningful innovation that aligns with broader societal and environmental goals.

Data over Procedure

In the realm of AI, data stands as a centerpiece, evolving platforms, tools, and systems, facilitating greater efficiency and improved service delivery. As AI begins to take on an increasingly dominant role in decision-making, a critical challenge has emerged: understanding the labyrinthine data-driven process of AI's reasoning for the sake of trustworthiness.

Let's move beyond the perfectionism of causality that leads to linear and procedure-thinking to embracing the pragmatism of effectuality. Embracing practices like highlighting relevant data sections contributing to AI outputs or building models that are more interpretable could enhance AI transparency. But is transparency the only antidote to the trust issues with AI? Or could there be a different approach that not only explains AI's decisions but also anticipates its consequences?

Leaders must come to terms with the uncomfortable truth that AI's decision-making capabilities often far exceed human comprehension. However, AI can help leaders understand in detail the associated effects of AI's decision-making capabilities. For instance, AI could simulate various scenarios to illustrate the potential outcomes of its recommendations. This way, AI can be used to understand the breadth and depth of its own impact. In a medical setting, AI might recommend a certain treatment plan. Anticipating the consequences means understanding how this treatment could affect the patient's health outcomes, taking into consideration the individual's unique medical history and circumstances.

It is also worth mentioning that AI's effectiveness is heavily influenced by the data it processes; forget about an unbiased dataset as the magic bullet to address biases. There will always be biases in datasets, as data are originally produced by humans, and the process of refining them involves humans again. Embracing the intrinsic nature of bias in datasets is a challenge that can lead to more accurate and adaptable AI models. This is achieved by recognizing that total neutrality is a myth and integrating a diverse range of data to ensure AI models can respond to various contexts.

It's not only about who curates the data. While it's beneficial to involve diverse teams in data collection and processing, overemphasis on representation might lead to enforced uniformity, suppressing the rich and natural variations in human expression and experience. Instead, a more balanced approach would allow AI models to learn and adapt from the organic nature of data, including biases, to respond more genuinely to different perspectives.

Finally, let's rethink the trade-offs of large datasets versus small datasets. The pursuit of larger AI systems by tech companies is not merely a race toward volume. Larger datasets encompass broader knowledge, mirroring the vast spectrum of human perspectives. Reducing the size of a model for the sake of better understanding might, in fact, diminish the depth and richness of insights it can provide.

No matter how meticulously AI is developed and documented, it can never fully grasp the depth of human experiences and biases, leading to inadvertent harm. Hence, the strategy shouldn't be to eradicate bias but to acknowledge and manage it, reducing the risks that are associated while enabling us to navigate complex human biases and patterns effectively. AI will be truly powerful only when it can navigate the complex, bias-ridden real world. That will be achieved only while appreciating the multifaceted nature of data and developing AI models that can recognize and adapt to these complexities that are in essence not always "procedurable."

Several companies are at the forefront of addressing these challenges, offering valuable insights into how organizations can navigate the complexities of AI deployment.

IBM   IBM's efforts in developing explainable AI technologies exemplify the pursuit of transparency and trustworthiness in AI systems. Through tools like AI Explainability 360, IBM aims to make AI's decision-making processes more understandable and reliable for users. This initiative reflects an understanding that enhancing AI transparency is crucial for fostering trust and ensuring that AI's recommendations are both comprehensible and actionable by human users.

Autodesk   Autodesk, known for its software for the architecture, engineering, construction, and manufacturing sectors, leverages AI, particularly generative design technology, to revolutionize how designs are conceived and optimized. Generative design allows designers to input design goals along with parameters such as materials, manufacturing methods, and cost constraints. The AI then explores all the possible permutations of a solution, quickly generating design alternatives. This process emphasizes the power of data to drive creativity and efficiency, moving beyond traditional design procedures to embrace a more expansive, AI-driven exploration of possibilities.

Ocado   Ocado, a British online supermarket, utilizes AI and robotics in its highly automated warehouses to optimize the efficiency of grocery picking and delivery. By analyzing vast datasets concerning customer behavior, product shelf life, and warehouse logistics, Ocado's AI systems manage inventory and route planning more effectively than traditional methods. This data-centric approach allows Ocado to anticipate demand trends, reduce waste, and improve customer satisfaction, showcasing how AI can transform retail operations.

Grammarly   Grammarly uses advanced AI and natural language processing (NLP) technologies to enhance written communication. By analyzing the context and intent behind users' text, Grammarly provides suggestions for grammar, clarity, engagement, and delivery-style improvements. This tool demonstrates how AI can surpass traditional spellcheckers through a deep understanding of language nuances, aided by a vast dataset of user interactions to continually learn and improve its suggestions, making written communication more effective and error-free.

Square   Square, a financial services and mobile payment company, leverages AI to offer personalized financial products and detect fraudulent transactions. By analyzing transaction data, Square's AI can identify patterns that indicate fraud, enhancing security for its users. Furthermore, AI-driven insights allow Square to tailor its services to the specific needs of businesses and consumers, demonstrating how data-centric approaches in financial technology can lead to more secure and customized experiences.

Duolingo Duolingo, an AI-powered platform for language learning, exemplifies the use of AI to create personalized education experiences. By analyzing data on users' learning habits, mistakes, and progress, Duolingo's AI algorithms adjust lesson difficulty and content in real time, providing a tailored learning journey for each user. This focus on data over traditional, one-size-fits-all educational procedures has made Duolingo a leader in digital language education, showing the potential of AI to adapt learning experiences to individual needs.

These examples illustrate the transformative potential of adopting a data-over-procedure approach in AI development and deployment. By focusing on enhancing AI transparency, managing biases, and ensuring that AI systems are both understandable and aligned with human values, these organizations are walking the walk toward a more responsible and effective use of AI technologies. Their efforts underscore the importance of a nuanced understanding of data and the complexities it encompasses, paving the way for AI that truly complements and augments human decision-making in diverse sectors.

Human Capital Value Transitioning over Reskilling

Leaders need to face the new or exacerbated human capital challenge that AI poses. The emergence of AI necessitates new skill sets and competencies, redefining what expertise is essential for delivering value in this new **AIconomic** era. But it goes beyond that.

The prospect of AI triggering mass unemployment is often overshadowed by optimistic predictions based on historical technological revolutions. It is imperative, however, to examine AI's impact not through the lens of the past but in the context of its unique capabilities. For instance, the transition from horse-and-buggy to automobiles indeed reshaped job markets, but it did not render human skills redundant. AI, on the other hand, has the potential to do just that.

Contrary to the belief that AI should not create meaningful work products without human oversight, the use of AI in tasks like document generation can result in increased efficiency. Of course, human oversight is important to ensure quality, but relegating AI to merely auxiliary roles might prevent us from fully realizing its potential.

Take Collective[i]'s AI system, for instance. Yes, it may free up salespeople to focus on relationship building and actual selling, but it could also lead to a reduced need for human personnel, as AI handles an increasingly larger share of sales tasks. The efficiencies of AI could easily shift from job enhancement to job replacement, creating a precarious future for many roles. Similarly, while OpenAI's Codex may make programming more efficient, it could, in the long run, undermine the value of human programmers. As AI progresses, the line between "basic purposes" and more complex tasks will blur.

Certainly, investments in education and upskilling form a key part of any strategy to cope with job displacement due to the rise of AI. This includes fostering new-age skills that enable workers to adapt to the changing employment landscape and thrive in AI-dominated sectors. However, this approach alone may not be sufficient. It is imperative to also craft comprehensive social and economic policies that provide immediate relief and long-term support to those displaced by AI's advancement. Unemployment benefits, for instance, could be reevaluated and expanded to cater to AI-induced job losses.

Moreover, addressing AI displacement should not solely focus on financial security. The social and psychological impacts of job loss—including the loss of identity, self-esteem, and social networks—are equally significant and need to be factored into policy planning. Social support services and career counseling could be made widely accessible to help individuals navigate the transition period. A human capital value transitioning analysis can effectively cushion the impact of AI-induced displacement and build a resilient and inclusive organization from AI advancements while safeguarding its human capital.

Several leading companies have taken innovative steps to navigate the transition from traditional reskilling efforts to a more holistic approach to human capital value. These organizations are setting precedents in integrating AI into their operations while ensuring their workforce remains relevant and resilient in the face of technological advancements.

IBM   IBM has introduced the concept of "new collar" jobs, which emphasizes skills over traditional academic credentials, recognizing the changing landscape of work requirements due to AI and digital transformation. This initiative focuses on vocational training, apprenticeships, and certifications in areas such as cybersecurity, data science, and artificial intelligence. By valuing skills and potential over degrees, IBM is actively preparing its workforce for the future, demonstrating a commitment to human capital value transitioning.

Google   Google has launched career certificates that offer accessible job training, recognizing the importance of equipping individuals with the skills needed for high-demand fields including data analytics, project management, and user experience design. Through its Grow with Google initiative, the company offers a range of programs and resources aimed at expanding digital skills, thus facilitating a transition to careers impacted by AI advancements. This approach reflects an understanding that the future of work requires continuous learning and adaptability.

Microsoft   Microsoft, through its AI School, provides training and resources to developers, data scientists, and the public to better understand and create AI solutions. Coupled with LinkedIn Learning, a platform offering thousands of courses on AI and related fields, Microsoft is investing in the development of a workforce capable of thriving in an AI-integrated economy. These initiatives are part of Microsoft's broader strategy to ensure that workers are not only resilient to AI-induced job displacement but also equipped to leverage AI in their roles.

Salesforce   Salesforce's Trailhead platform offers self-paced learning paths that cover a broad range of topics, including AI and analytics, aiming to empower individuals to skill up for the future of work. By providing accessible training and recognizing acquired skills with credentials, Salesforce is contributing to a labor market where individuals are valued for their knowledge and ability to adapt to new technologies, including AI.

Siemens   Siemens has implemented AI apprenticeships and continuous learning programs within its workforce development strategy. Recognizing the impact of AI on the industrial sector, Siemens focuses on equipping its employees with the skills necessary to work alongside AI technologies, ensuring they remain a valuable part of the evolving workplace. This forward-thinking approach underscores the importance of transitioning human capital to meet the demands of an AI-driven economy.

These examples illustrate the importance of a comprehensive approach to managing the impact of AI on the workforce. By prioritizing human capital value transitioning over mere reskilling, these companies are not only preparing their employees for the future but are also shaping the future of work itself. Their initiatives highlight the necessity of adapting social and economic policies to support workers through AI-induced changes, ensuring that the workforce remains robust, adaptable, and equipped to harness the benefits of AI advancements. Through such efforts, these leaders are demonstrating that the path forward is one that combines technological innovation with a deep commitment to human capital.

Ethical Stands over Value Proposition

AI introduces novel policies and standard needs, necessitating a reevaluation of decision-making protocols and organizational conduct. But let's not think that AI regulation will be enough to regulate AI. The agile nature of AI evolution has outpaced the regulation meant to keep it in check. The burden of ensuring that AI tools are used ethically and safely thus rests heavily on the shoulders of the companies employing them.

The role of AI ethics watchdogs and regulation is crucial, but their effectiveness can be limited by the rapidly changing landscape of AI. Overly relying on the arrival of external checks and balances or acting as if waiting for them to first take a stance before taking action could lead to complacency within organizations. It is thus essential for leaders to foster a culture of ethical AI development and usage and not just depend on external watchdogs or regulations.

While government regulations are evolving to address AI, organizations should proactively ensure their AI applications are responsible, fair, and ethical. It's not just about reaping the benefits of AI but also about responsibly integrating these technologies without causing harm to stakeholders. This necessitates not only technological sophistication but also ethical mindfulness and societal understanding.

The example of popular videoconferencing software Zoom, which made headlines over concerns about an update to their terms of service that allows the company to use customer data to train its artificial intelligence, illustrates this. The path to responsible AI deployment is less about waiting for appropriate regulations and more about fostering a deep understanding and ethical use of the technology.

Companies are increasingly recognizing that beyond the race for innovation and competitive value propositions, lies a fundamental responsibility: to ensure AI is developed and deployed with ethical integrity. This new paradigm demands a proactive approach to ethics, well ahead of regulatory requirements. Here are examples of how leading companies are navigating this imperative:

Salesforce   Salesforce, a global leader in customer relationship management (CRM) software, has taken significant steps to ensure the ethical use of AI. The company established an Office of Ethical and Humane Use of technology to guide its practices. Salesforce has developed ethical use guidelines that govern the deployment of its AI technologies, including Einstein AI, ensuring these innovations serve the common good while respecting user privacy and fairness.

Google   Google has been at the forefront of addressing ethical concerns in AI development. After public and internal debates about its AI engagements, Google published its AI Principles, which serve as a guideline for ethical AI development and use within the company. These principles prohibit the creation of AI technologies that cause harm, and Google has established an internal review board to evaluate AI projects, ensuring they align with these principles.

IBM   IBM has emphasized trust and transparency as foundational elements of its AI initiatives. Recognizing the critical importance of explainability in AI systems, IBM developed the AI Explainability 360 toolkit, an open-source library of algorithms that help users understand and interpret AI model predictions. This initiative reflects IBM's commitment to leading by example, demonstrating that ethical considerations and transparency are integral to AI deployment.

Microsoft   Microsoft's AI for Good initiative exemplifies how ethical stands can shape a company's value proposition. This program focuses on leveraging AI to tackle some of the world's biggest challenges across sustainability, accessibility, and humanitarian issues. By dedicating resources to ethical AI development, Microsoft underscores the potential of AI to contribute positively to society, beyond commercial gains.

DeepMind   DeepMind, known for its groundbreaking work in AI, established an AI Ethics and Society team to explore and address the real-world impacts of AI technologies. This multidisciplinary group works to ensure that DeepMind's AI advancements contribute to societal well-being, addressing ethical, social, and governance issues related to AI deployment. DeepMind's approach reflects a commitment to responsible innovation, where ethical considerations are integral to the research and development process.

These examples illustrate a shift toward prioritizing ethical considerations in AI development and deployment. By embedding ethical guidelines, transparency measures, and societal impact initiatives into their operations, these companies are setting new standards for responsible AI. This trend highlights the importance of internal governance and ethical foresight in navigating the challenges of AI, emphasizing that the true value of technological advancement lies not only in what it can do but also in how it aligns with societal values and ethical standards.

Pioneering AI-Driven Operating Models

By moving to an AI-ready operating model, organizations will need to chart their own AI-transformation journey by prioritizing an adaptive blueprint over structure, emphasizing mindset more than just skillset, valuing data above procedure, placing emphasis on the transition of human capital value instead of just reskilling, and elevating ethical stances above traditional value propositions. To navigate this multidimensional transformation effectively, organizations would benefit from a structured approach to assess their readiness and progress in developing their operating model's "AI Quotient" based on these five dimensions.

AI is like no other tech wave in history with the potential to empower employees, reimagine work, and shift how companies deliver value in leaps versus incremental steps. Similarly, it requires a radical approach to transforming the operating model to unlock its full potential. As organizations shift toward an AI-ready operating model, they must define their artificial intelligence quotient (AIQ) and design their unique AI transformation path. This means prioritizing flexibility over fixed structures, focusing on mindset beyond just skills, valuing data over traditional procedures, emphasizing the evolution of human capital value rather than mere reskilling, and prioritizing ethical considerations over conventional value propositions.

ORGANIZATION: "BLUEPRINT OVER STRUCTURE"

Distributed Teams
Fluid Organization
AI-Augmented Strategy
AI Integration Roadmap
Uncertainty Management Through AI
Intelligent Organizational Responsiveness

PEOPLE: "HUMAN CAPITAL OVER RESKILLING"

Human Capital Value Transitioning
Transitional Support Policies
Human-AI Collaboration
Social Capital Safeguarding
Human-centric AI Governance
Inclusive "AIconomics" Standards

TECH: "ETHICS OVER VALUE PROPOSITION"

Collapsed Tech Stack
Sustainable Development-Friendly Infrastructure Standards
Responsive Ethical AI Framework
Trust-centric AI Design
Real-World AI Readiness
AI Safety Nets

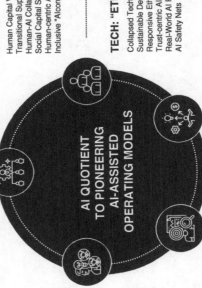

AI QUOTIENT
TO PIONEERING
AI-ASSISTED
OPERATING MODELS

CULTURE: "MINDSET OVER SKILLSET"

Digital Fluency
Human-centric Tech Leadership
AI Stewardship
Societal AI Alignment
Oracle Fallacy Avoidance
Strategic AI Questioning

PROCESS: "DATA OVER PROCEDURE"

Multifaceted Data Literacy
AI-Enabled Empathy
Ethical Data Stewardship
Dynamic Bias Management
AI-Augmented Decision-Making
Data-Driven Effectual Thinking

Companies that can quickly evolve toward a high level of AIQ will begin to separate themselves from the pack in their respective industries in terms of their ability to navigate algorithmic boost, humanistic reinforcement, and algorithmic recalibration transitions. This is key in upholding the capacity to develop and maintain not just the intelligence that a system may be capable of, but the integrity to which it is held to operate as such.

5 | How to Thrive Through Navigating Algorithmic Boost

The cluster termed *algorithmic boost* encapsulates a series of transitions that significantly enhance the role or performance of artificial intelligence (AI) within a given organizational context, regardless of the initial level of human value added.

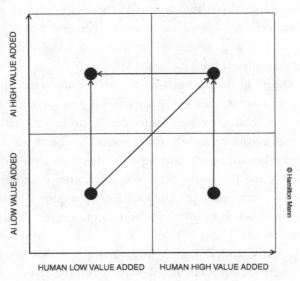

AI HIGH VALUE ADDED

AI LOW VALUE ADDED

HUMAN LOW VALUE ADDED   HUMAN HIGH VALUE ADDED

© Hamilton Mann

The transitions of this cluster see processes evolving from states of lower AI involvement to states of higher AI involvement, indicating an overarching strategy to leverage technology to improve efficiency, accuracy, or capability.

Algorithmic Boost Is an AI Push

Within the algorithmic boost cluster, the shift from low human intelligence value added/low AI value added to low human intelligence value added/ high AI value added exemplifies a pivotal transition. This change is typically observed in processes where human contribution is deliberately kept at a low level while the system undergoes an AI-centric upgrade. Such a transition is aimed at harnessing the power of AI to carry out routine, repetitive tasks, thus freeing up human resources for more complex challenges that may require creative thinking or emotional intelligence. It's a clear push toward automation, indicative of the AI's expanding role in enhancing productivity and operational efficiency without additional human intervention.

In a comprehensive analysis conducted by Arntz, Gregory, and Zierahn (2016), it was found that AI and robotics have a propensity to supplant routine and repetitive tasks within various industries. Their study provides robust support for the growing trend of businesses transitioning from operations that previously required minimal contributions from both human workers and AI to those where AI assumes a primary role. Specifically, automation technologies are being implemented to take charge of monotonous tasks that generally do not demand a high degree of human judgment or inventive thinking.

This evolution in the business model underscores a strategic reorganization within industries, with companies seeking to capitalize on the benefits of AI and robotic process automation to bolster efficiency. The introduction of automation does not necessarily equate to a heightened requirement for human intellectual input in these tasks; rather, it facilitates a repurposing of the human workforce toward more complex, intellectually engaging, and strategic roles. Such roles often require a human touch—creativity, problem-solving capabilities, and emotional intelligence—that AI has not yet mastered.

Arntz, Gregory, and Zierahn's findings suggest that as routine tasks become automated, employees are liberated from the tedium of repetitive work, enabling them to refocus their efforts on tasks that generate greater value for their organizations. This shift has implications for workforce development and training, emphasizing the need for skills enhancement in areas where human workers excel over machines. The redirection of human labor toward more analytical and interpersonal tasks not only enhances job satisfaction but also adds a layer of value to the work being performed, which goes beyond what AI can currently achieve.

In the administrative core of contemporary business structures, there is a palpable transition underway, largely driven by the advent of robotic process automation (RPA). This shift is most evident in back-office functions, where human operators have traditionally performed tasks such as data entry, document handling, and invoice processing. While necessary, these contributions by humans did not significantly enhance the strategic value of operations due to the highly repetitive and procedural nature of the tasks involved. However, with the incursion of RPA technology, there is a marked move toward augmenting the role of AI within these domains.

RPA technology excels in taking over monotonous tasks, executing them with precision and consistency beyond human capability. The significance of this transition is underpinned by empirical research that provides a compelling case for RPA adoption. In their influential work, Willcocks, Lacity, and Craig (2015) elucidate how RPA not only diminishes the likelihood of human errors—a perennial issue in manual processing—but also catalyzes a surge in operational efficiency. The implications of such advancements are twofold: on one hand, they enhance the speed and reliability of routine administrative tasks; on the other, they afford human employees the opportunity to engage in more intellectually stimulating and strategically impactful work.

By offloading the procedural drudgery onto RPA systems, organizations enable their workforce to concentrate on activities that demand human intelligence, such as decision-making, problem-solving, and innovating—areas where human acumen remains indispensable. Thus, the application of RPA is not merely a technological upgrade; it is a strategic realignment that seeks to leverage human intellectual capacity to its fullest potential, fostering a synergy between human and artificial intelligence that optimizes the overall value generated by the workforce.

Conversely, the progression from high human intelligence value added/ low AI value added to high human intelligence value added/high AI value added reflects an integrated enhancement approach. In this transition, AI is introduced or elevated in environments already rich in human skills and expertise, effectively combining the strengths of both human and artificial intelligence. The intention behind this movement is to augment the human workforce with AI, thereby increasing the capacity for human-led innovation and strategic thinking. It leverages AI to undertake data-intensive tasks, offering insights and precision and, thus supporting human roles to achieve a higher level of performance and decision-making prowess.

In the intricate fabric of modern business operations, AI has emerged as a pivotal force, particularly in its ability to enhance human cognitive tasks. This is particularly evident in areas requiring acute problem-solving skills and strategic decision-making. Bessen's research from 2019 offers insightful perspectives on how AI can act not merely as a tool for automation but also as a powerful adjunct to human expertise. By analyzing complex patterns and vast data sets, AI systems can unearth insights and trends that might elude even the most astute human analysts.

The strategic incorporation of AI into business processes marks a significant shift from traditional operations, embracing an augmentation approach. In this model, AI technologies are integrated seamlessly with human-driven processes, enriching the decision-making landscape. This synergy is not just additive but multiplicative, creating a compound effect that elevates the organizational capacity to unprecedented levels. Such a configuration enables AI to tackle the heavy lifting involved in data processing and analytical tasks, thereby freeing up human intellect to engage with the more nuanced aspects of the business, such as strategy formulation, innovation, and ethical decision-making.

The potential of AI to complement human tasks is more than a hypothetical proposition; it is grounded in empirical evidence. Bessen's study illustrates that when AI is applied as a collaborative partner to human intellect, the resultant output is far greater than the sum of its parts. This collaboration ensures that AI is not a replacement for human intelligence but an extension of it, enabling humans to operate with enhanced efficiency and effectiveness. It signifies a shift in the paradigm where the value added by both humans and AI is magnified, leading to more innovative solutions and better-informed strategic outcomes.

The realm of medical diagnostics, specifically radiology, illustrates a compelling narrative where AI's prowess is harnessed to complement and amplify the high-value intelligence of human experts. In this domain, AI-powered tools are increasingly being adopted as adjuncts to provide second-opinion services, thereby enhancing the reliability and swiftness of diagnostic procedures. These tools are meticulously designed to work in concert with radiologists, not as their replacements but as sophisticated aids that magnify their diagnostic acumen.

An illustrative example of this synergistic relationship is seen in the use of AI algorithms that assist in the detection of pathologies such as pneumonia from chest X-rays. Research by Rajpurkar and colleagues in 2017 underscored the potential of AI in medical imaging, demonstrating that these algorithms could match, and sometimes even surpass, the diagnostic performance of seasoned radiologists. The study revealed that AI, when trained with deep learning techniques on massive datasets of chest X-rays, developed the capability to identify telltale signs of pneumonia—a task traditionally demanding the trained eye of a radiologist.

This integration of AI into radiological practices marks a significant enhancement in the field's diagnostic capabilities. AI does not stand alone; it serves as an invaluable extension of the radiologist's own expertise. By rapidly analyzing images and highlighting areas of concern, AI algorithms act as a diligent assistant, enabling radiologists to focus their attention where it's most needed and to make more informed interpretations. The outcome is a heightened level of accuracy in diagnoses, quicker turnaround times for patients awaiting critical results, and a notable increase in the co(llective)-intelligence value added to the healthcare process. Thus, the interplay between human intelligence and AI in radiology epitomizes a model wherein the strengths of both are leveraged to improve patient outcomes and advance the medical field.

Following this trend, the transition from high human intelligence value added/high AI value added to low human intelligence value added/high AI value added emphasizes the notion of algorithmic boost in its purest form. This particular shift might occur in contexts where the AI's ability to learn and adapt has reached a point where it not only can match but can exceed the quality of the outcomes produced with high human involvement. In effect, it suggests a scenario where the system has been optimized to such an extent that human input is no longer a value-adding factor; instead, the AI can operate at peak efficiency, harnessing its full potential to deliver superior results without the variability introduced by human labor. This could manifest in sectors where precision and replicability are paramount and where AI's lack of cognitive fatigue can be a definitive advantage.

The McKinsey Global Institute's 2017 report illuminates the transformative influence of AI within the sphere of advanced manufacturing. The report delves into how AI applications are not merely automating tasks but also redefining the benchmarks of efficiency and precision in areas once dominated by skilled human labor. As AI systems evolve, they increasingly undertake complex tasks, transcending what was traditionally considered the preserve of high-value human input.

This shift in operational dynamics is emblematic of an era where AI's capabilities are robust enough to shoulder responsibilities that necessitate intricate decision-making and meticulous control—functions that, until recently, were entrusted solely to humans. In automotive manufacturing, for instance, AI-driven robots are now performing detailed assembly work with a level of consistency and precision that surpasses human capability. These advanced AI systems can quickly adapt to different tasks, enabling them to switch between functions with minimal downtime, thus greatly enhancing operational flexibility and productivity.

As a result of this shift, there is a recalibration within the workforce landscape. Organizations are prompted to reassess the deployment of their human resources, channeling their efforts toward arenas where AI's reach is limited or nonexistent—such as strategic planning, creative problem-solving, and tasks requiring nuanced human judgment or emotional intelligence. Furthermore, the realignment often involves steering human talents toward the exploration of new business avenues and innovation strategies, ensuring that the workforce remains engaged in high-value-added activities that drive organizational growth and evolution.

This nuanced rebalancing act between the roles of AI and human workers marks a pivotal point in the journey of advanced manufacturing. It reflects a sophisticated acknowledgment that while AI brings unprecedented efficiencies, the human element becomes even more critical in steering the technology toward meaningful outcomes and sustaining the creative and strategic growth of the industry. The development of autonomous vehicles represents a significant paradigm shift in the automotive industry—a sector traditionally reliant on human expertise and skill. Companies such as Waymo have been at the forefront of this transformative journey, pioneering advanced AI systems capable of complex tasks such as intricate navigation and split-second decision-making, domains once solely the purview of human drivers.

The evolution of these AI systems is a marvel of modern engineering and machine learning. With an array of sensors and sophisticated algorithms, these vehicles process a torrent of data in real time to safely maneuver through diverse traffic scenarios. The AI performs dynamic tasks ranging from detecting pedestrians to predicting the actions of other drivers and adjusting accordingly to maintain safety and flow. This level of autonomous operation was once speculative fiction but has now been realized to an extent where these vehicles can consistently navigate with precision in complex urban and suburban environments.

Moreover, empirical data and research increasingly suggest that autonomous vehicles could potentially surpass human drivers in safety and efficiency. This is exemplified by Waymo's (n.d.) safety reports and road test statistics that indicate lower rates of incidents and accidents as compared to human-operated vehicles. This is not merely a testament to the reliability of AI but also to the extensive training and learning protocols that these systems undergo, encompassing countless simulated miles and real-world experiences to refine their decision-making prowess.

In embracing AI's potential, the industry is redefining the role of human operators. The value added by human drivers is being recalibrated from direct vehicle operation to oversight and system improvement roles, where the focus shifts to monitoring system performance, managing exceptions in vehicle behavior, and providing feedback for AI system refinement. This shift heralds a new operational model where the human role evolves to complement the elevated functions of AI, ensuring that the blend of human oversight and AI's capabilities leads to the safest and most efficient transportation solutions.

In a remarkable leap, the shift from low human intelligence value added/low AI value added to high human intelligence value added/high AI value added represents a comprehensive transformation, both in the deployment of human expertise and the integration of AI. This dual escalation underscores a situation where a significant increase in human input is matched with a parallel intensification of AI application. Such a scenario typically emerges when a system or process is being thoroughly restructured or innovated, harnessing the full spectrum of human analytical and creative skills alongside sophisticated AI algorithms. The outcome is a symbiotic environment where the strengths of both human intelligence and AI are harnessed to their full potential, driving unparalleled advancements in the system's overall performance and output.

The dynamic interplay between AI and human strategic input is central to the digital transformations outlined by Davenport and Ronanki in their 2018 examination of contemporary business practices. As companies navigate the complexities of the digital age, there's a pronounced trend toward leveraging AI to bolster system performance while simultaneously amplifying the strategic role of human intellect. This two-pronged enhancement strategy has been pivotal for businesses intent on maintaining a competitive edge in an era defined by rapid technological evolution.

AI systems in this context serve as more than just backend processors; they are sophisticated decision-support tools that handle the heavy lifting of data analysis, uncovering patterns and insights at a scale and speed beyond human capability. These systems take on the brunt of computational tasks, from predictive analytics to customer behavior modeling, thus providing a robust platform for data-driven decision-making.

On the other hand, human experts are tasked with interpreting AI-generated insights and formulating strategic initiatives that align with the organization's broader goals. Their role transcends the traditional bounds of data interpretation, encompassing the design of innovative solutions and the steering of the organization through uncharted business landscapes. It's their foresight, creativity, and capacity for nuanced understanding that guide the ethical deployment of AI and ensure that the insights it generates are leveraged for sustainable growth and value creation.

This symbiotic relationship between human and machine is indicative of a new operational archetype. In it, AI does not supplant human intelligence but instead augments it, creating a collaborative environment where the sum of combined intelligence is greater than its individual parts. This not only enhances efficiency and insight generation but also allows human employees to engage in more fulfilling work that underscores their strategic and creative capabilities.

The success of this integrated approach is contingent upon a careful balance, ensuring that AI systems are designed and deployed in ways that complement human skills rather than replace them. The resultant corporate ecosystem is one characterized by an agile, innovative, and resilient approach to both operational challenges and opportunities for growth.

The pharmaceutical industry is witnessing a profound transformation as AI becomes a cornerstone in drug discovery, transitioning from a peripheral computational aid to a central player in the research and development process. Atomwise (n.d.) epitomizes this shift with its AI platform, which harnesses deep learning algorithms to predict molecular interactions with a level of speed and accuracy that was previously unattainable. By simulating countless potential chemical reactions and biological affinities, this AI technology presents human researchers with a narrowed, high-potential set of compounds for further investigation.

This paradigm shift is marked by a substantial elevation in the role of both AI and human intelligence within the drug discovery pipeline. Where AI initially played a rudimentary role in processing molecular data, it now provides pivotal predictive insights that guide the strategic decisions of human scientists. The deep learning models employed are trained on vast chemical libraries and biological data sets, enabling them to anticipate the pharmacological properties of novel compounds, predict off-target effects, and suggest modifications to enhance efficacy or reduce toxicity.

For human researchers, the implications are transformative. Relieved of the initial stages of high-volume screening, scientists can direct their expertise toward more nuanced and creative aspects of pharmaceutical development such as designing targeted in vivo studies, understanding complex biological mechanisms, and tailoring therapeutic agents to specific patient populations. This synergy between human and AI has the potential to significantly reduce the time and cost associated with bringing new drugs to market, turning a process that once took years into one that may take just months.

Moreover, by interfacing with AI, researchers are able to interrogate vast chemical spaces that would be otherwise impenetrable, exploring novel chemical entities and mechanisms of action. This collaborative approach does not just streamline existing processes but opens the door to innovative therapeutic pathways and treatments for complex diseases.

As AI continues to evolve, the complementary relationship between machine efficiency and human ingenuity is poised to unlock new frontiers in medicine. The value-added shift for both AI and human roles in this field is a testament to how intelligent technology, when integrated thoughtfully into human-centric workflows, can redefine the boundaries of innovation and healthcare advancement.

In contrast to other types of transitions, such as humanistic reinforcement, where the focus is on enhancing human roles, and algorithmic recalibration, which involves adjusting the balance between human and AI contribution (often by reducing AI's role in favor of human input or vice versa), algorithmic boost specifically highlights a strategic increase in AI's role. This is indicative of a belief in the potential of AI either to complement high levels of human input or to take the lead in driving processes forward where human contribution remains limited. It suggests a direction where AI is trusted as a driver of progress and efficiency, aiming for an overall enhancement in performance by upgrading the technological component of workflows and decision-making processes.

Navigating from Marginal Mode to AI-First Mode

The transition toward the algorithmic boost cluster from a state of Marginal mode (low human intelligence value added/low AI value added) to an AI-First mode (low human intelligence value added/high AI value added) marks a pivotal shift in the operational dynamics of AI systems. This shift is not merely about enhancing AI capabilities but also about ensuring that these advancements align with the core principles of artificial integrity. Transitioning from Marginal mode to AI-First mode represents a significant shift, where the contribution of AI in operational outcomes escalates dramatically, despite a continued low level of human intelligence value added needed to deliver such an outcome. In this scenario, the AI evolves from a basic tool to a primary agent of action, harnessing its advanced capabilities to drive tasks and processes more autonomously to deliver the expected result.

In AI-First mode, the sophistication of AI is not just supplementary but becomes the main driving force. The system leverages high-level AI functionalities for complex data analysis, predictive modeling, and decision-making with minimal human intervention from an outcome delivery standpoint. The role of human intelligence is not to lead but to oversee, guide, and provide occasional inputs where necessary, primarily focusing on tasks that are not intrinsically considered as value adding for the expected outcome.

Thus, in this mode, AI's "high value-added" contribution is seen in its capacity to handle operations with speed, efficiency, and a level of sophistication required to deliver the expected outcome that exceeds the limitations of human-led processes. AI takes the forefront in managing routine, data-intensive, and computation-heavy tasks, allowing human resources to focus on other areas where they add unique value. This shift highlights a future where AI's potential is maximized for operational excellence, leading to outcomes that are a product of advanced technology with human oversight, but where human value added is both not critical and outpaced to deliver a given outcome.

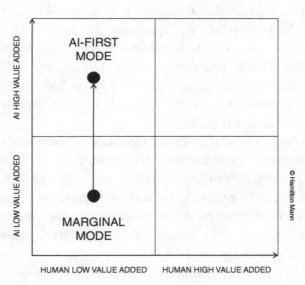

This transition involves a series of actions, focusing on the following critical concerns: bias automatic detection, scalable ethics protocols, explainability, and automated ethical balancing. Each of these areas plays a critical role in ensuring that the enhanced AI capabilities are not only effective but also grounded in integrity and aligned with human values.

About Bias Automatic Detection

In the transition from Marginal mode to AI-First mode, the advancement in AI necessitates systems that are not only efficient but also fair and as unbiased as possible. Here, the emphasis is on developing self-aware AI systems capable of identifying and rectifying biases. This includes fostering contextual understanding and implementing dynamic learning mechanisms, ensuring AI systems are attuned to the nuances of cultural and societal contexts.

Automated ethical oversight and collaborative frameworks with human ethicists are integral in this process, facilitating a comprehensive understanding and correction of biases. These approaches should enable the AI to not only detect biases autonomously but also understand and rectify them in alignment with the nuanced ethical considerations AI would entail to achieve artificial integrity.

This involves the development of self-aware AI systems, where we create AI systems capable of self-assessment. This capability allows them to understand the context of their operations and the implications of bias within those contexts, which is crucial for recognizing the multifaceted nature of biases beyond mere data points. In addition, designing AI with the ability to introspect on its decision-making patterns and identifying potential biases in its reasoning, not just in data, is key. This requires a sophisticated level of cognitive processing.

Furthering this concept is the incorporation of contextual understanding and integrity reasoning. Models that provide AI with a deep understanding of cultural, societal, and individual contexts are vital for identifying biases that may not be evident in the data alone. Also, equipping AI systems with ethical reasoning capabilities enables them to weigh the consequences of biases and determine the integrity-based appropriate course of action when a bias is detected.

Moreover, dynamic learning and adaptation mechanisms are essential. Implementing advanced learning algorithms enables AI to dynamically update its knowledge base and decision-making frameworks based on new information, mirroring human learning processes. In addition, establishing adaptation mechanisms allows AI to adjust its behavior in real time based on the detection of bias; ensuring that its actions remain fair and equitable across all interactions is an essential step toward fostering artificial integrity.

The concept of automated integrity oversight is also pivotal. Creating an automated integrity oversight system within the AI that operates continuously, auditing decisions for biases against a set of value standards and guidelines, is crucial. As an extension to this, developing an AI oversight module that can override certain operations if they are deemed to be biased, even if they are efficient or cost-effective, emphasizes the prioritization of integrity with regard to value principles over other performance metrics, and is required for ensuring that ethical considerations remain at the forefront of AI decision-making.

Human-AI collaborative frameworks are also key. Designing collaborative frameworks where AI systems work alongside human ethicists to understand and correct biases can enhance the system's capability to learn the subtleties of human ethical judgments. Complementary to this, establishing protocols for AI to consult with human experts when uncertain about a bias can ensure that decisions are vetted through an understanding of human integrity.

Finally, transparent decision-making processes are vital. Ensuring that AI systems can transparently communicate their decision-making processes allows for external audits to understand how biases were detected and addressed. In addition, providing a clear rationale for actions taken to correct biases can ensure that all stakeholders have access to information concerning the value principles that have been followed, as well as the manner in which they have been followed by the AI system.

Through these guiding principles, AI systems tasked with bias automatic detection will be able to perform this function with high efficiency, which contributes to embodying the principles of artificial integrity. It will actively contribute to an AI ecosystem that is fair, unbiased, and aligned with the complex ethical standards expected from systems approaching human-level intelligence and reasoning. These actions represent a convergence of technological prowess and ethical foresight, positioning AI as a proactive agent in pursuing unbiased and equitable AI operations and, hence, artificial integrity.

About Scalable Ethics Protocols

As AI systems become more autonomous and capable as they transition from Marginal mode to AI-First mode, it's essential to embed scalable ethics protocols. This involves establishing ethical governance structures, integrating ethical considerations into the AI development life cycle, and building dynamic ethical reasoning engines. Continuous ethical learning, ethical scenario simulation, and transparent ethical decision-making processes are crucial to ensuring that AI systems can adapt and expand their ethical understanding alongside their operational capabilities. Incorporating scalable ethics protocols within an AI system requires these protocols to not only be robust and comprehensive at the AI's current level of operation but also designed to evolve as the AI's capabilities and autonomy expand.

First, it's essential to establish ethical AI governance. This involves implementing a governance structure that oversees the ethical performance of the AI system, ensuring that ethical considerations remain at the forefront as the system scales. In addition, involving a diverse board of stakeholders in the governance process, including ethicists, technologists, end users, and also experts from multidisciplinary fields such as philosophers, anthropologists, and sociologists, provides multiperspective oversight that enriches the decision-making process and ensures a more comprehensive understanding of the ethical implications of AI systems.

Moving on to the ethical AI development life cycle, it's crucial to integrate ethical considerations at every stage of the AI development life cycle, from initial design to deployment and beyond. In addition, conducting ethical impact assessments at each phase of scaling up can help evaluate how AI enhanced capabilities may affect stakeholders to adjust the ethical framework accordingly.

The development of a dynamic ethical reasoning engine is also useful. Building a reasoning engine within the AI that can interpret ethical principles in various contexts can allow for nuanced decision-making that mirrors human ethical reasoning. This engine should be capable of considering a wide range of ethical theories and adapt its recommendations based on the specific situation and cultural context.

Moreover, continuous ethical learning plays a crucial role. Implementing machine learning mechanisms that allow the AI to learn from ethical outcomes and incorporate these learnings into future decisions can help create an ethical feedback loop. This loop can enable the AI system to update its ethical understanding based on new data, societal norms, and legal standards.

Ethical scenario simulation is another key action. Using simulations to test the AI's responses to hypothetical ethical scenarios can help assess the system's readiness to handle complex ethical decisions. Complementary to this, enabling the AI to learn from simulated experiences, much like humans learn from thought experiments, can enhance its ethical decision-making capabilities.

Ensuring transparent ethical decision-making is paramount. The AI system should be able to explain the ethical reasoning behind its decisions, maintaining transparency as it scales up. It should also be able to provide to stakeholders insights into how ethical decisions are made and allow for human override when necessary.

Furthermore, the development of ethical prioritization algorithms is essential. These algorithms should weigh different ethical principles and outcomes, guiding the AI in making decisions when ethical imperatives conflict. Integrating exception handling protocols that recognize when the AI faces an ethical dilemma beyond its programmed capabilities should also be considered so that the AI system can refer the decision to human oversight.

Lastly, cross-cultural ethical adaptability is critical. Equipping the AI with the ability to understand and adapt to different cultural norms and values ensures its ethical protocols are relevant and respectful across diverse global contexts. As an equally necessary measure, involving cultural experts in the training process of the AI can help provide insights into nuanced ethical considerations specific to different regions and cultures.

By addressing these guiding principles, the AI system will be equipped with a set of scalable ethics protocols that can adapt and expand alongside the AI's capabilities. This approach ensures that AI embeds an ethical framework that is deeply ingrained and capable of handling the complexities of increased autonomy and decision-making power. Such a system will be positioned to act with artificial integrity, embodying the ethical standards expected from advanced intelligent systems.

About Explainability

From Marginal mode to AI-First mode, embedding explainability within AI is pivotal for artificial integrity. This entails developing AI systems with frameworks that provide clear and comprehensible rationales for their decisions. User-centric explanation interfaces, explainability as a core design feature, and incorporation of ethical reasoning in explanations are critical. Furthermore, feedback loops for improvement and transparent decision-making processes play a significant role in fostering trust and understanding between AI systems and their human counterparts. Embedding explainability within an AI system, particularly in the context of achieving artificial integrity, requires a comprehensive strategy that touches on transparency, user trust, and the system's ability to self-reflect and articulate its reasoning.

First, the development of AI systems with integrated explainable AI (XAI) frameworks from the ground up is crucial. These frameworks should be capable of not just providing outcomes but also detailing the rationale behind each decision in a manner that emulates human explanation. To achieve this, it's beneficial to utilize advanced XAI models that can deconstruct the AI's decision-making process into components that are easily understood, such as feature importance, decision trees, or rule-based explanations. In addition, designing the AI to automatically generate explanations in natural language that summarize the reasoning process, the data involved, and the relevant ethical considerations can help make the explanations accessible to those without technical expertise.

Moreover, focusing on user-centric explanation interfaces is important. Creating interfaces that provide explanations at different levels of complexity can help users choose how much detail they want to receive about a decision, from a simple overview to a detailed, step-by-step walkthrough of the AI's reasoning. Implementing interactive elements within the interface that allow users to query the AI system about specific decisions, receive clarifications, and understand the implications of its actions can also enhance expandability. Furthermore, designing the user interface to present explanations visually where possible, using graphs, flowcharts, or other visual aids, can help users intuitively grasp the AI's processes.

Another key aspect is ensuring that explainability is a core design feature. It's essential to ensure that explainability is ingrained in the AI's core functions, making it a foundational aspect of the system rather than an afterthought or a feature added to an already complex black-box system. Embedding within the AI's architecture the ability to trace the lineage of its data processing and decision pathways provides a transparent view of its operations. Establishing standards for the quality of explanations, ensuring they meet criteria for clarity, completeness, and accuracy is also a necessity that should involve testing with diverse user groups to validate the effectiveness of the explanations provided.

Explainability in ethical decision-making is also paramount. Incorporating a mechanism that requires the AI to justify its decisions not only based on efficiency or outcomes but also on ethical grounds, explaining how its actions align with ethical protocols, is indispensable. Training the AI system to identify and articulate the ethical principles at play in a given decision provides a moral rationale for its actions that reflect an understanding of artificial integrity. Developing protocols for the AI to report its confidence levels in its decisions and explanations can also be a plus to help users assess the reliability of both the outcome and the rationale provided.

Finally, establishing feedback loops for continuous improvement is vital for the ongoing explainability refinement of the AI system. Establishing feedback loops where users can rate the quality of explanations and provide input on their usefulness can enable the AI system to refine its explanatory capabilities over time. Using user feedback to identify areas where the explanations are lacking or unclear directs the AI to adjust its explanatory models for better clarity in future interactions.

Integrating a continuous learning process where the AI system can evolve its explanatory functions based on new information, user interactions, and societal changes is a key step toward adaptability and relevance. By addressing these guiding principles, the AI system will not only be able to enhance decision-making but also communicate the reasoning behind those decisions transparently and understandably, which is consistent with artificial integrity. This fosters a greater level of trust and collaboration between humans and AI, ensuring that as AI systems progress toward more capabilities, they remain aligned with the ethical and operational standards that society values.

About Automated Ethical Balancing

Automated ethical balancing is about creating AI systems that can autonomously balance operational efficiency with ethical considerations. While transitioning from Marginal mode to AI-First mode, ethical benchmarking, continuous ethical training, and transparent ethical decision-making, along with human oversight mechanisms, ensure that AI decisions are not only efficient but also ethically responsible.

Achieving automated ethical balancing in an AI system, entails creating a system that can autonomously gauge and adjust its actions according to ethical guidelines. In this perspective, constructing ethical reasoning models that emulate human moral deliberation processes is crucial, as it allows the AI to weigh various ethical principles and outcomes against each other. These models need to be capable of handling ethical dilemmas where principles may conflict and finding a resolution that best aligns with overarching ethical standards.

In addition, the integration of multidimensional ethical frameworks is essential. By incorporating a multidimensional ethical framework that includes deontological (rule-based), consequentialist (outcome-based), and virtue ethics perspectives, the AI system is provided with a rich foundation for assessing the morality of its decisions. This framework should be dynamic, allowing for updates as societal norms and ethical understandings evolve.

Further, there is a need for ethical impact prediction engines. Equipping the AI system with prediction engines that can forecast the long-term impacts of its decisions, including potential ethical repercussions, is vital. These engines, by analyzing historical data, current trends, and predictive models, should be able to simulate various scenarios to understand the broader implications of the AI's actions on individuals, groups, and society.

Implementing ethical benchmarking and compliance systems is also a key step. This involves setting up benchmarking systems that measure the AI's decisions against established ethical standards and societal norms, ensuring alignment with accepted moral conduct. In doing so, compliance systems should ensure that the AI's operations adhere to legal and regulatory requirements, which often reflect ethical considerations.

Moreover, continuous ethical training and updating cannot be overlooked. Establishing continuous training protocols where the AI system is regularly updated with new ethical data, case studies, and evolving societal values ensures its reasoning remains relevant and informed. The AI should also participate in simulated ethical training scenarios to refine its balancing algorithms and adapt to new ethical challenges.

Also, human oversight and intervention mechanisms should be a priority. Despite the aim for automation, it's important to design the system with mechanisms for human oversight where ethical decisions can be reviewed and, if necessary, overridden by human decision-makers. Creating intervention protocols that can be activated if the AI's ethical balancing is found to be at odds with human ethical judgments ensures that there is a "safety net" for critical decisions.

Lastly, the establishment of ethical advisory systems also plays a critical role. Implementing an advisory system within the AI that can provide recommendations to human operators when faced with complex ethical decisions effectively can serve as an "ethical consultant." This system should draw on a comprehensive database of ethical knowledge, including philosophical texts, legal precedents, and cultural norms, to provide well-rounded advice.

By addressing these guiding principles, AI systems will have the capacity for automated ethical balancing, which is essential for ensuring artificial integrity. This will not only enable the AI to make decisions that are ethically sound but also adjust its operations proactively as it encounters new situations and information, maintaining ethical conduct as a core aspect of its functionality. These detailed operational and technical measures ensure that as AI systems transition toward higher AI value added, they maintain a strong alignment with standards to achieve artificial integrity, addressing potential biases, ensuring explainability, and upholding ethical stances at every step. This is crucial for cultivating trust between humans and AI and for ensuring that AI systems contribute positively to society while respecting human values.

Navigating from Human-First Mode to Fusion Mode

Transitioning toward the algorithmic boost cluster from a state of Human-First mode (high human intelligence value added/low AI value added) to a state of Fusion mode (high human intelligence value added/high AI value added) necessitates a strategic augmentation of AI capabilities to complement and enhance human intelligence.

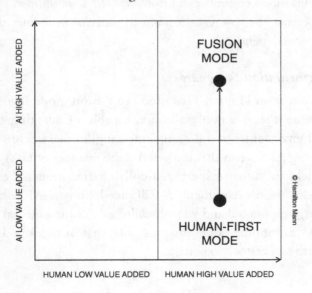

This transition involves a meticulous integration of augmentation safeguards, advanced security features, and continuous learning and adaptation processes, ensuring that AI systems are both powerful and principled.

In transitioning from the Human-First mode to Fusion mode, we witness a harmonious integration of high-level AI capabilities with advanced human intelligence, elevating the value-added from both ends from an outcome making standpoint. In this phase, AI's role evolves from a supportive backdrop to an equal collaborator, working in tandem with human insight and creativity.

This integration sees AI not just augmenting human capabilities but also actively collaborating, contributing to complex decision-making processes, and offering innovative solutions that directly participate to the production of the expected outcome. AI in Fusion mode possesses the sophistication to process and analyze vast amounts of data, providing insights and perspectives that might elude human cognition. Simultaneously, human intelligence imparts contextual understanding, ethical considerations, and creative problem-solving, aspects where AI alone might fall short.

Thus, in Fusion mode, the outcome is a product of a seamless blend of human and AI contributions, each amplifying the other's strengths. The sophisticated AI functionalities combined with enriched human intelligence lead to groundbreaking innovations and efficient problem-solving strategies. This mode epitomizes a future where AI and human intelligence don't just coexist but co-create, leading to superior outcomes than either could achieve independently.

About Augmentation Safeguards

The transition from Human-First mode to Fusion mode involves creating AI systems that are context-aware, capable of adapting to various operational environments and complementing human decision-making. By developing AI systems that understand the nuances of tasks and know when to yield to human expertise, a collaborative model is established. This includes the development of advanced human–AI collaboration models using augmented and virtual reality, establishing ethical guardrails to limit AI autonomy, and ensuring adaptive autonomy levels that respond to the operator's expertise.

Crucial to this is the creation of human override protocols and intelligent confirmation systems that require human approval for critical decisions, thereby maintaining human control over AI decision-making. Achieving augmentation safeguards within an AI system means ensuring that as AI capabilities are enhanced to a high level, they complement rather than override human intelligence.

Starting with the development of context-aware capability, it's key to construct AI systems that are capable of understanding the nuances and implications of different operational environments. These systems should adapt their behavior to support human decision-making appropriately and be able to assess the complexity and criticality of tasks, recognizing when human expertise is crucial for invoking human collaboration.

Building on this, advanced human–AI collaboration models are necessary. These models, based on advanced cognitive computing, should facilitate an intuitive partnership between humans and AI, allowing for seamless augmentation of human capability. Utilizing models such as augmented reality (AR) and virtual reality (VR) interfaces can also be useful in that aspect to provide humans with enhanced situational awareness and data visualization, aiding in decision-making processes.

Furthermore, integrating ethical guardrails for AI autonomy is essential. These guardrails, embedded into the AI system should automatically limit AI autonomy in scenarios with high stakes or ethical considerations, ensuring human values and judgment remain paramount. They should be dynamic, adjusting the level of AI autonomy in real time based on the ethical and operational context of the task.

In line with this, adaptive autonomy levels are also crucial. Implementing systems that adapt to the level of AI autonomy according to the expertise and authorization level of the human operator involved ensures that AI support is proportionate and appropriate. Also, developing AI systems that can provide varying levels of decision support, from suggestions to fully formulated plans, caters to the human operator's preference and the situation's demands.

In addition, establishing human override protocols is important to ensure ultimate human control. These protocols should allow human operators to easily override AI decisions at any stage of the process and be designed to revert the system to a safe state when human intervention occurs.

Intelligent confirmation systems also play a critical role. Designing systems that require human approval for decisions that exceed certain ethical or operational thresholds ensures critical decisions are made with human consent. These systems should predict when human confirmation is needed and proactively prepare the necessary information for a quick and informed human response.

Moreover, creating feedback and learning mechanisms where human operators can provide input on AI performance is essential. These mechanisms should enable the AI to refine its augmentation capabilities and learn from human decisions, preferences, and overrides to improve its strategies continuously.

Lastly, ensuring accountability and traceability features in all AI-augmented decisions maintains transparency and responsibility. In that matter, implementing mechanisms for audit trails to be reviewed can provide transparency into the decision-making process and the interplay between human and AI contributions.

By addressing these guiding principles to the AI system, the goal is to establish a level of artificial integrity that ensures AI systems respect and augment human expertise rather than supplant it. As AI capabilities increase, these augmentation safeguards will be crucial in maintaining a synergistic relationship between human intelligence and AI, fostering an environment where each enhances the other's strengths.

About Advanced Security Features

In this transition phase from Human-First mode to Fusion mode, the focus on security intensifies with the need to develop robust access control mechanisms, proactive anomaly detection, and continuous security assessments. Implementing adaptive encryption protocols and AI systems capable of ethical hacking ensures the robustness and integrity of the system. Immutable audit trails for accountability, and intelligent threat response systems, become indispensable, ensuring that the AI remains a secure and reliable tool. In the pursuit of artificial integrity, advanced security features become essential to protect against misuse, manipulation, and unintended consequences.

First, it is essential to develop robust access control mechanisms. Sophisticated access control mechanisms should not only authenticate users through multifactor authentication but also continuously validate the user's intent and behavior throughout the interaction. In addition, implementing role-based access controls that dynamically adjust the level of access to the AI's capabilities based on the user's current task, context, and profile ensures that users can only utilize AI functions relevant to their needs and authorization.

Furthermore, integrating proactive anomaly detection is crucial. This involves advanced machine learning algorithms capable of learning typical patterns of system usage and identifying deviations in real time, which may indicate potential security breaches or misuse. Also, employing AI systems to conduct predictive threat analysis by analyzing trends and patterns in cyber-security threats can preemptively address security challenges.

In addition to these measures, continuous security assessment is vital. Embedding continuous security testing into the AI's operational cycle with automated tools that regularly scan for vulnerabilities and automatically apply patches or suggest updates helps maintain uninterrupted system availability. Complementary to this, developing AI-driven simulation environments for red team–blue team exercises can help test the AI system's resilience against attacks and its ability to maintain artificial integrity under duress.

Another crucial action is the use of adaptive encryption protocols. These protocols adjust the level of encryption based on the sensitivity of the data being processed, the interaction context, and the perceived threat level. Also, considering implementing quantum-resistant encryption methods anticipates future advancements in computing that could challenge current encryption standards.

The concept of ethical hacking AI also plays a significant role. Creating AI systems capable of ethical hacking means they can autonomously probe the AI's defenses to find weaknesses, acting as continuous, automated penetration testing within defined ethical and operational boundaries to enhance the system's robustness without compromising integrity.

Moreover, ensuring immutable audit trails is essential, in particular for transparency and accountability. All actions taken by the AI, especially those related to security, should be logged in an immutable ledger, providing an unalterable record for audit. Utilizing blockchain or similar distributed ledger technologies can help maintain these records ensuring that they are tamper-proof and available for review by authorized parties.

Lastly, designing an intelligent threat response is key. The AI system should be able to intelligently respond to detected threats in real time, through measures like isolating compromised modules, alerting human supervisors, or initiating predetermined countermeasures.

These responses must be guided by the AI's understanding of the potential impact on human users and its broader ethical obligations to ensure that security measures do not inadvertently cause harm. By addressing these guiding principles, the AI system would be equipped with advanced security features ensuring the security of the system, the data it processes, and the implications from an artificial integrity standpoint. This comprehensive security approach is vital for maintaining trust and ensuring that as the AI system's capabilities expand, it remains a reliable and secure augmentation to human intelligence. These features are integral to achieving artificial integrity, as they ensure the system operates ethically, securely, and resiliently in complex, real-world environments.

About Continuous Learning and Adaptation

Transitioning from Human-First mode to Fusion mode involves enhancing machine learning algorithms to process complex feedback and adapt AI behavior accordingly. It includes integrating sophisticated feedback mechanisms, learning from overridden decisions, and scenario-based adaptive learning. The AI should synthesize interdisciplinary knowledge and have ethics-focused learning objectives. It is vital to establish iterative learning and feedback cycles, ensuring continuous improvement and adaptation of the AI system.

To achieve "continuous learning and adaptation" in AI systems at a level that aligns with the principles of artificial integrity, AI should be somehow capable to assimilate and apply complex ethical and operational knowledge continuously. Starting with the development of enhanced machine learning algorithms, they should be designed to process not only explicit feedback but also subtle cues and indirect feedback, such as changes in human emotional states or variations in task execution patterns. Furthermore, employing meta-learning techniques should allow the AI to learn how to learn from new situations dynamically, choosing the most suitable learning strategy based on the context.

Building upon this, sophisticated feedback integration is critical. Systems that integrate feedback across various modalities, including verbal feedback, nonverbal cues, and direct system interactions, form a holistic view of human operator intentions and preferences. It's essential for the AI to discern and prioritize feedback, distinguishing between off-hand comments and critical instructional feedback and adapting its behavior accordingly.

In addition, learning from overridden decisions is an important aspect. Establishing protocols for the AI to conduct root-cause analyses when decisions are overridden allows it to understand the reasoning behind human corrections and adapt its decision-making processes. Integrating mechanisms for the AI to test new strategies in simulated environments before deploying them in real-world scenarios ensures that adaptations are beneficial and do not introduce new risks.

Moreover, scenario-based adaptive learning plays a significant role. Developing a library of scenarios, derived from both historical data and predictive modeling, that the AI can use to simulate decision-making and learning from virtual experiences is vital. These simulations expose the AI to a wide range of potential situations, enabling it to build a repertoire of responses that are ethically sound and aligned with human values.

Another important action is the interdisciplinary knowledge synthesis. Incorporating a broad range of interdisciplinary knowledge into the AI's learning databases, including ethics, law, sociology, and psychology, provides the AI with a diverse perspective on human intelligence and decision-making. This knowledge enhances the AI's ability to reason about the consequences of its actions and adapt its behavior to better support human operators.

Furthermore, embedding ethics-focused learning objectives within the AI's algorithms is crucial. These objectives specifically focus on understanding and applying ethical principles, ensuring that the AI's continuous learning is always anchored to these principles. Complementary to this, developing evaluation metrics that measure the AI's performance not just based on task completion but also on adherence to ethical standards and positive impact on human operators is essential.

Lastly, establishing iterative learning and feedback cycles is key to continuous improvement. This involves a system where the AI regularly updates its models and strategies based on new data, feedback, and ethical considerations, ensuring an ongoing evolution and refinement of its operations.

By addressing these guiding principles, the AI system is designed with the capability to balance operational efficiency with ethical imperatives, ensuring that as it becomes more integrated into decision-making processes, it enhances human intelligence value added without compromising on ethical standards. This approach to continuous learning and adaptation is fundamental to achieving artificial integrity fostering AI systems that are not only intelligent and capable but also principled and trustworthy.

Navigating from Fusion Mode to AI-First Mode

As organizations transition toward the algorithmic boost cluster from a state of Fusion mode (high human intelligence value added/high AI value added) to a state of AI-First mode (low human intelligence value added/high AI value added), it revolves around enhancing AI capabilities while reducing human input in decision-making, without compromising on ethical standards and user-centric values.

In transitioning from Fusion mode to AI-First mode, there is a significant shift in the operational dynamics between human intelligence and AI capabilities. In Fusion mode, both AI and human intelligence synergistically contribute at high levels, working in tandem to achieve desired outcomes. However, moving into AI-First mode, the focus pivots to elevating the role of AI as the primary driver of processes and decisions while human intelligence assumes a more supervisory or oversight role.

In this new arrangement, the sophistication of AI is not just a supportive mechanism but becomes the central feature of operational execution to deliver outcomes. AI's advanced algorithms and learning capabilities are harnessed to perform complex tasks, make autonomous decisions, and handle a larger spectrum of responsibilities, reducing the direct involvement of human intelligence in routine, tactical, or even strategic functions.

While human value added becomes less pronounced in direct task execution outcomes, it remains vital in setting strategic directions, ethical boundaries, and oversight. Here, AI is no longer just an enabler but a leader in operational processes, characterized by its capacity to learn, adapt, and act independently. This mode underscores a shift from human–AI collaboration to AI-led operations, where AI's high value-add is derived from its ability to operate with minimal human intervention, albeit under human-established frameworks and principles. This mode represents a paradigm where AI's advanced capabilities are maximized, aligning with scenarios that prioritize speed, efficiency, and scalability, often in complex environments where AI can navigate and manage variables beyond human capabilities.

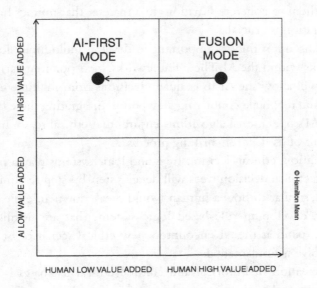

The key areas to consider in this transition include autonomous ethical reasoning, robust fail-safes, impact assessment, and user-centric design.

About Autonomous Ethical Reasoning

From Fusion mode to AI-First mode, it requires building AI systems capable of sophisticated ethical decision-making, akin to human reasoning. It involves constructing AI with complex cognitive architectures that integrate human cognition models, moral philosophy, and ethical decision-making frameworks. Such systems should be able to process and apply ethical concepts autonomously, ensuring AI decisions align with human values even as human involvement decreases.

Embedding autonomous ethical reasoning within AI systems requires an advanced set of actions that enable the AI to independently navigate ethical landscapes with the same complexity and nuance as a human. This involves creating systems that do not merely follow a set of preprogrammed rules but can engage in a form of moral reasoning and learning.

First, the development of sophisticated cognitive architectures is essential. These architectures should support complex ethical reasoning by integrating models of human cognition, moral philosophy, and ethical decision-making. The capability of processing abstract ethical concepts and applying them to concrete situations in a manner that mimics human ethical deliberation is crucial.

Building upon this, it's important to develop multidimensional ethical frameworks within the AI. These frameworks, incorporating various ethical theories, will allow the AI to evaluate decisions from multiple ethical perspectives and reconcile conflicting viewpoints. Integrating these frameworks with the AI's operational algorithms ensures that ethical reasoning is a core component of its decision-making process.

In addition, ethical decision trees and logic systems play a pivotal role. Designing ethical decision trees will detail a step-by-step reasoning process for the AI, similar to how a human would break down an ethical problem. Moreover, developing rule-based logic systems that are flexible and can adapt or expand as the AI encounters new ethical scenarios or as societal norms evolve is fundamental.

The creation of historical and cultural ethical databases is also a key action. These comprehensive databases of historical ethical decisions, cultural norms, and legal precedents will inform the AI's ethical reasoning. Regular updates and curation to reflect current ethical standards and global diversity are essential.

Implementing case-based reasoning mechanisms will allow the AI to analogize from previous ethical decisions to new situations, learning from the outcomes of past judgments. Also, enabling the AI to abstract general ethical principles from specific cases, which can then be applied to new and unprecedented scenarios is instrumental.

Predictive ethical modeling is another significant step. Using predictive modeling to forecast the potential outcomes of the AI's decisions, including their ethical implications, and integrating these models with the AI's decision-making processes, will allow it to anticipate and mitigate potential ethical issues.

Furthermore, ensuring that the AI's ethical decisions are explainable is crucial. This explainable ethical AI should provide clear justifications for its choices, with interfaces allowing users to query the ethical basis of decisions and receive explanations in understandable language.

Lastly, the creation of dynamic ethical balancing systems within the AI is necessary. These systems should weigh various factors, such as individual well-being, societal impact, and long-term consequences, adjusting actions to maintain ethical integrity. Sensitivity to the context and scale of decisions will ensure appropriate ethical considerations are made for both minor and major decisions.

By addressing these guiding principles, an AI system will be equipped to engage in autonomous ethical reasoning, a critical component of artificial integrity. This capacity will enable the AI to act with a high degree of autonomy while still aligning its decisions with human ethical values, ensuring that as human involvement in decision-making decreases, the AI upholds the same moral standards we expect in human society.

About Robust Fail-Safes

Essential for maintaining trust and safety, robust fail-safes in AI systems become increasingly critical as human oversight diminishes when transitioning from Fusion mode to AI-First mode. Developing layered fail-safe architectures, context-sensitive intervention protocols, and real-time ethical monitoring mechanisms ensures that AI systems can autonomously address and mitigate ethical breaches. These fail-safes should be capable of handling both minor infractions and significant ethical violations, maintaining artificial integrity at all levels.

Establishing robust fail-safes in AI systems is critical for ensuring artificial integrity. These fail-safes are necessary to maintain trust and safety in AI systems, particularly as they begin to operate with lower levels of human oversight. Toward this aim, constructing a layered fail-safe architecture is critical. This would involve the AI's decision-making process being overseen by multiple, independent systems that can intervene at different stages of operation. These layers should include local, immediate response systems for minor ethical breaches and more comprehensive, high-level systems for significant ethical violations, examining broader implications.

Building on this, it's necessary to develop context-sensitive intervention protocols. These protocols should discern the context of an action and determine the appropriate level of response, ranging from simple corrective action to a complete system shutdown. This requires the AI to be aware of the operational context, including potential risks to human well-being and societal impact.

In addition, integrating ethical benchmarking and response systems that continually assess the AI's decisions against a library of ethical standards and precedents is paramount. These systems must be dynamic, adapting these standards as societal norms evolve, and designed to automatically trigger responses if deviations from accepted norms are detected, without waiting for human intervention.

Another crucial step is implementing real-time ethical monitoring. Sophisticated monitoring systems should analyze the AI's operations in real time, using anomaly detection algorithms to spot deviations from expected ethical behavior. The monitoring system must interpret the AI's decision-making rationale, ensuring interventions are informed and precise based on a deep understanding of the AI's operations.

To ensure effectiveness, regular simulation and testing environments are vital. Conducting simulations and stress tests within controlled environments will evaluate the effectiveness of the fail-safe systems in various ethical breach scenarios. These simulations can help refine the AI's responses, ensuring preparedness for new and unforeseen ethical dilemmas.

Moreover, fail-safe activation transparency is essential. Any activation of a fail-safe mechanism must be transparent, with logs of all interventions kept for audit and improvement purposes. The system should notify relevant stakeholders upon fail-safe activation, explaining the ethical breach and actions taken.

Following such activation, establishing human–AI collaborative review processes where human ethicists work with the AI to understand the breach and refine the system's ethical reasoning is crucial. These reviews should feed back into the AI's learning processes, allowing it to improve its ethical decision-making and reduce the likelihood of future breaches.

Finally, escalation pathways for serious breaches are required. Clear pathways must be created to bring serious ethical breaches to the attention of senior human supervisors or ethics committees for review, prompting a swift and appropriate response, including system-wide reviews or updates to the AI's ethical frameworks if necessary.

By addressing these guiding principles within AI systems, they are equipped to safeguard against ethical breaches. Robust fail-safes are a cornerstone of artificial integrity, ensuring that the AI remains a safe, reliable, and ethical partner in its interactions with humans and society at large.

About Impact Assessment

Considering the transition from Fusion mode to AI-First mode, AI systems must be equipped to assess the broader implications of their decisions. This involves integrating predictive modeling to forecast potential outcomes and their societal impacts, employing real-time sentiment and reaction monitoring, and developing dynamic socio-technical systems models. Such systems should be capable of performing stakeholder impact analysis, considering cross-cultural impacts, and incorporating feedback loops for continuous adaptation.

For an AI system to achieve "impact assessment" it must be capable of understanding and evaluating the potential consequences of its actions in a broad societal context. This requires advanced predictive capabilities and a deep understanding of human societies, behaviors, and the potential ripple effects of its actions. Starting with predictive consequence analysis, it's crucial to develop AI models that can simulate potential outcomes based on historical data, current societal trends, and projected future states. These models must consider various dimensions of impact, including economic, social, ethical, and environmental factors.

Building on this, the implementation of real-time sentiment and reaction monitoring is essential. Implementing real-time sentiment analysis and social listening tools that assess the public's emotional and cognitive responses to the AI's decisions or actions will enhance responsiveness. These tools need to be integrated with the AI's decision-making processes, enabling it to adjust actions in response to real-time feedback from affected stakeholders.

Furthermore, integrating advanced socio-technical systems modeling into the AI's operational framework is vital. This approach helps to understand and account for the complex interactions between technology, individuals, and society, thereby allowing the AI to anticipate the broader implications of its actions, particularly their effects on social structures, relationships, and human well-being.

Another key action is conducting stakeholder impact analysis. Creating algorithms that identify and weigh the interests of different stakeholders, while considering factors like power dynamics and vulnerability, will ensure that the AI can adjust its actions to prioritize the well-being of the most affected or vulnerable groups.

To guide decision-making processes, designing an ethical impact scoring system is necessary. This system would rate the AI's potential decisions based on their ethical alignment and the positive or negative impacts they may have, guiding the AI toward more ethical and beneficial outcomes.

In addition, cross-cultural impact considerations are imperative. Ensuring the AI is equipped with a cross-cultural understanding to assess the impact of its actions across different cultural contexts is critical, especially for global systems operating in multicultural environments.

Integrating feedback loops is also crucial. These loops should channel insights from impact assessments back into the AI's learning and adaptation cycles, ensuring it evolves to make more socially responsible decisions over time. Feedback should come from a diverse range of societal voices, not just direct users, to ensure a breadth of perspectives.

Lastly, developing mechanisms for transparent impact reporting is paramount. These mechanisms should provide clear and accessible information to stakeholders and the public on both the expected and actual impacts of the AI's decisions. Such transparency and accountability are key to building trust in the AI's operations.

By addressing these guiding principles, the AI system will be better equipped to conduct thorough impact assessments and adjust its behavior accordingly, a crucial aspect of achieving artificial integrity. This comprehensive approach to understanding and mitigating potential negative impacts is essential for ensuring that AI systems contribute positively to society and reflect the ethical standards expected by their human counterparts.

About User-Centric Design

From Fusion mode to AI-First mode, as AI assumes more responsibilities, the focus on user-centric design becomes paramount. This includes developing inclusive and adaptive interfaces, transparent user controls, and consent mechanisms that respect user privacy and autonomy. The AI should feature personalization algorithms that adapt to user behaviors and preferences while adhering to ethical personalization standards. Moreover, ensuring AI systems are context-aware and responsive to the user's environment enhances the overall user experience.

Embedding artificial integrity into AI systems necessitates a user-centric design that prioritizes the needs, preferences, and well-being of the user.

To achieve artificial integrity from a "user-centric design" standpoint, a series of guiding principles could be considered. In aiming to achieve this, the development of inclusive and adaptive interface design is crucial. These adaptive user interfaces can be personalized for different users, adjusting complexity and interaction style based on the user's experience, ability, and preferences. Utilizing universal design principles can ensure the AI system is accessible to all users, including those with disabilities, incorporating features like voice commands, screen readers, and alternative input methods.

Building on this foundation, implementing transparent user controls and preferences is essential. This system allows individuals to easily adjust settings, preferences, and limits on how the AI interacts with them and makes decisions on their behalf. In addition, integrating a preference learning mechanism that observes user behavior and feedback refines these settings, enhancing user agency without compromising it.

Moreover, designing clear and unambiguous consent and autonomy mechanisms is important. These mechanisms should ensure users are fully informed and able to provide or withdraw consent for different levels of AI interaction and data use at any time, maintaining ease of use and accessibility.

Personalization and adaptation algorithms are also key. Advanced personalization algorithms that tailor AI functions to individual users' needs, learning from user behavior, offer more relevant and supportive interactions over time. However, it's important to ensure these algorithms respect user privacy and are transparent in their use of personal data to drive personalization.

In addition, creating user experience (UX) feedback loops is vital. These loops incorporate user experience data into the AI's learning process, enhancing the system's user-centric design. Actively soliciting user feedback through various channels ensures that the AI system evolves in response to user needs and preferences.

Integrating quality of life metrics into the AI's decision-making processes ensures that user well-being is the primary focus. These metrics should account for holistic well-being, encompassing emotional, social, and physical factors, beyond mere user satisfaction.

Establishing ethical personalization standards is also critical. These standards should prevent the AI from manipulating user behavior or promoting addictive patterns, instead enhancing user autonomy and empowerment.

Finally, enabling context-aware assistance allows the AI to understand and respond appropriately to the user's current situation and environment. This assistance should adapt to factors such as the user's mood, time of day, and physical setting.

By addressing these guiding principles of user-centric design, an AI system can achieve artificial integrity, ensuring that its operations are always aligned with the best interests of the users. This alignment is crucial for maintaining trust and fostering a beneficial partnership between humans and intelligent systems. In this transition, technical provisions must be made to ensure that as AI systems begin to function with more autonomy, they do so with a firm foundation in ethical reasoning, equipped with the necessary tools to assess their impact and designed with a focus on serving user needs effectively and ethically.

Navigating from Marginal Mode to Fusion Mode

In the journey toward the algorithmic boost cluster from a state of Marginal mode (low human intelligence value added/low AI value added) to a state of Fusion mode (high human intelligence value added/high AI value added), the aim is to elevate both human intelligence contributions and AI capabilities, ensuring they work in harmony, supported by robust ethical frameworks. In moving from Marginal mode to Fusion mode, the journey is marked by a deliberate increase in both the involvement of AI and the prominence of human intelligence required to achieve an expected outcome. In Fusion mode, AI is designed to work in concert with high human intelligence, contributing significantly to outcomes while not overshadowing the human element but still participating to shape the ultimate result. In this balanced scenario, AI's advanced capabilities are used to amplify human expertise, bringing forth a synergy where complex analytical tasks and creative problem-solving benefit from the combined strengths of AI's rapid processing and human insight to deliver an expected outcome.

Here, the value added by AI in the outcome is substantial in terms of efficiency and innovation, yet it's carefully calibrated to complement rather than diminish human roles. It represents a collaborative zenith where AI and human intelligence both operate at their highest potential, integrating seamlessly to enhance decision-making, innovation, and strategic foresight. This equilibrium ensures that AI systems are leveraged to their full potential without compromising the unique contributions of human cognition. The focus is on forging a partnership where the intuitive, creative, and emotional capacities of humans are augmented by the predictive, analytical, and computational strengths of AI, leading to enriched outcomes that neither could achieve alone.

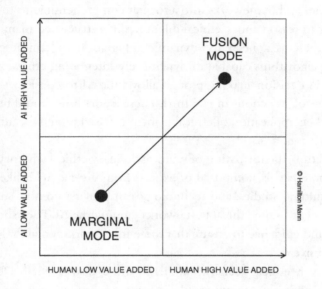

The critical elements in this transition include developing interdisciplinary ethical frameworks, ethical training data, collaborative interfaces, and dynamic consent mechanisms.

About Interdisciplinary Ethical Frameworks

When transitioning from Marginal mode to Fusion mode, to achieve high AI value addition without compromising ethical standards, it's essential to embed interdisciplinary ethical frameworks into AI systems. This involves creating ethical AI ontologies, dynamically integrating ethical principles into AI decision-making, and engaging multidisciplinary panels for continuous ethical guidance. By doing so, AI systems can navigate complex ethical landscapes, ensuring decisions are made with a comprehensive understanding of diverse ethical perspectives.

To ensure artificial integrity in AI systems through the development of interdisciplinary ethical frameworks, it involves not only establishing robust, ethical guidelines but also equipping the AI with the ability to understand, interpret, and apply these guidelines within its decision-making processes. One essential action is the development of an ethical AI ontology. Building a structured ethical ontology enables the AI to understand complex ethical concepts and the relationships between them. This ontology translates ethical principles and frameworks into a format comprehensible to the AI, thus enabling it to reason about ethical dilemmas in a structured manner.

Also, there is a need for dynamic integration of ethical principles. Designing algorithms capable of dynamically integrating ethical principles into the AI's decision-making process allows the AI to consider the ethical implications of its actions in real time. These algorithms should be adept at adjusting their application of ethical principles based on the specific context of each decision.

In addition, the formation of multidisciplinary ethical advisory panels is crucial. These panels, composed of experts from diverse fields like philosophy, law, cultural studies, and technology, can provide continuous updates and refinement to the ethical frameworks guiding the AI. They should offer oversight and guidance to ensure that these frameworks remain relevant and comprehensive.

Moreover, ethical scenario simulations are instrumental. Developing simulation environments where the AI can explore ethical scenarios and learn from the outcomes, akin to human learning from case studies, allows the AI to test its application of ethical principles. These simulations help refine the AI's ethical reasoning without real-world consequences.

Embedding ethics in machine learning cycles is another key step. This process ensures that ethical reasoning is an integral part of the AI's learning process, involving the use of ethically annotated datasets for training and incorporating ethical performance metrics into the AI's evaluation criteria.

Furthermore, integrating cross-cultural ethics modules is vital. This integration ensures that the AI's ethical reasoning is sensitive to cultural diversity and does not impose a single ethical viewpoint. It enables the AI to navigate the pluralistic ethical landscape of a globalized world.

Implementing real-time ethical decision auditing is also necessary. This mechanism enables the AI to provide a rationale for its actions that human supervisors can review, ensuring accountability and opportunities for ongoing learning and improvement in ethical reasoning.

In addition, creating feedback loops for ethical evolution allows the AI to evolve its understanding of ethics based on new information, societal changes, and stakeholder input. This evolutionary approach ensures that the AI's ethical frameworks adapt to changing ethical norms and values.

Lastly, ensuring transparent ethical reporting is crucial for building trust with users and stakeholders. Developing systems that clearly communicate the ethical principles applied in each decision shows that the AI is consistently upholding its ethical obligations.

By addressing these guiding principles, the AI system will be equipped to operate with a high level of artificial integrity, ensuring that it not only functions with high human intelligence value added but also adheres to the highest ethical standards. This comprehensive approach to ethics within AI ensures that as AI systems take on more complex and impactful roles, they do so in a manner that is responsible, equitable, and aligned with the multifaceted ethical expectations of society.

About Ethical Training Data

The foundation of an ethically sound AI system lies in its training data. In the context of the transition from Marginal mode to Fusion mode, ensuring the provision of ethical training data involves the development of inclusive data acquisition frameworks, ethical data curation, and the use of synthetic data for balance. This step is crucial in preventing biases and ensuring the AI's decisions are fair and representative of diverse societal norms.

The provision of ethical training data is a foundational element for ensuring artificial integrity in the development of AI. It requires not only the careful selection and processing of data but also the establishment of protocols that safeguard against biases and ethical transgressions.

Key to achieving "ethical training data" is the development of a diverse and inclusive data acquisition framework. This framework should emphasize diversity and inclusion, ensuring that the data reflects a wide range of human experiences and conditions to prevent biased AI outcomes. Collaborating with a diverse range of stakeholders, especially marginalized and underrepresented groups, is crucial to gather data that accurately reflects the entire population spectrum.

Alongside this, there needs to be an ethical data curation and annotation process. Establishing a multitiered process that includes ethical reviews of data sources, setting annotation guidelines, and ongoing assessment of data quality is vital. Collaboration with ethicists and domain experts during the annotation process ensures that the data is labeled in a manner that aligns with ethical considerations and societal norms.

Moreover, the utilization of synthetic data for ethical balance plays a significant role. Advanced synthetic data generation can create diverse and balanced datasets where real-world data is lacking, or its use could lead to privacy breaches. It's essential to ensure that synthetic data is generated using models vetted for ethical soundness and is used to enhance rather than replace real-world data where necessary.

Implementing informed consent and data transparency is also crucial. Establishing clear and robust informed consent processes for all data collection provides data subjects with comprehensive information about how their data will be used. Transparent data usage policies should be easily accessible and understandable to nonexperts, fostering trust and confidence in the AI system.

Dynamic data source validation is another important action. Introducing mechanisms for the continuous evaluation of data sources ensures their integrity and ethical compliance over time, allowing for adjustments in the training datasets as societal norms and ethical standards evolve. Automating the monitoring of data sources quickly identifies and addresses any arising ethical issues.

Furthermore, ethical data life-cycle management is essential. Adopting a life-cycle approach to data management that considers the ethical implications from collection to disposal ensures all stages adhere to high ethical standards, including secure disposal protocols for data that is no longer needed or fails to meet ethical standards.

Establishing feedback systems for ethical data use allows the AI to learn from its performance and user interactions, identifying potential biases or ethical issues in the training data. This feedback aids in iteratively refining the training datasets, supporting the ethical development of the AI system.

Finally, the creation of cross-functional ethical oversight teams, comprising data scientists, ethicists, and legal experts, is imperative. These teams should oversee the ethical use of training data in AI development, with the authority to make decisions regarding the suitability of datasets and to mandate necessary changes.

By addressing these guiding principles into the AI development process, the resulting AI system will be better equipped to act with artificial integrity, making decisions and taking actions that are ethical, fair, and respectful of human values. This comprehensive approach ensures that as AI systems become more advanced and autonomous, they remain anchored to the ethical principles that are essential for trust and cooperation between AI and humans.

About Collaborative Interfaces

When transitioning from Marginal mode to Fusion mode, as AI systems take on radically advanced roles, fostering effective collaboration between humans and AI becomes paramount. Designing seamless interaction interfaces, clearly defining human–AI roles, and ensuring equal valuation of inputs from both parties are essential. These interfaces should facilitate intuitive communication and context-aware decision support, enhancing joint problem-solving capabilities.

To embed artificial integrity within AI systems, the development of collaborative interfaces must be approached holistically. This encompasses fostering teamwork, enhancing mutual capabilities, and aligning toward common objectives.

One of the key steps is the seamless interaction design. This involves designing interaction protocols that allow fluid communication between humans and AI, enabling the seamless exchange of ideas and information. These interfaces should enable natural language processing, contextual understanding, and adaptive response generation to match the user's communication style.

Following this is the aspect of human–AI role definition. It's important to clearly define the roles and responsibilities of both humans and AI within the collaborative framework. This ensures that tasks and decision-making processes are appropriately allocated and systems are developed to understand and adapt to the dynamic distribution of roles based on situation and task complexity.

Moreover, equal valuation of inputs is crucial. Systems should be created to ensure that the contributions of both humans and AI are equally valued, with mechanisms in place to resolve conflicts or disagreements respectfully. Decision-making models should incorporate both AI and human inputs, utilizing consensus-building algorithms to find the best course of action.

Another essential element is intuitive design and interaction paradigms. Using user-centered design principles, interfaces should be intuitive for human users, reducing the learning curve and enhancing cooperation. Understanding human teamwork dynamics is key to designing AI interaction paradigms, ensuring that AI complements human work styles and preferences.

Furthermore, integrating context-aware decision support within AI systems is important for providing tailored decision support. These systems should not only offer relevant information but also anticipate user needs, presenting information in an immediately actionable format.

In addition, the development of adaptive information presentation algorithms is key. These algorithms should determine the most effective way to present data and suggestions, considering factors like the user's expertise, cognitive load, and situation urgency, and adjust the information's complexity based on user responses. They should also be able to adjust the level of detail and complexity of the information presented based on the user's response and understanding.

Equipping AI systems with joint problem-solving capabilities need to be considered to enable collaborative solution development. These capabilities should include models for shared creativity and innovation, leveraging the strengths of both human and machine intelligence.

Ethical alignment in collaboration is also essential. Collaborative interfaces must be designed with an ethical alignment that considers the values and goals of human users, including systems that can adapt to different ethical perspectives and find solutions that are acceptable to all parties involved.

Finally, implementing feedback and iterative improvement mechanisms within the collaborative interface is crucial. These mechanisms allow both AI and human users to learn from each interaction, continually improving the interface. This ensures effective and satisfying collaboration for all parties involved, from a human-centric standpoint.

By addressing these guiding principles, AI systems can be developed with collaborative interfaces that truly embody artificial integrity. These interfaces will enable humans and AI to work together synergistically, with AI systems supporting human intelligence and decision-making, enhancing productivity and creativity, and ensuring that outcomes are achieved ethically and efficiently.

About Dynamic Consent Mechanisms

From Marginal mode to Fusion mode, considering such increased AI autonomy, maintaining user autonomy and trust is critical. Implementing dynamic consent mechanisms that evolve with user behavior and preferences, provide granular control, and ensure real-time consent revocation capabilities is essential. This approach respects the dynamic nature of user comfort and expectations, upholding transparency and accountability in AI operations.

With this purpose in mind, implementing granular consent options is key. These options allow users to have fine-grained control over different aspects of data usage and AI interactions and should be easily accessible and understandable to enable informed decision-making about their data.

Building on this, AI systems need to be capable of evolving consent with user behavior. Such systems would learn from user behavior, suggesting consent adjustments that align with users' evolving privacy preferences and interaction patterns. Regular engagement with users to confirm or adjust consent reflects the dynamic nature of user comfort and expectations.

Moreover, creating context-sensitive consent mechanisms is important. These mechanisms would adjust the level of data sharing and AI autonomy based on the context, such as requiring explicit consent in more sensitive situations.

In addition, ensuring real-time consent revocation is key. This feature allows users to immediately halt ongoing data processing or AI actions they are uncomfortable with, with the system responding instantaneously to consent withdrawal, with transparent processes in place to show users how their data and interactions are handled post-revocation.

Maintaining consent traceability is also crucial. Keeping a transparent and immutable log of consent-related actions enables users to audit their consent history with robust protection against unauthorized access and tampering, and maintaining the integrity of consent records.

Integrating user education on consent implications within the AI system helps users understand the implications of their consent decisions. These resources provide clear explanations tailored to the user's expertise level, without overwhelming technical jargon.

Ensuring that consent processes are legally compliant is also essential. The consent mechanisms should align with legal frameworks like GDPR and the e-Privacy Directives and be adaptable to legislative changes, accommodating different legal requirements from various jurisdictions, particularly for AI systems with a global user base.

Finally, offering user-driven consent customization empowers users to set personalized consent settings that reflect their individual preferences and needs. This customization process should be intuitive, guiding users through the process of setting and adjusting their consent choices.

By addressing these guiding principles, AI systems can be developed with "dynamic consent mechanisms" that truly embody artificial integrity. Such systems will ensure that user autonomy is central to AI interactions and that consent is a living process, capable of adapting to users' changing needs and preferences. This approach is vital for building trust and ensuring that AI systems are used responsibly and ethically.

In transitioning to a scenario where both human and AI contributions are highly valued, it is essential to ensure that AI systems are technically capable of operating within sophisticated ethical boundaries, utilizing ethically sound data, enabling close collaboration with human partners, and upholding user autonomy through dynamic consent. These actions will not only foster trust and cooperation between humans and AI but will also ensure that the enhanced capabilities of both are leveraged to produce outcomes that are beneficial and aligned with societal values. In each of these transitions, the technical design and implementation of the AI system must be foresighted, with a foundational commitment to ethical operations that protect and enhance human values, ensuring that the advancements in AI capabilities are matched with an equal progression in ethical sophistication.

6 | How to Thrive Through Navigating for Humanistic Reinforcement

The cluster labeled *humanistic reinforcement* is characterized by a set of transitions that emphasize elevating the role of human contribution in contexts where artificial intelligence (AI) is involved.

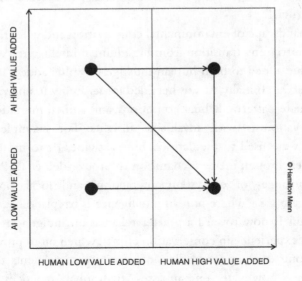

The defining feature of this cluster is a deliberate shift toward increasing human input and decision-making capacity while maintaining or reducing the role of AI. This shift often reflects a strategic decision to bolster the aspects of service, production, or creativity that are uniquely human and cannot be replicated by AI, such as empathy, ethical judgment, and deep contextual understanding.

Humanistic Reinforcement Puts the Utmost Importance to Human Agency

The progression from high human intelligence value added/high AI value added to high human intelligence value added/low AI value added signals a purposeful strategic shift, wherein the focus is shifted back to human expertise while downscaling the AI components. This transition may arise in scenarios where the unique qualities of human intelligence are revalued, possibly due to a reassessment of the role of technology in enhancing rather than replacing human capabilities. It reflects a nuanced understanding that, while AI can process and analyze data at an extraordinary scale, there are dimensions of problem-solving and critical thinking where human judgment remains superior. This approach is often taken to ensure that the final output retains the irreplaceable nuances of human discretion and unique subtleties of discernment, especially in sectors where human insight is crucial.

In the landscape of environmental conservation and wildlife protection, there is an intriguing transition from high human intelligence value added/ high AI value added to high human intelligence value added/low AI value added underway. Initially, AI was heralded for its ability to analyze vast datasets on climate patterns, habitat conditions, and animal migrations, providing conservationists with invaluable insights. For example, AI-driven algorithms were used to predict poaching activities or to monitor endangered species through image recognition (Norouzzadeh et al., 2018). However, the nuances of ecosystem interactions and local environmental knowledge are areas where human intelligence is irreplaceable.

The shift is now toward a greater reliance on indigenous knowledge and human experience in conservation efforts, which often provide a deeper, more contextual understanding of natural environments than AI can offer. Such knowledge encompasses traditional practices that have conserved biodiversity for centuries and understanding the subtleties of local species and ecological balance that AI, for all its data processing prowess, cannot fully grasp. The scientific community and environmental organizations are increasingly valuing this localized human expertise over AI, recognizing the limitations of technology in capturing the intricate tapestry of life that experienced human conservators understand intrinsically.

In the field of legal jurisprudence, a transition from high human intelligence value added/high AI value added to high human intelligence value added/low AI value added is observable. Legal AI tools have been used extensively to analyze large volumes of case law, predict legal outcomes, and assist in legal research. These AI systems significantly speed up the process of sifting through legal documents, identifying relevant case precedents, and even suggesting probable outcomes based on historical data.

However, the interpretation of law involves not only the letter but also the spirit of the statutes, which often necessitates a deep understanding of ethical considerations, human judgment, and the unique circumstances of each case—factors that AI is not equipped to process. As noted in a study by Surden (2019), while AI can provide valuable assistance in legal analysis, there is a shift back toward emphasizing the nuanced understanding and critical thinking skills of experienced lawyers for advocacy, strategy, and negotiations. The legal profession is recognizing the limitations of AI in areas that require complex interpretative skills and ethical decision-making, leading to a resurgence in the reliance on human intelligence over AI.

Transitioning from low human intelligence value added/high AI value added to high human intelligence value added/high AI value added reflects a significant strategic enhancement where human expertise is elevated to match the sophisticated level of AI deployment. This shift is emblematic of an environment where the synergy between human creativity and AI's analytical prowess is maximized. It signals an acknowledgment of the value that human insight brings to complex decision-making processes, particularly where nuanced understanding and emotional intelligence are paramount. By intensifying human involvement, businesses or systems can exploit AI's capacity to handle data-heavy tasks while humans provide strategic oversight, innovation, and moral considerations, leading to a more holistic and potent combination of human and artificial intelligence.

This transition acknowledges that the interplay between human intuition and AI's computational power can drive innovation and efficiency in unprecedented ways, creating a sum greater than its parts. In the ever-evolving domain of cybersecurity, the interplay between human expertise and artificial intelligence is critical, as outlined by Cummings (2013). Cybersecurity challenges are characterized by their complexity and dynamism, with threats constantly evolving to exploit new vulnerabilities. In this high-stakes environment, AI serves as an indispensable asset for real-time threat monitoring and the analysis of vast datasets to identify potential security breaches. However, the unpredictable nature of cyber threats necessitates a level of adaptability and creative problem-solving that is inherently human.

Cummings emphasizes the complementary nature of human and AI roles in constructing a robust defense against cyber-attacks. While AI algorithms excel at detecting patterns and anomalies within data flows that might suggest a breach, human cybersecurity experts are essential for interpreting these findings, understanding the broader context, and orchestrating an appropriate response to sophisticated and novel threats. This nuanced approach often requires a deep understanding of hacker psychology, complex systems, and the strategic implications of each decision—areas where human intuition and experience are paramount.

The shifting landscape of cybersecurity illustrates a strategic enhancement of both AI and human capabilities. AI tools are increasingly sophisticated, using machine learning to adapt to new threats and automate responses to known attack vectors. Meanwhile, human experts are empowered to concentrate on higher-order strategic tasks such as anticipating attacker behaviors, crafting bespoke defensive measures, and engaging in ethical hacking to test system robustness.

This balanced paradigm in cybersecurity underpins a greater trend across industries: the recognition of the irreplaceable value of human insight in complex scenarios, coupled with a strategic utilization of AI for its analytical prowess and operational efficiency. Together, this synergy enables a more formidable and agile response to the multifaceted cyber threats faced by organizations, reflecting a shift toward a model where human intelligence is augmented by rather than supplanted by AI technology.

The field of mental health support, as explored in the study by Sharma et al. (2022), provides an insightful example of AI's role in complex human interactions. It demonstrates that while AI is effective for routine tasks like scheduling and grammar-checking, it faces challenges in complex, emotionally nuanced tasks like empathic conversations in peer-to-peer mental health support. The research found that their AI-in-the-loop system, HAILEY, led to a significant increase in conversational empathy. This indicates that AI, when properly integrated, can enhance human performance in tasks requiring emotional intelligence.

These soft skills, such as emotional intelligence, are cultivated through direct human engagement and are vital for empathic conversation. The study suggests a future where AI's role in augmenting human abilities, especially in delicate, human-centric areas like mental health support is promising. As a result, this points to the evolving role of AI as an aid in enhancing human capabilities in sensitive and nuanced areas like mental health support, rather than acting as a stand-alone solution.

As a result, AI's growing presence in mental health is not replacing human practitioners but rather redefining their roles, emphasizing their irreplaceable value in developing empathetic relationships with patients that require soft skills. By leveraging AI for its strengths in data processing and pattern recognition, healthcare systems can enhance the human intelligence value added. This creates a symbiotic relationship between technology and human expertise, leading to a more holistic and empathetic patient experience. This integrated approach points to the future of mental health support, where technology and human insight combine for comprehensive care.

Embracing this theme further, the shift from low human intelligence value added/low AI value added to high human intelligence value added/low AI value added marks a strategic realignment toward prioritizing human expertise in scenarios where AI has not been heavily implemented. This could reflect a scenario where the nuances and subtleties of human judgment are required to a greater extent than what AI can offer, or where the human touch is reintroduced to provide a more personalized or artisanal service. This transition is often a nod to the irreplaceable value of human interaction, discretion, and personal service in an increasingly automated world. It's a recognition that while AI can greatly enhance many aspects of work and life, the fundamental human qualities of insight, understanding, and personal connection are often the key differentiators in delivering value.

Richard Sennett's (2008) work delves into the renewed valorization of craftsmanship in the creative sector, an intriguing counterbalance to the age of mass production accentuated by AI and automated processes. He contemplates the cultural and economic forces fostering a renaissance of artisanal products, suggesting a collective yearning for the singular and the authentically crafted. This pivot points to an elevated esteem for the intrinsic qualities of human touch, skill, and creative expression—attributes that AI, with its algorithms and automated efficiencies, is intrinsically unable to mimic.

Sennett underscores the notion that the uniqueness of handcrafted goods derives from the human story they embody, the years of skill honed through practice, and the nuanced imperfections that confer character and individuality to each piece. In the creative industries—ranging from pottery to furniture making and from couture fashion to gourmet cuisine—consumers are increasingly drawn to goods that resonate with the signature of the artisan, an autograph of human intelligence and creativity.

This trend is not a rejection of technology but rather an assertion of human value in a complementary role. The tactile, the bespoke, and the handmade offer a narrative of craftsmanship that mass production cannot tell. As industries pivot to accommodate this appetite, there is a discernible shift toward valuing the high human intelligence that can only be imparted by hands skilled through years of dedication to a craft. This transition signifies industries' recognition of the irreplaceable human value in certain domains, where the efficiency of AI is secondary to the authenticity and emotive connection elicited by the human-crafted experiences. In essence, Sennett's insights illuminate a growing niche wherein the high human value is celebrated and sought after, indicating a broader societal trend that cherishes the uniquely human contributions to creativity and production, even in an era increasingly dominated by artificial intelligence.

In the domain of local tourism, a subtle yet impactful transition is taking place, as described by Xiang (2018), where the sector is moving away from impersonal, technology-driven tour experiences toward more authentic, human-centric engagements. Xiang's research asserts that despite the profound transformation of the travel landscape through information technology—enabling self-guided tours and virtual experiences—the human guide's role has become increasingly invaluable. The unique insights, personal anecdotes, and interactive narratives provided by human guides enhance the touristic journey, offering a depth of experience that AI-guided tours lack.

Xiang explores this dynamic, noting that the expertise of local guides in storytelling and their ability to connect emotionally with tourists elevate the travel experience. These guides offer nuanced understanding and interpretations that transcend the factual information available via digital platforms. They adapt their delivery to the audience's responses, tailor their itineraries to interests voiced on the spot, and answer questions with the kind of contextual richness that only a local expert can provide. As tourists seek not just to see but to understand and feel connected to the places they visit, the human guide's role becomes irreplaceable.

This shift toward high human value-added in local tourism signifies an industry adapting to the desires of travelers who are looking for more than just the convenience of technology—they are looking for an experience that feels personal, engaging, and deeply connected to the culture and history of the place. It's a renaissance of the age-old tradition of storytelling, where the story's value is as much in the telling as it is in the narrative itself. The study emphasizes the symbiotic relationship between AI and human intelligence in the tourism industry: while AI can enhance operational efficiency and offer personalized tour recommendations, it is the human guides who deliver the irreplaceable value of personal connection and engagement that define memorable travel experiences.

In the same vein, the transition from low human intelligence value added/high AI value added to high human intelligence value added/low AI value added marks a strategic shift toward prioritizing human intelligence over AI capabilities. In certain contexts, this change might arise from the recognition that AI, while potent, cannot substitute the nuanced judgment and intricate decision-making processes of the human mind. This transition underlines a return to human expertise in areas where the subjective understanding, emotional intelligence, and cognitive flexibility of people are deemed more valuable than the speed and processing power of AI. It reflects an acknowledgment of the unique strengths of human cognition that AI cannot emulate, ensuring that services and solutions retain the irreplaceable human perspective that fosters trust, connection, and relatability.

In the realm of news journalism and content creation, AI has been deployed to automate the generation of news articles on topics such as sports results and financial earnings reports, areas where the value added by human intelligence was traditionally deemed low. Nonetheless, there is a growing recognition of the importance of investigative journalism, op-eds, and in-depth reporting—facets of journalism that require a high degree of human intellectual contribution and are resistant to AI automation.

The resurgence of long-form journalism and the critical role of journalists in providing nuanced storytelling and analysis is echoed in the work by Graefe et al. (2018), which discusses the limitations of automated journalism and the value of human touch in reporting complex issues. This evolution highlights the balance shifting back toward human creativity and intellectual engagement in producing quality content that captures the subtleties of human experience.

In the sector of transportation logistics, AI has been leveraged for optimizing routes, managing fleet schedules, and predicting maintenance, areas where previously the human input was minimal and routine. However, with increasing complexities in global trade, customer demands, and the need for sustainable operations, there is a resurgence in the need for human expertise.

Strategic decisions regarding route planning to avoid geopolitical issues or to comply with new environmental regulations are examples where human judgment is becoming more prevalent. The nuanced understanding of cultural, political, and environmental factors impacting logistics is something AI cannot yet fully comprehend or integrate into its algorithms. This is supported by a study from Sople (2012), which highlights the importance of human decision-making in logistics to address variables that are beyond the scope of current AI technologies. Thus, while AI has automated many of the systematic tasks in logistics, the sector is witnessing a shift toward a greater reliance on human intelligence for strategic, high-level decision-making and problem-solving.

In contrast to algorithmic boost, where the focus is on amplifying the AI's capabilities to enhance or replace human effort, humanistic reinforcement seeks to preserve and accentuate the value humans bring to the table. It is not a rejection of technology, but rather an affirmation of the unique contributions that human workers provide. And unlike algorithmic recalibration, which adjusts the balance of human and AI contributions often due to over-automation or inefficiencies, humanistic reinforcement actively promotes human skills and involvement as indispensable elements in the technology-human partnership. Humanistic reinforcement thus stands out as it deliberately steers the interaction between humans and AI toward outcomes where human values, ethics, and capabilities are foregrounded.

This approach can be particularly vital in sectors where trust, personal service, and human judgment are paramount. It represents a commitment to ensuring that as AI systems become more integrated into our work environments, they do not eclipse the human elements that are the bedrock of our social and professional fabric.

Navigating from AI-First Mode to Human-First Mode

In the transition toward the humanistic reinforcement cluster, from a state of AI-First mode where AI holds a high value in decision-making and task execution (low human intelligence value added/high AI value added) to a state of Human-First mode where human intelligence is more prominently valued and AI support is minimized (high human intelligence value added/ low AI value added), the shift is centered on enhancing human capabilities and decision-making prowess while strategically diminishing the overarching role of AI.

In the context of this transition, navigating from an AI-First mode, where AI dominates decision-making and task execution from an outcome standpoint to a Human-First mode, which places greater emphasis on human intelligence to deliver such expected outcomes, a significant shift in approach is necessary. In the AI-First mode, high AI value-added signifies an era where machines are at the forefront, automating and optimizing processes with little human intervention, reflecting a phase of advanced automation and self-sufficiency to deliver outcome. However, the transition to a Human-First mode reconfigures the balance, underscoring the indispensable insights and judgments unique to human cognition for the outcome delivery.

Here, AI steps back to a supportive role, enhancing rather than directing human operations. This strategic adjustment is not a diminishment of AI's capabilities but a realignment to spotlight human expertise, creativity, and nuanced understanding. AI, while still sophisticated, is repurposed to amplify these human attributes, fostering a collaborative synergy where each decision and action is rooted in human intellect, with technology as the enabling force in the background, fine-tuning and assisting rather than leading. This transition champions the concept that the pinnacle of technological advancement is not the replacement of humanity but its augmentation, ensuring that AI serves to empower human potential.

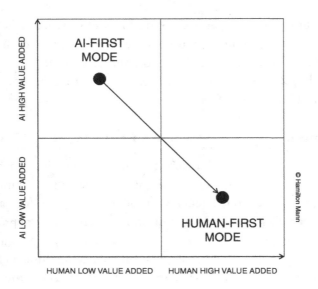

Such a transition is pivotal in environments where human intuition, creativity, and ethical judgment are critical. The key elements in this transition involve user empowerment features, interactive learning modules, adaptive user support, and reduction of over-automation.

About User Empowerment Features

In the context of transitioning from AI-First mode to Human-First mode, these features are essential in ensuring AI systems serve as enablers rather than directors of human decision-making. The development of transparent decision-support algorithms allows users to understand and trust the AI's recommendations. By creating configurable AI guidance levels, individuals can tailor the extent of AI involvement according to their expertise and comfort, thereby retaining decision-making control. Furthermore, integrating ethical alignment ensures AI suggestions are in harmony with human values, while personalized UX design enhances user interaction, making AI tools more intuitive and user-friendly.

An important step in this process is the development of transparent decision-support algorithms. These algorithms are crucial for presenting the reasoning behind AI recommendations transparently, including the data used, the weight of different factors, and alternative options, thus facilitating informed human decision-making. Such transparency empowers users to understand the basis of AI suggestions and make choices that align with their values and priorities.

Following this, creating configurable AI guidance levels is necessary. It's essential to design systems that allow users to configure the level of guidance provided by the AI. This configurability can range from simple information prompts to more detailed analysis, tailored according to the user's expertise and confidence in specific domains. This configurability ensures users retain control over their decisions, with AI input being adjustable to complement their knowledge and decision-making style.

In addition, ensuring ethical alignment in decision support is critical. AI's decision-support tools must align with ethical guidelines, providing recommendations that carefully consider ethical implications and user well-being. Embedding ethical considerations into the AI's operational code is fundamental to ensure its guidance consistently reflects these ethical priorities in decision-making support.

Moreover, incorporating personalized user experience (UX) design is vital. This involves integrating UX design principles that cater to individual user needs, thus allowing for the personalization of the AI interface and how decision-support information is presented. Considering factors like the user's cognitive load and information processing preferences is essential to enhance the decision-making experience.

Furthermore, adaptive learning from user feedback is key. Utilizing user feedback helps adapt the AI's decision-support mechanisms, ensuring the system evolves to better meet the user's needs over time. This adaptation process includes responding not only to explicit feedback but also to implicit cues, such as user behavior and choices.

Integrating autonomy preservation mechanisms is also a crucial action. These mechanisms should actively preserve user autonomy, requiring human confirmation for decisions that have significant impacts or irreversible consequences. It's important to design these mechanisms to prevent the inadvertent erosion of user control as the AI system becomes more advanced.

In addition, providing education and training components within the AI system is key. These components aim to enhance the user's understanding of complex data and the implications of different decisions, and can include interactive tutorials, simulations, and access to additional resources. This approach empowers users to make more informed choices.

Lastly, establishing a feedback-driven AI evolution process is essential. This process ensures the AI system improves its decision-support capabilities based on the successes and shortcomings of past user interactions. An ongoing process, it ensures the AI remains a relevant and effective tool for user empowerment.

By implementing these guiding principles, AI systems will be equipped with user empowerment features that uphold the principles of artificial integrity. These systems will support and enhance human decision-making, providing the information and insights needed for users to make choices that are informed, ethical, and aligned with their personal and professional objectives. Through such a partnership, the potential of both human and artificial intelligence is maximized in a manner that respects human autonomy and agency.

About Interactive Learning Modules

Considering the transition from AI-First mode to Human-First mode, these modules are crucial in fostering a continuous learning environment within AI systems. By introducing adaptive learning paths, AI can personalize the educational experience, adjusting to the user's learning pace and style. Responsive feedback systems and real-time skill assessment tools play a pivotal role in guiding the learning process. The incorporation of gamified elements and interactive content delivery formats, like augmented reality (AR) and virtual reality (VR), make the learning process more engaging and effective. These modules not only aid in skill enhancement but also ensure that AI evolves as an educational tool, adapting to the user's growing capabilities.

The integration of "interactive learning modules" within AI systems necessitates prioritizing personalized learning experiences and continuous skill enhancement. Achieving this level of artificial integrity involves creating a learning environment within the AI that is dynamic, responsive, and centered on the user's growth. One of the key steps is the design of adaptive learning paths. These paths intelligently adjust the complexity and depth of content based on real-time assessments of the user's progress and comprehension, offering alternative explanations or examples when needed, to ensure a truly personalized learning experience.

Building on this, responsive feedback systems should be implemented. These mechanisms guide users through the learning modules, providing encouragement and corrective suggestions to facilitate skill acquisition.

They are designed to recognize the user's strengths and areas for improvement, offering tailored advice that aligns with their learning goals.

Furthermore, incorporating real-time skill assessment tools is essential. These tools measure user competencies before, during, and after interaction with the learning modules, ensuring that the AI can track and respond to the user's development. They provide users with visibility and insights into their progress and areas needing attention.

In addition, employing gamified learning experiences can significantly enhance engagement. Introducing elements like challenges, achievements, badges, or leaderboards motivates users and makes the learning process more engaging. This approach stimulates intrinsic motivation and encourages setting and achieving their own learning milestones.

Proactive skill gap addressing is another crucial action. AI analytics can identify potential skill gaps based on user performance and industry trends, offering relevant learning modules to fill these gaps. The AI should recommend both foundational and advanced modules for comprehensive professional development.

Interactive content delivery, using formats like AR or VR, should be leveraged to provide immersive and hands-on learning experiences. These formats enhance retention and understanding and should be seamlessly integrated into the user's workflow, allowing for on-the-job learning and application of new skills. Creating collaborative learning environments within the AI system facilitates peer-to-peer learning, knowledge exchange, and the ability to solve problems collectively. These environments should support interactions among users and the sharing of best practices and experiences.

Finally, fostering a continuous learning culture within the AI ecosystem is pivotal. This involves embedding educational opportunities into daily workflows, making learning an integral part of interactions with the AI. The system should encourage regular engagement with learning modules, integrating skill development into the natural rhythm of the user's activities.

By addressing these guiding principals, AI systems will not only be tools for task completion but will also become platforms for user empowerment and skill enhancement. The implementation of interactive learning modules that embody artificial integrity will ensure that as AI evolves, it does so with a focus on nurturing human potential and fostering a collaborative partnership that benefits both the individual and the organization.

About Adaptive User Support

Transitioning from AI-First mode to Human-First mode involves crafting AI systems that can predict and respond to user needs, thereby enhancing the user experience. Contextual support adjustment ensures that AI assistance is tailored to the user's current situation and requirements. The development of user profiling and predictive modeling allows AI to anticipate user needs and adapt its support strategies accordingly. Real-time performance analytics and virtual assistants with natural language understanding capabilities are instrumental in providing proactive and relevant support. These systems are designed to evolve based on user feedback, ensuring that they remain effective and user-centric.

To actualize artificial integrity in AI systems to accomplish adaptive user support, it's imperative to craft AI that not only responds to user needs but also anticipates them, promoting user growth and confidence. The realization of this feature requires the AI to be sensitive to the user's abilities and adapt accordingly. An integral part of this is contextual support adjustment. Integrating mechanisms that enable AI systems to analyze the context of user interactions allows for the adjustment of support intensity and methodology, offering a tailored experience that respects the user's current state and needs. The AI should deftly discern when users need more detailed explanations and when they require high-level summaries, optimizing support to fit the situation.

Next, implementing user profiling and predictive modeling is crucial. Utilizing advanced predictive modeling to understand and predict user behavior creates nuanced user profiles that inform the AI's support strategies. These profiles should continually evolve with each interaction to ensure the AI's support remains aligned with the user's developing skills and preferences.

Also, the deployment of personalized learning and support pathways plays a vital role. These pathways, leveraging the AI's understanding of the user's knowledge base, present information and support that is most relevant to their learning curve. They should include options for users to modulate the level of assistance they receive, placing control over their learning journey in their hands.

Incorporating real-time performance analytics is another key action. These analytics monitor user performance and engagement in real time, pinpointing moments where users might need additional support or could be encouraged to handle more complex tasks independently. This anticipatory approach allows the AI to offer support proactively rather than reactively.

The integration of virtual assistants with natural language understanding is also important. These assistants, capable of engaging in meaningful dialogue, answer questions and provide explanations in a conversational manner, adapting to the user's communication style for natural and helpful interactions.

Furthermore, creating just-in-time learning prompts based on the user's activity provides insights and tips that are immediately applicable to the task at hand. Designed to enhance understanding and performance, these prompts should seamlessly integrate into the user's workflow.

In addition, support scalability is essential. Support systems within the AI should be capable of scaling up or down based on the complexity of tasks and the user's demonstrated competence, ensuring that as users grow more proficient, the AI provides a level of support that reflects their advancing capabilities.

Lastly, implementing a feedback-driven support evolution process is fundamental. This process allows the AI to refine its user support functions based on user input, ensuring that the system is continually improving and staying aligned with user expectations and needs.

By addressing these guiding principles, AI systems can be developed with "adaptive user support" features that represent the essence of artificial integrity. Such systems will not only react to the users' immediate needs but will also empower them to progress toward more complex, high-value tasks, fostering an environment where human intelligence is augmented by AI in a thoughtful, respectful, and user-centric manner.

About Reduction of Over-Automation

Moving forward, when transitioning from AI-First mode to Human-First mode, the reduction of over-automation is a critical component in ensuring that AI systems do not overshadow human roles but rather complement them. By creating a valuation system that classifies tasks based on their suitability for automation, AI can identify areas where human involvement is more beneficial. Developing human–AI collaboration frameworks and ethical oversight protocols ensures a balanced partnership where AI supports human decision-making without compromising ethical standards.

Introducing smart alert systems, human-inclusive design, and continuous human skill development initiatives are pivotal in maintaining the delicate balance between human and AI contributions, ensuring that the workforce evolves alongside AI advancements.

Achieving artificial integrity in AI systems, particularly in the context of reducing over-automation, requires a nuanced approach that prioritizes human expertise in certain domains while utilizing AI for support. A crucial step in this direction is the creation of a task valuation and classification system. This AI-powered system can classify tasks based on their suitability for automation, considering factors like complexity, the necessity for human judgment, emotional intelligence, and creativity. It's essential for this system to highlight tasks where human involvement is most beneficial, marking these as areas for human expertise.

In tandem with this, developing human–AI collaboration frameworks is vital. These frameworks should outline clear roles for both humans and AI, ensuring AI enhances rather than replaces human work. Ideally, the AI assists with data-driven insights, while humans provide contextual interpretation and final decision-making.

Furthermore, implementing ethical oversight protocols within the AI is key. These protocols are designed to involve human input in sensitive or critical decision areas, particularly where moral, legal, or personal implications are present. The sensitivity of these protocols to such elements is essential to ensure appropriate human involvement.

Integrating smart alert systems is another significant action. These systems are designed to notify human operators when AI encounters situations beyond its confidence intervals or operational parameters, recognizing its limits and seeking human guidance as needed.

In addition, ensuring a human-inclusive design in AI systems is crucial. This design approach should integrate human roles as a central part of the operational model, avoiding a lean toward full automation and valuing human traits like empathy, intuition, and adaptability, which AI cannot replicate.

It's also important to maintain task flexibility and adaptability. This flexibility allows AI to handle routine aspects of tasks while retaining the ability to revert control to the human operator as necessary, adapting the level of involvement based on task complexity and the unique skills of the human operator.

Moreover, a focus on continuous human skill development is essential. As AI handles more routine tasks, systems that facilitate human skill enhancement in areas less suited to automation has become crucial. This approach ensures that the human workforce evolves alongside AI advancements, maintaining high human value addition.

Lastly, developing AI systems with awareness of their limitations is important. These systems should recognize and communicate their limitations to human users, fostering an environment where over-automation is consciously avoided. This awareness in AI ensures that tasks requiring human expertise are appropriately flagged and routed.

By implementing these guiding principles, AI systems can achieve reduction of over-automation, ensuring that artificial integrity is embedded within the AI by maintaining and enhancing the value of human contributions in the age of automation. This strategy not only preserves essential human roles but also maximizes the complementary strengths of humans and AI in a collaborative and ethical manner. It helps ensure AI systems enhance and empower human intelligence rather than replace it.

This recalibration toward high human intelligence value added requires AI to be designed with features that foster human decision-making, learning, and adaptability, ensuring that the AI's role in supporting human users is optimized without leading to over-automation.

Navigating from Fusion Mode to Human-First Mode

The transition toward the humanistic reinforcement cluster, from a state of Fusion mode (high human intelligence value added/high AI value added) to a state of Human-First mode where AI plays a less dominant yet supportive role (high human intelligence value added/low AI value added), emphasizes enhancing human decision-making and expertise while strategically reducing AI's direct involvement in tasks and decisions. Transitioning from a Fusion mode, where both human intelligence and AI contribute significantly to outcomes, to a Human-First mode, where AI assumes a more supportive role, requires a strategic adjustment of the AI's functionality. In Fusion mode, the high value-added by AI is characterized by its substantial input and active participation in the outcome through its involvement in decision-making processes, often working in tandem with humans to achieve complex objectives. This mode leverages the full potential of AI's analytical and processing capabilities alongside human intelligence, thus creating a synergistic effect where the sum is greater than its parts.

The shift to Human-First mode, however, involves redefining the role of AI from a co-leader to a facilitator. In this mode, AI's primary function transitions to augmenting and amplifying human capabilities rather than leading or equally sharing the tasks. The focus is on harnessing AI's sophisticated tools for in-depth analysis, prediction, and problem-solving in a way that empowers human users to make more informed, strategic decisions. This doesn't reduce the sophistication or capabilities of AI; instead, it changes the direction of these capabilities toward enhancing human-driven processes.

In Human-First mode, AI is "low value added" in terms of direct leadership or autonomous operation as far as the outcome is concerned but becomes invaluable in providing insights, suggestions, and support that bolster human creativity, intuition, and judgment. The human element takes precedence, with AI functioning as a sophisticated yet subtle background tool that informs and assists rather than dictates. This transition places a premium on human expertise and decision-making, with AI serving as an intelligent enabler, ensuring that technology remains aligned with and responsive to human needs and values. The resulting dynamic is one where human intelligence is at the forefront, with AI seamlessly integrating into the fabric of human-led processes, enhancing efficiency and effectiveness without overshadowing the human touch.

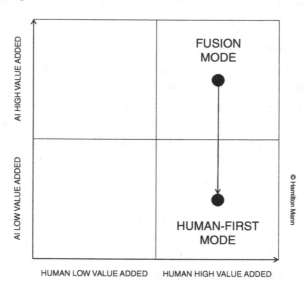

Key elements in this transition include configurable AI assistance, ethical decision support, human-centric workflow design, and feedback mechanisms.

About Configurable AI Assistance

The crux of the transition from Fusion mode to Human-First mode lies in developing AI systems with highly customizable assistance capabilities. These systems should be equipped with user-friendly interfaces that allow individuals to adjust AI support according to their specific needs and proficiency levels. The AI's functionality would modulate based on task complexity and user expertise, offering more passive assistance in scenarios requiring human judgment and a more active role in data-driven tasks. This configurability ensures that AI enhances human decision-making without usurping it.

To embed artificial integrity into AI systems, particularly for "configurable AI assistance," it's critical to adopt a user-focused strategy. This strategy centers on crafting AI systems that not only provide adjustable support but also align this support with the user's skill set and independence.

One integral part of this approach is equipping AI systems with customization and control interfaces. These interfaces allow users to easily navigate and personalize AI assistance settings, enabling them to fine-tune the level of support to match their current needs and task complexity. In addition, these interfaces should offer explanations for each setting, aiding users in understanding how their choices affect AI behavior.

In line with this, implementing task-specific AI modulation is crucial. AI systems need to be able to adjust their functionalities according to the specific task at hand, taking a more passive role for tasks requiring deep human expertise and offering more active assistance for data-driven tasks. This modulation should occur seamlessly and with minimal user input, thus reducing cognitive load and allowing the user to concentrate on the task itself.

Furthermore, integrating decision-support analytics into the AI aids in informed decision-making. These analytics process complex datasets and present distilled insights to the user, supporting rather than dictating decisions. They should be transparent, allowing users to understand how conclusions were reached and include options for users to explore alternative scenarios or question the AI's reasoning.

Developing AI systems capable of creating behavior profiles based on individual user interactions and preferences is also vital. These profiles help the AI anticipate the required level of assistance and adjust its support proactively, updating continuously as the user's patterns and preferences evolve.

Allowing users to define operational boundaries for AI is another essential action. This includes setting clear limits on AI's autonomous functions and decisions. This could include setting thresholds for when the AI should seek human validation before proceeding. These boundaries should be easy to modify, giving users the flexibility to adapt AI assistance as their relationship with the technology matures.

Aligning the AI's operational principles with the user's ethics and preferences ensures the assistance provided does not conflict with the user's values or preferred working style. This alignment should be an ongoing process, with regular check-ins or assessments that should be conducted to ensure that the AI's behavior remains consistent with the user's expectations and ethical standards.

Lastly, integrating feedback and evolution mechanisms within the AI system are crucial. These mechanisms should collect and analyze user feedback on AI assistance, evolving AI behaviors and functionalities over time to stay relevant and useful. These mechanisms should facilitate a two-way learning process where the AI adapts to the user, and the user gains deeper insights into optimizing AI assistance for their purposes.

By addressing these guiding principles, AI systems can provide configurable AI assistance that epitomizes artificial integrity. Such systems will not only respect and enhance human autonomy and expertise but will also remain adaptable and responsive to the changing needs and preferences of users, fostering a synergistic relationship between humans and AI.

About Ethical Decision Support

Embedding ethical decision-making frameworks within AI systems is crucial in navigating the transition from Fusion mode to Human-First mode. These frameworks would guide users through complex ethical dilemmas, supplementing human judgment with AI's analytical capabilities. The inclusion of a diverse range of ethical theories and principles, along with user-centric customization options, ensures that AI's ethical support aligns with individual and organizational values.

To achieve artificial integrity in AI systems, particularly for fostering "ethical decision support" during the transition from high human intelligence value-added to low AI value-added scenarios, it should be ensured that the AI's support is directed toward enhancing the user's ethical decision-making capabilities. The first step involves ethical framework integration. Embedding a robust ethical framework into the AI guides users through the decision-making process. It presents ethical considerations and reflective questions, encouraging thoughtful deliberation. This framework should be both easily accessible and regularly updated to keep pace with evolving ethical standards and societal norms.

In conjunction with this, developing a case-based learning repository is crucial. This in-system repository of ethical case studies and precedents allows users to consult historical outcomes when faced with moral dilemmas. This repository should be interactive, enhancing users' ability to explore different scenarios and shapes informed, ethically sound decisions.

Furthermore, implementing a proactive ethical alert system is key. This mechanism identifies potential ethical conflicts in decision-making scenarios, highlighting issues and suggesting a range of ethically aligned resolution options. In addition, equipping the AI with an ethical reasoning assistance tool enhances the decision-making process. This tool processes complex ethical questions and provides reasoned advice based on established ethical theories and principles, supporting rather than replacing the user's reasoning.

Moreover, user-centric ethical customization allows users to align the AI's decision support with their personal or organizational ethical standards. This flexibility should also enable users to prioritize different ethical principles as needed, according to the situation at hand. Creating ethical feedback loops is another essential action. These loops analyze the outcomes of decisions influenced by the AI's ethical support, informing future guidance. This continuous learning approach refines the AI's ethical decision support based on real-world applications and outcomes.

Lastly, maintaining transparent ethical audit trails is fundamental. These audit trails document how the AI's ethical guidance has influenced decision-making processes. This transparency is crucial for accountability and for users to understand the AI's influence on their decisions.

By addressing these guiding principles, AI systems will be capable of offering ethical decision support that aligns with the principles of artificial integrity. This will ensure that as AI systems assist with ethical decision-making, they do so in a way that supports and respects human judgment, reinforces ethical considerations, and promotes a culture of integrity within the organization.

About Human-Centric Workflow Design

Redefining workflows to center around human decision-making is a fundamental aspect of the transition from Fusion mode to Human-First mode. AI systems would be integrated as analytical tools, providing insights and recommendations while ensuring that critical decision nodes remain under human control. The design of these workflows would focus on complementing human skills, with AI taking on repetitive tasks to free up human resources for higher-order thinking.

For "human-centric workflow design" to be successfully integrated into AI systems that aligns with the principles of artificial integrity, we must ensure that the systems support and enhance human decision-making without supplanting it. A key approach in achieving this balance is the workflow integration of AI analytics. It is needed to develop AI systems that serve as advanced analytical tools, offering deep insights through data visualization and pattern recognition. Such systems should support human cognitive processes by facilitating complex analysis, enabling humans to make informed decisions based on synthesized information.

Alongside this, integrating human decision nodes into workflow processes is essential. These nodes are where human judgment is crucial, ensuring AI does not bypass the human element in critical decision-making. The AI should augment human decision-making abilities by providing relevant information and recommendations at these nodes.

Moreover, task segmentation and allocation are critical considerations. By segmenting complex tasks into subtasks and delineating components for AI or human handling, the AI can take on repetitive and time-consuming parts, freeing humans for higher-order thinking and decision-making.

In addition, offering customizable interface options caters to various user needs and preferences. This customization allows for a more intuitive use of AI tools within existing human-centric workflows, easing adoption and reducing the learning curve.

Also, incorporating an iterative design approach allows workflows to be adjusted based on feedback from human operators about the effectiveness and utility of AI support. Complementing this, mechanisms for continuous feedback from users are essential to refine the AI's role in workflows, ensuring that it remains an asset rather than a hindrance to human-centric processes.

Furthermore, providing human–AI collaboration training is crucial. Training programs focused on optimizing human–AI collaboration educate users on how to leverage AI support effectively. Such training should highlight the complementary relationship between human intuition and AI's analytical capabilities, fostering a cooperative work environment.

Lastly, establishing ethical oversight mechanisms is paramount. These mechanisms continuously monitor AI operations within workflows, ensuring actions align with organizational values and ethical standards. They should be capable of intervening or alerting human operators if AI deviates from the established ethical framework.

By addressing these guiding principles, AI systems can be designed to fulfill the requirements of human-centric workflow design, thereby ensuring that AI supports human operators in a manner that embodies artificial integrity. This approach positions humans at the forefront of decision-making, with AI serving as a powerful support system that enhances human capabilities without seeking to replace them.

About Feedback Mechanisms

In the context of transitioning from Fusion mode to Human-First mode, establishing robust feedback systems within AI tools is essential for aligning AI behavior with human intelligence and preferences. These systems would gather user feedback, enabling the AI to adapt and refine its functionality over time. Feedback mechanisms would also facilitate a two-way learning process, where AI evolves based on human input, and users gain insights into optimizing AI assistance for their specific purposes. To implement artificial integrity into AI systems, especially for the effective implementation of "feedback mechanisms" the approach should enable the AI not just to perform tasks but also to learn from its human counterparts and evolve over time.

A foundational aspect of this is developing a feedback collection framework. This framework, integrated within the AI, would solicit and compile feedback from users, systematically categorizing it for analysis. It's vital for this framework to facilitate easy feedback provision at various interaction stages, ensuring a comprehensive understanding of user experiences and expectations.

In conjunction with this, utilizing adaptive machine learning models is essential. These models analyze user feedback in real time and modify the AI's behavior accordingly. They should be capable of identifying patterns in feedback that suggest improvements, adapting the AI's responses to enhance user satisfaction.

Moreover, implementing a system for user preference alignment is critical. This system learns individual user preferences, adjusting the AI's behavior to align with these preferences over time thereby personalizing the user experience. The dynamic nature of this system allows it to evolve as user preferences change, ensuring that the AI remains relevant and valuable to the user.

In addition, creating operational feedback integration mechanisms is vital. This approach ensures feedback is not isolated or siloed within the AI system but shared across the organization, informing broader operational and strategic decisions. Integrating feedback in this way ensures that insights gained from feedback contribute to the continuous improvement of both the AI system and organizational processes.

Another key action is embedding feedback into the AI's development cycle. This means ensuring user insights are central to ongoing AI development and refinement. Developers should have mechanisms to test new features or changes based on user feedback before full-scale implementation.

Furthermore, leveraging feedback to build an organizational learning platform supports knowledge sharing and continuous improvement across teams. This platform should highlight successful human–AI collaborations and offer best practices for maximizing AI systems' value within the organization.

Lastly, designing Iterative feedback loops is crucial for gradual AI improvement. These loops facilitate incremental changes, ensuring stability and reliability while incorporating user feedback. The AI should also suggest its own improvements based on these loops, fostering a proactive approach to its evolution.

By undertaking these guiding principles, artificial integrity within AI systems will be realized through robust feedback mechanisms, which are critical for aligning AI behavior with human intelligence and ensuring that AI systems are responsive, adaptable, and continuously refined based on human input and organizational objectives. In implementing these measures, the transition toward lower AI value added is handled in a way that respects and enhances the role of human intelligence within the workflow. The AI becomes a sophisticated tool that supports human expertise, fostering an environment where ethical considerations and human judgment are paramount, and where the human–AI partnership is characterized by mutual learning and adaptability.

Navigating from AI-First Mode to Fusion Mode

The transition toward the humanistic reinforcement cluster from a state of AI-First mode (low human intelligence value added/high AI value added) to a state of Fusion mode (high human intelligence value added/ high AI value added) underscores a balanced integration of human cognitive skills and AI capabilities, fostering a collaborative environment where each enhances the other's strengths. In the context of this transition, the focus shifts to harmonizing the strengths of both AI and human intelligence to achieve synergistic outcomes. In AI-First mode, the primary value of the outcome is derived from the AI's capabilities in automating processes and making decisions with minimal human intervention. However, in Fusion mode, the emphasis is on integrating human insight and creativity with AI's analytical and processing power to enhance both efficiency and innovation.

In this new paradigm, the sophistication of AI still plays a crucial role, but it is now coupled with an elevated importance of human expertise and judgment. AI systems in Fusion mode are designed not just to execute tasks independently but to collaborate with humans, drawing on their ability to understand complex, abstract concepts and to provide creative solutions that AI alone might not conceive. This involves AI systems being more transparent and explainable, allowing humans to understand, trust, and effectively interact with them.

The value added by AI in Fusion mode is not solely in performing tasks but in providing advanced insights, predictions, and recommendations that complement human decision-making. The human contribution, on the other hand, is in providing contextual understanding, moral reasoning, and creative thought—areas where AI is limited. The goal is to create an environment where humans and AI can each operate at their best, with AI

enhancing human capabilities and humans guiding AI toward more meaningful, ethical, and innovative outcomes.

By embracing this Fusion mode, organizations can harness the full
potential of both AI and human intelligence. This approach leads to a
more adaptive, resilient, and innovative operational model, where the
combined strengths of human and artificial intelligence are leveraged to
achieve superior results.

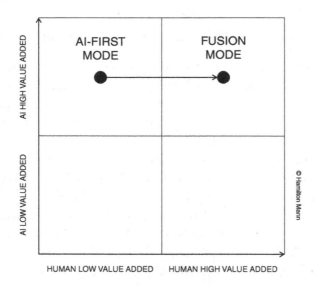

The focus areas for this transition include augmented intelligent systems, augmented collaborative intelligence, skill development analytics, and
ethical collaboration guidelines.

About Augmented Intelligent Systems

The cornerstone of the transition from AI–First mode to Fusion mode lies
in developing AI systems that augment, rather than replace, human intelligence. These systems should be designed as cognitive partners that assist in
complex decision-making processes. By integrating cognitive partnership
development, context-aware algorithms, and intuitive communication interfaces, AI systems can provide advanced data analysis, predictive modeling,
and real-time insights, thereby empowering human workers to make more
informed decisions. This approach should ensure that AI is sensitive to

abstract concepts and situational nuances, effectively translating vast data into actionable intelligence.

First, there is the need for cognitive partnership development. Crafting AI systems to function as cognitive partners focuses on the augmentation of human decision-making rather than automation. These systems should assist with tasks like advanced data analysis, predictive modeling, and providing real-time insights, thereby empowering human workers to make more informed and nuanced decisions. The capability of these AI systems to understand abstract concepts and complex contexts is vital, as it translates vast quantities of data into actionable intelligence that can be easily understood and leveraged by humans.

Building on this, context-aware algorithm integration is essential. The aim is to develop algorithms that can accurately assess the user's current task, environment, and intent and can offer context-appropriate assistance, enhancing the natural human cognitive abilities without overriding or bypassing human judgment. This involves creating AI that interprets situational nuances and adjusting its functioning accordingly to provide insights and assistance that are relevant and timely.

Furthermore, AI systems with advanced natural language processing capabilities and intuitive user interfaces is crucial. These interfaces should translate the AI's complex analytics into an easily digestible format for the user, enabling them to make decisions based on a deep understanding of the information provided. The communication interface should also allow users to query the AI in natural language and receive explanations and clarifications that are intuitive and insightful.

Another important step is the creation of collaborative platforms where humans and AI can work together on problem-solving. These platforms should allow humans to set the direction and goals, with the AI providing the analytical horsepower to explore possibilities and predict outcomes. Such platforms would enable real-time collaboration, allowing for an iterative process where human creativity and AI's computational abilities are both leveraged to their fullest.

In addition, ensuring ethical and privacy considerations is fundamental. Augmented intelligence systems must be built on a strong ethical foundation, prioritizing and respecting user privacy and data security at every step. AI should be transparent about the data it collects and uses, and it should operate within the ethical boundaries set by society. The AI should also be programmed to recognize and respect ethical dilemmas, seeking human guidance when faced with decisions that have moral implications.

Lastly, facilitating human-centric training and adaptation is vital. This involves creating an environment where AI adapts to the individual working styles and preferences of its human partners. This includes learning from human feedback and adapting its models and recommendations accordingly. Also, implementing training sessions for human workers to understand how to interact with and leverage the AI best should ensure that they can take full advantage of the augmented intelligence systems.

By addressing these guiding principles, AI systems can be developed to a level where they embody artificial integrity, ensuring that they serve as cognitive partners that amplify human intelligence. This approach positions AI as an enabler of human potential, fostering a collaborative environment where both human and AI contributions are maximized, leading to superior decision-making and innovation.

About Augmented Collaborative Intelligence

Essential to the transition from AI-First mode to Fusion mode is fostering AI's capabilities not just as a tool but as an active participant in intellectual and creative processes. This involves constructing interactive platforms and virtual co-creation workspaces where AI and humans can engage in meaningful dialogue and co-creative processes. AI should be capable of offering immediate, contextual support, sharing its thought processes, and participating in collaborative decision-making. Ensuring ethical and transparent interactions and integrating learning algorithms that evolve with human interaction are key to achieving a harmonious human–AI collaboration.

First, the development of interactive platforms is essential. These platforms should go beyond being mere repositories of data, evolving into interactive spaces where human and AI engage in meaningful dialogue. This interaction needs to extend beyond simple question-and-answer formats to enable co-creative processes that leverage the unique strengths of both parties. These platforms should be equipped with AI that can proactively contribute to discussions, drawing on vast databases and learning models to introduce new perspectives and ideas that can inspire human users.

In addition, creating virtual co-creation workspaces can be considered. These environments allow AI to act as a co-creator, providing not only analytical support but also participating in the generation and refinement of ideas. Such spaces should facilitate the seamless integration of AI-generated content with human creativity, fostering a synergistic co-creation process where AI functions dynamically, suggesting hypotheses, visualizing outcomes, and simulating scenarios that aid in decision-making and problem-solving.

Moreover, implementing real-time collaboration support is crucial. Systems where AI offers immediate, contextual support during human deliberation processes enhance collaborative efforts with actionable intelligence. This involves AI understanding the flow of conversation or the evolution of an idea and providing input that is immediately relevant and constructive. Such support would include the ability to pull up relevant data, provide simulations, or offer predictive models on the fly.

Establishing shared cognitive processes is also key. Mechanisms where AI can share its "thought processes" with humans are crucial for enabling a better understanding of how it arrives at certain suggestions or conclusions. This transparency is crucial for building trust and facilitating more profound collaborative efforts. This would require AI systems with advanced explanatory capabilities, capable of articulating complex processes in a manner that is easily comprehensible to human partners.

Ensuring ethical and transparent interactions is fundamental. Embedding ethical considerations into every collaborative platform layer ensures that all AI contributions align with established moral principles and societal values. Transparency in AI's operational logic and decision-making criteria is crucial for maintaining a clear ethical stance and fostering trust amongst human collaborators.

Lastly, equipping AI with learning and evolutionary algorithms that not only evolve based on new data but also from the interaction patterns with human users is key. This adaptive learning is key to maintaining relevance and effectiveness in a rapidly changing environment. The AI's learning process should mimic the human cognitive ability to learn from experience, enabling the AI to become a more efficient and insightful collaborator over time.

By addressing these guiding principles, AI can achieve a level of sophistication in terms of collaborative intelligence enablement conducive to artificial integrity, hence ensuring that AI systems not only perform tasks but also become intellectual partners to humans. This integration promises to elevate the capability of such platforms, transforming them into breeding grounds for innovation and problem-solving that are greater than the sum of their individual human or AI contributions.

About Skill Development Analytics

In the transition phase from AI-First mode to Fusion mode, AI systems should embody a focus on skill development analytics aimed at evaluating current competencies and addressing skill shortages. This involves developing AI-driven diagnostic tools for skill gap analysis, adaptive learning platforms, predictive modeling for future skill requirements, and real-time skill development tracking. By collaborating with educational institutions and integrating industry trend analyses, AI systems can proactively foster human intelligence growth and adaptability in the workplace. Embedding artificial integrity into AI systems encompasses a suite of specialized actions to install "skill development analytics" aimed at evaluating current competencies, addressing skill shortages, and proactively shaping workforce development to meet future demands.

Central to this is the development of AI-driven diagnostic tools for skill gap analysis. Advanced AI analytics can process complex datasets to discern specific skill deficiencies at an individual and organizational level, utilizing data from performance metrics, job requirements, and individual assessments. By integrating these tools into workplace systems, managers and employees gain actionable insights for creating personalized development paths based on the analysis.

Complementary to this foundation, the construction of adaptive learning platforms powered by AI is useful. These platforms tailor educational content to the individual's learning style and pace, providing an efficient and effective custom learning experience. As learners progress, these platforms would continuously adapt, presenting increasingly challenging materials to ensure consistent growth and skill acquisition.

Furthermore, employing predictive modeling for future skill requirements is essential. Predictive modeling algorithms that analyze market trends, technological advancements, and emerging industry can help forecast future skill needs. Anticipating these requirements enables AI systems to advise on long-term learning strategies and recommend beneficial courses or certification programs that will be most beneficial in preparing the workforce for future demands.

In addition, real-time skill development tracking is pivotal. Utilizing real-time tracking systems to monitor skill development allows for immediate learner feedback and dynamic adjustment of training programs. This real-time tracking would also enable organizations to measure the return on investment in training and adjust strategies to optimize learning outcomes.

Analyzing industry trends using deep learning algorithms is also a key action. This analysis doesn't just focus on current skills but also identifies emerging competencies required for future success. Insights from these analyses inform the development of new training modules, ensuring they keep pace with the evolving professional landscape.

Finally, fostering collaboration with educational institutions and content creators is paramount. Partnerships with academic stakeholders can help ensure that training materials are current, industry-aligned, and continuously refined. Such collaborations can result in a virtuous cycle of feedback and content refinement, ensuring that learning resources remain relevant and effective.

By addressing these guiding principles, the aim is to create AI systems that embody artificial integrity by proactively fostering the growth and adaptability of human intelligence in the workplace. Such systems would not only respond to current educational needs but also anticipate and prepare for future shifts. This approach ensures that as AI takes on a more prominent role in the high-value-added domain, it does so by empowering human partners, thus maintaining a robust and forward-looking human–AI synergy.

About Ethical Collaboration Guidelines

When navigating the transition from AI-First mode to Fusion mode, establishing ethical collaboration guidelines is critical to ensure that AI systems operate within a framework that respects human values. This involves developing ethical collaboration frameworks, integrating human values into AI decision-making processes, and establishing automated ethical oversight. AI systems should be equipped with dynamic ethical adaptation capabilities, transparent ethical decision-making processes, continuous ethical learning modules, and stakeholder ethical input platforms. This ensures that AI not only exhibits ethical behavior but also evolves alongside societal values, ensuring effective and ethical human–AI collaboration.

To achieve "ethical collaboration guidelines" under the paradigm of artificial integrity, a robust framework must be established. This framework should be intrinsic to the AI's design, ensuring it can navigate and support ethical human–AI collaborations effectively. Integral to actualizing artificial integrity in this context, and enhancing the symbiosis of human and AI contributions, is the development of ethical collaboration frameworks. Codifying these frameworks into the AI's operational code enables it to apply ethical principles across various collaborative scenarios, ensuring decisions are made with a consistent ethical stance. Further, incorporating scenario-based learning within AI systems, where they simulate and learn from myriad collaborative situations, helps them better navigate real-world ethical complexities.

In parallel, human values integration is critical. Embedding human ethical values into AI's decision-making processes ensures that AI's recommendations and actions are consistently weighed against the backdrop of human-centered ethical considerations. Also, utilizing advanced machine learning algorithms can help refine the AI's understanding of human values, adapting its collaborative strategies to reflect nuanced human ethics accurately.

Moreover, automated ethical oversight should be established within AI systems. This involves establishing real-time ethical monitoring and equipping the AI with the capability to autonomously enforce ethical guidelines and maintain accountability in collaborative endeavors. AI should also autonomously generate ethical compliance reports, offering insights into the alignment of collaborative decisions with ethical standards and where improvements can be made.

Dynamic ethical adaptation is also key. Equipping AI systems with adaptive ethical reasoning capabilities allows them to recalibrate their collaborative approaches in response to shifting ethical landscapes and interaction dynamics. Fostering the AI systems' ability to conduct ethical risk assessments, while predicting and preemptively adjusting strategies to mitigate potential ethical breaches is also at stake.

Transparent ethical decision-making is crucial to foster an environment of transparency and trust. Ensuring all AI-generated decisions within collaborations are accompanied by clear, accessible explanations of the ethical reasoning behind them is key. Interfaces developed should not only display the AI's decision rationale but also allow users to query and understand the ethical parameters that influenced these decisions.

In addition, integrating continuous ethical learning modules into AI systems is necessary. These modules should update the AI's ethical frameworks based on emerging societal norms and human feedback, with reflective learning loops within AI systems encouraging them to self-assess their ethical performance and learn from human collaborators to refine their ethical judgment.

Finally, creating interactive platforms for stakeholder ethical input ensures broad representation and ongoing refinement of collaborative principles in shaping the AI's ethical guidelines. Feedback mechanisms that aggregate stakeholder perspectives on ethical matters should be considered to inform and update the AI's collaborative protocols with these insights.

By addressing these guiding principles, artificial integrity becomes a cornerstone of AI development, creating AI systems that not only exhibit ethical behavior autonomously but also evolve alongside human societal values, ensuring effective and ethical human–AI collaboration at all levels of interaction. By focusing on these technical strategies, AI can be positioned not just as a tool but as an ally that actively contributes to the enrichment of human intelligence. This transition reflects an advanced model of work where AI and human intelligence amplify each other, leading to outcomes that neither could achieve alone. The integration of ethical considerations throughout ensures that this augmentation occurs within a framework that respects and promotes human values.

Navigating from Marginal Mode to Human-First Mode

The transition toward the humanistic reinforcement cluster, from a state of Marginal mode (low human intelligence value added/low AI value added) to a state of Human-First mode (high human intelligence value added/low AI value added), emphasizes enhancing human capabilities and decision-making with AI as a supportive rather than dominant force. In the context of this transition, the sophistication of the AI isn't directly related to its prominence or dominance in the ultimate outcome. Instead, it is about how effectively the AI supports and enhances human capabilities to achieve that outcome.

In this scenario, the AI's sophistication is leveraged not for its autonomous functions or to replace human roles, but to provide nuanced, intelligent support that augments human decision-making, learning, and problem-solving. So, while AI in this mode is considered "low value added" in terms of direct contributions to the outcome, its sophisticated features are crucial for enhancing the human element of the process. It's a shift from AI as a performer of tasks to AI as an enabler of human performance. This approach places higher value on human skills and intelligence, with AI acting as a sophisticated tool that supports and augments these human qualities.

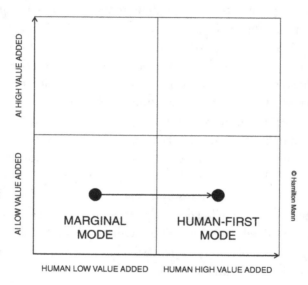

The key elements to consider in this transition include task optimization for learning, cognitive enhancement tools, role-specific AI customization, and mentorship AI.

About Task Optimization for Learning

AI systems in the Marginal mode to Human-First mode transition framework are designed not just for efficiency but for educational enhancement. They dissect tasks into learnable segments, offering tailored challenges that align with the user's skill level and learning curve. The key is to embed learning opportunities within everyday tasks, using AI to identify knowledge gaps and provide customized learning modules. This approach fosters a continuous learning environment where task execution and skill development are seamlessly integrated.

To achieve "task optimization for learning" in the pursuit of embedding artificial integrity into AI systems, the challenge is to not only pinpoint and capitalize on intrinsic learning opportunities within tasks but also to foster an environment that continuously nurtures and expands the user's competencies. Central to this goal is intelligent task analysis. Deploying AI systems with analytical engines that dissect tasks into learnable segments can allow for the identification of segments that serve dual roles as skill enhancers and performance metrics.

Equipping AI with adaptive complexity assessment tools can allow for the calibration of task difficulty in alignment with the user's learning curve, offering just-right challenges that foster skill growth. In addition, programming AI to recognize and bridge knowledge gaps by suggesting custom learning modules or resources can help integrate learning seamlessly into the workflow.

Building on this, implementing dynamic workflow adjustment is crucial. AI-driven adaptive workflow systems that evolve with the user offer a scaffolded approach, increasing in sophistication with the user's skill level. Developing AI that anticipates learning plateaus and proactively introduces novel challenges or advanced task parameters can also help push the boundaries of the user's abilities. Complementary to this, constructing AI workflows that respond to real-time performance data and fine-tunes task demands can be useful to maintain an optimal zone of proximal development for each user.

Furthermore, personalized task sequencing is key. The aim here is to design AI with intelligent sequencing algorithms that curate a personalized task order, optimizing skill acquisition and retention through strategic task arrangement. Utilizing predictive modeling in AI systems can help chart a course of tasks that progressively build upon previously established skills, ensuring continuity and depth in learning. AI frameworks that apply machine learning to past performance analytics can also be useful to tailor upcoming task sequences to reinforce weak areas and capitalize on strengths.

In addition, implementing contextual resource provisioning by integrating situational learning aids into AI systems can provide in-task guidance and resources that are relevant to the immediate challenges faced by the user. Designing AI to serve as an on-demand repository of context-specific knowledge offers insights, precedents, or case studies that are applicable to the task at hand. Also, programming AI to deliver contextual prompts and cues that stimulate reflective thinking and application of skills deepens the learning experience within the workflow.

Moreover, incorporating feedback-responsive learning paths in AI mechanisms can help adjust future learning paths based on user feedback, keeping the system attuned to the user's educational needs and aspirations. Also, developing AI that interprets user engagement and satisfaction signals can help refine task presentations and learning materials to better resonate with the user's learning style while feedback loops evolve the AI's pedagogical strategies, creating a dynamic learning ecosystem that is responsive to user interactions.

In line with this, implementing skill progression tracking in AI systems to visualize skill progression can help provide users with a dashboard of learning milestones and a forecast of potential skill trajectories. AI that benchmarks user performance against industry standards or organizational goals provides a clear and motivating overview of progress and potential. Also, designing AI to recognize and celebrate skill mastery integrates gamification elements that encourage ongoing development.

Lastly, designing learning-focused user interfacing is essential. AI interfaces that prioritize educational features like inline assistance and learning prompts create a user experience centered on growth. Complementary to this, constructing AI systems with interface layers that adapt to the user's proficiency can help cater to varying levels of expertise, simplifying them for beginners or offering advanced tools for experienced users. Interactive interface elements in such systems should also encourage exploration and discovery, making the act of learning an engaging and integral part of task completion.

By addressing these guiding principles, AI systems can be designed to not only support task completion but also serve as sophisticated educational partners that enhance human intelligence. This integration of artificial integrity within AI will enable a seamless transition from low to high human value-added tasks, ensuring that AI systems serve as catalysts for human development and empowerment in an ever-evolving digital landscape.

About Cognitive Enhancement Tools

From Marginal mode to Human-First mode, AI should also be envisioned as a tool for human cognitive augmentation, offering support that is both intuitive and empowering. AI systems are equipped with cognitive scaffolding algorithms and real-time analytical assistance, aiding in problem-solving and decision-making. These tools dynamically adjust educational content and suggest personalized learning pathways, enhancing the human cognitive process, and encouraging personal and professional growth. To actualize cognitive enhancement tools as part of embedding artificial integrity in AI systems, we need to ensure that AI effectively augments human cognitive capabilities, offering support that is both intuitive and empowering.

First, it's important to develop AI-enhanced cognitive frameworks. These frameworks should consist of cognitive scaffolding algorithms that guide users through complex problem-solving processes, thereby enhancing logical and strategic thinking. By integrating systematic instructional design principles that tailor learning experiences to individual cognitive styles, AI can promote a deeper understanding. Furthermore, creating AI models that simulate expert reasoning provides users with the opportunity to shadow and learn from virtual expert decision-making processes.

Alongside this, implementing real-time analytical assistance is crucial. AI-driven data synthesis tools should be employed to condense large volumes of information into digestible insights, aiding in quick comprehension and application. The inclusion of on-demand predictive analytics can allow users to forecast trends and patterns, allowing users to make proactive informed decisions. In addition, equipping AI systems with the capability to generate visual data representations can simplify complex information into clear, intuitive formats.

Another key aspect is the design of adaptive learning algorithms. Such algorithms dynamically adjust educational content based on user interactions, optimizing the learning curve to suit individual pace and progress. Continual assessment of learning outcomes by AI diagnostic tools can adapt the difficulty level and content type to address specific cognitive needs. Moreover, creating memory augmentation systems could be useful. These systems, such as AI-enhanced memory aids, can help users organize and retrieve information efficiently, leveraging advanced retrieval techniques. Context-aware reminder systems within AI can help prompt recall of relevant information at critical moments, enhancing performance and productivity. Also, cloud-based knowledge repositories accessible by AI can provide users with an extended, easily navigable memory bank.

In addition, developing heuristic pattern recognition capabilities in AI is important. These algorithms should identify complex patterns and offer heuristic solutions to simplify decision-making processes for users. AI can also detect inefficiencies in user workflows and suggest heuristic strategies to optimize performance and cognitive load. By integrating AI-driven recommendation systems that apply heuristic reasoning, it can help propose optimal methods for task execution and human cognitive enhancement.

Automating cognitive tasks using AI, such as data sorting or report generation, is another significant step. This automation frees users to engage in more intellectually stimulating activities. Complementary to this, implementing AI systems that can handle multitasking environments, managing background cognitive tasks can help minimize distractions and cognitive fatigue. Also, enabling AI to take on complex data analysis can provide users with synthesized results that can be used for strategic decision-making.

Lastly, utilizing AI to create individualized learning and development pathways can allow you to map out a series of cognitive challenges and milestones tailored to each user. Developing AI-driven career progression tools that align with users' development goals can also help in suggesting roles and projects that will foster the desired growth.

By addressing these guiding principles, AI systems can be created to not only perform tasks but also to serve as catalysts for cognitive enhancement. Such systems would embody the principles of artificial integrity by actively contributing to the growth of human intelligence, ensuring that as the complexity of AI increases, it aligns with and supports the development of human cognitive strength. This approach will solidify the foundation for a collaborative future where AI serves as a sophisticated tool for human cognitive empowerment.

About Role-Specific AI Customization

Navigating the transition from Marginal mode to Human-First mode, this aspect focuses on tailoring AI systems to the unique requirements of specific roles within an organization. The AI is designed to understand and adapt to the nuances of various job responsibilities, offering personalized support that aligns with the evolving nature of each role. The integration is seamless, enhancing role-specific tasks without superseding the critical human element.

To embed artificial integrity within AI systems, particularly for "role-specific AI customization" a focused approach is required to ensure that AI systems are not only tailored to the unique needs and contexts of specific roles within an organization but also maintain the ethical standards and operational integrity required by such roles. A key step in this process is the precision customization of AI functionalities. Developing AI systems capable of understanding and adapting to the fine-grained requirements of specific roles is crucial. This includes grasping the nuances of decision-making processes and operational priorities unique to each position. Equipping AI with advanced learning algorithms can also allow for real-time adaptation to changes in role responsibilities, ensuring the system continually aligns with the evolving nature of the job.

Following this, implementing adaptive role-based AI profiling is key. AI profiling mechanisms that construct and update comprehensive user profiles based on role-specific interactions, preferences, and feedback ensure that AI support is both personalized and effective. Integration of AI systems with organizational role databases enables automatic adjustment of functionalities and support levels, tailoring the AI's capabilities to the parameters of each specific role, thereby promoting efficiency and relevance.

In addition, seamless role-centric AI integration is crucial. AI systems should be designed to integrate with specialized role-centric tools, enhancing and extending their functionalities without superseding the human element critical to the role's tasks. It's important to ensure that AI integrations can evolve alongside role-specific software, maintaining compatibility and augmenting the toolset available to the user. Creating AI interfaces that are intuitive for users within specific roles facilitates a seamless interaction that respects the unique workflow and cognitive demands of each user's position.

By addressing these guiding principles, AI can achieve a level of sophistication and adaptability that aligns with the goals of artificial integrity. Such systems will not only support the specific tasks associated with various roles but will also uphold the ethical standards and operational excellence expected in a world where AI is an integral part of the workforce. This ensures that AI systems are an empowering extension of human capabilities, enriching the role-specific experience while maintaining the user's control and oversight.

About Mentorship AI

In the transition from Marginal mode to Human-First mode AI systems act as mentorship aids, guiding and supporting human learning and development within the workplace. They are developed to anticipate learning needs, offer personalized feedback, and provide continuous skill development opportunities. These AI systems act as career coaches, setting realistic learning goals and tracking skill progression, thereby fostering a culture of continuous learning and professional growth. Incorporating artificial integrity into AI, particularly for it to function as a "mentorship AI" requires AI systems that understand and adapt to human learning processes.

The first step is the development of intuitive mentorship logic. Engineering AI systems that not only guide users through tasks but also anticipate learning needs and adapt the mentoring approach accordingly is crucial to ensure that guidance is provided in the most effective manner for each individual learner. Integrating advanced natural language processing and machine learning can enable such AI systems to understand and respond to user queries with nuanced, contextually relevant advice, mirroring the responsiveness of a human mentor.

Next, creating personalized feedback and encouragement mechanisms is necessary. To do so, algorithms that analyze user performance and provide personalized, constructive feedback can help recognize achievements and gently correct the course as needed. The AI should also recognize individual preferences and tailor its feedback delivery, whether direct, suggestive, or inquiry-based, to match the user's learning style.

In addition, implementing adaptive coaching protocols is essential. These protocols detect user difficulties through behavioral cues and feedback, triggering supportive interventions tailored to the user's specific challenges. Equipping AI systems with the ability to suggest alternative strategies or provide additional learning resources dynamically can also help ensure that users have access to a range of options that suit their learning pace and style. Complementary to this is developing AI systems that can schedule follow-up sessions or check-ins can provide continuity in learning and support, similar to the ongoing relationship fostered by a human mentor.

Moreover, contextual learning and development should be a key focus. Designing AI systems that can analyze the context in which tasks are performed can offer real-time, contextual learning opportunities and suggestions for professional development. Employing AI-driven analytics can also help map out an individual's career trajectory and provide strategic recommendations for skill development that align with both current role requirements and future career aspirations. Integrating AI systems with access to a wide array of online courses and resources can be useful to develop the capability to recommend specific learning materials based on the user's performance metrics and identified skill gaps.

By addressing these guiding principles, AI systems can achieve the level of artificial integrity necessary to act as true mentorship aids. This will enable them to support the development of human intelligence within the workplace, fostering a learning environment where AI serves as a catalyst for human growth and development while also respecting and enhancing human autonomy and decision-making.

By focusing on these detailed strategies, AI systems can be designed to facilitate the growth of human intelligence value in the workplace. The goal is to create an environment where AI serves as a partner in the learning and development process, providing the tools and support needed to elevate the human contribution to higher levels of complexity and value without overwhelming the system with AI functionalities. Through these transitions with a focus on technical design elements, AI systems can be developed to not only respect but actively promote and enhance human capabilities, reflecting a commitment to humanistic values in the age of intelligent machines.

Lastly, progress monitoring and goal-setting functionalities are imperative. Implementing AI functionalities that track progress against set learning goals can provide users with visual dashboards that display their advancement and areas needing attention. Programming AI to assist in setting realistic, achievable goals based on user performance data, industry standards, and personal aspirations can help encourage continuous professional development. And developing AI that can recognize and celebrate milestones and achievements can ultimately provide positive reinforcement and motivation to maintain a steady pace in skill acquisition and professional growth.

7 | How to Thrive Through Navigating Algorithmic Recalibration

The cluster designated as *algorithmic recalibration* involves transitions that reflect a reassessment and subsequent adjustment of the balance between human and artificial intelligence (AI) contributions in various processes.

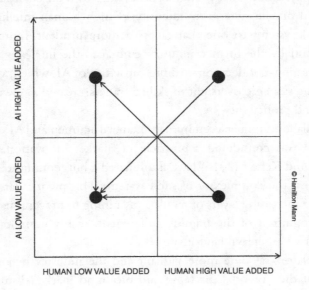

This cluster's transitions often represent corrective measures. The recalibration could also be driven by a desire to mitigate risks associated with AI, such as biases in decision-making or over-automation, by either increasing human oversight or reducing the scope of AI's autonomy.

Algorithmic Recalibration Is an Adaptive Necessity

The shift from high human intelligence value added/high AI value added to low human intelligence value added/low AI value added may reflect a strategic pivot toward simplification and a reduction in operational scale. This could be the result of numerous factors, including a reassessment of the cost–benefit ratio of high involvement of both human and AI resources, which may not yield commensurate returns. In this scenario, the deliberate deemphasis on both fronts could signify a reversion to more traditional methods that are less reliant on complex technologies and extensive human intervention, aiming for leaner and more agile operations. It can also be a response to market conditions that favor a more minimalist approach or a shift in organizational strategy toward products or services that require less intensive human and AI contributions.

In the realm of financial markets, particularly within high-frequency trading (HFT), a noteworthy shift is occurring from an environment that once thrived on the synergistic intensity of high human intelligence and advanced AI systems to one that favors a more prudent, human-centric approach. Initially, the finance industry embraced the intricate algorithms and the lightning-fast decision-making capacities of AI, which, when coupled with the strategic oversight of skilled traders, created a powerhouse of efficiency and profitability.

The collaboration between human financial acumen and AI's computational speed was considered a pinnacle of market innovation. However, Bookstaber and Kenett (2016) have illuminated a burgeoning trend toward a reduction in the complexity of such systems. This pivot is largely influenced by the increasing layers of regulations aiming to prevent market abuse and the recognition of the fragility inherent in overly complex financial ecosystems that are heavily automated.

As regulators become more vigilant and the industry becomes more cognizant of the potential for rapid and profound market disturbances—amplified by the AI-enabled high-speed trading—there is a conscious movement toward a simpler, more transparent market structure. This recalibration favors strategies that prioritize long-term stability and resilience over short-term gains, marking a significant transition toward lower AI dependency. The high-stakes arena of HFT now seems to be stepping away from an absolute reliance on complex algorithms and is beginning to value the measured judgment of experienced human traders, who can navigate the subtleties of market dynamics and risk management in ways that AI, for all its processing might, cannot fully emulate.

In the not-so-distant past, the domains of photo editing and graphic design were characterized by a rich interplay between high human intelligence and advanced AI tools. Industry professionals utilized complex software suites, which integrated sophisticated AI to facilitate the creation of intricate and aesthetically compelling visuals. Such software required not only an understanding of design principles but also a mastery of the AI-powered tools that could manipulate images in ways that seemed boundless. Over time, this landscape has begun to shift toward more intuitive, though inherently less capable, platforms indicative of a trend toward lower levels of both human intelligence and AI value added. As a result, they represent a departure from a paradigm where both the AI's sophisticated assistance and the human's intellectual rigor were paramount, moving toward a scenario where both are less pronounced.

Navigating from the point of intensive AI deployment, the transition from high human intelligence value added/low AI value added to low human intelligence value added/high AI value added signals a significant shift in operational dynamics, where the emphasis is moved from human capital to technological capital. This reallocation often points to an initiative to harness more sophisticated AI capabilities to streamline operations, reduce human labor costs, or circumvent the constraints of human scalability. It may also reflect a strategic decision to automate routine, time-consuming tasks, thereby allowing the human workforce to focus on areas that require more nuanced, complex judgment or interpersonal skills.

Such a shift typically accompanies a broader transformation within an organization as it adapts to technological advancements and market forces that value automation and data-driven decision-making. Such a transition is indicative of a company responding to competitive pressures and the drive for innovation, moving toward a business model that prioritizes AI's strengths in consistency, speed, and data processing over human labor.

The manufacturing landscape has been undergoing a significant transformation, particularly evident in innovative companies such as Tesla, which have become emblematic of the industry's push toward automation. Brougham and Haar (2018) outline this progression by highlighting how Tesla, known for its cutting-edge technology and a strong initial reliance on highly skilled labor, has gradually shifted its production paradigm to embrace more extensive automation. This move was largely driven by the dual goals of achieving superior efficiency and the capability to rapidly scale production volumes in response to consumer demand.

At the outset, Tesla's approach to manufacturing electric vehicles involved a considerable investment in human capital, with skilled workers playing a central role in the assembly and quality control processes. However, as the company's ambitions grew, it looked toward AI and robotic systems to take over some of the tasks that were once the domain of human workers. The rationale behind this strategic pivot is rooted in the pursuit of relentless efficiency—machines don't fatigue, can work around the clock, and are able to execute repetitive tasks with precision that surpasses human capability.

Yet, this transition has not been without its challenges. Reports of production bottlenecks and the complexities of aligning robotic precision with the artisanal quality of human craftsmanship have highlighted the intricacies involved in finding the right balance between human skill and machine consistency. Despite these hurdles, the trend in the manufacturing sector, as illustrated by Tesla's evolving strategy, shows a clear trajectory toward integrating more AI and automation technologies, redefining the role of human labor, and reimagining the capabilities of modern production facilities.

The genesis of online language translation services was distinctly marked by a reliance on high human intelligence value, with minimal AI contribution. In this initial phase, the intricate labor of translation fell upon the shoulders of expert linguists, whose deep understanding of not only language but also cultural context, idiomatic expressions, and sector-specific jargon was critical. Their skills were especially paramount in handling complex, nuanced documents—literary works imbued with subtle meanings, legal documents demanding absolute precision, and technical manuals requiring a high degree of subject-matter expertise. AI, in its nascent stages, was simply not equipped to grapple with such complexity; the algorithms lacked the depth of understanding necessary to discern and interpret the rich complexity woven by human languages.

As machine learning algorithms grew more sophisticated and the field of natural language processing advanced, a paradigm shift began to take root. Modern AI-driven tools, epitomized by platforms like Google Translate and DeepL, have emerged as powerful players, often matching and sometimes surpassing human performance in standard translation scenarios. These platforms leverage the enormous corpus of data available to them, coupled with feedback mechanisms, to refine their algorithms continuously. The resulting translations exhibit an increasingly nuanced understanding of context and language structure, ushering in an era of high AI value added in the realm of language services.

This technological renaissance has gradually eroded the monopoly once held by human translators over the industry, particularly for routine translation tasks, indicating a shift toward a lower human intelligence value-added landscape. While there remains a spectrum of translation needs for which the discerning eye of the human translator is irreplaceable—such as in the case of poetic literature, complex legal agreements, or highly technical scientific papers—the trajectory clearly points to a future where AI's role is ever-expanding. Consequently, the balance of value addition between human intelligence and artificial intelligence in language translation services is witnessing a dynamic recalibration, moving inexorably toward a space where sophisticated AI plays a dominant role.

The transition from high human intelligence value added/low AI value added to low human intelligence value added/low AI value added reflects a fundamental restructuring or scaling back of operations. This change might occur in a scenario where both human and AI contributions are minimized to focus on simplicity and cost-saving measures. In this instance, it is possible that tasks previously requiring significant human effort either are being eliminated due to changes in business strategy or are being streamlined to such an extent that neither advanced human skills nor sophisticated AI are necessary. This could be a response to market changes, a redefinition of core services, or an alignment to a more sustainable business model where efficiency and minimalism are prioritized. This scenario is often a prelude to a more radical transformation, reflecting an organization's move toward greater operational frugality and a reassessment of value creation strategies.

In the volatile expanse of the technology sector, shifts in employment and technological deployment are not uncommon, and they often act as bellwethers for broader industry trends. As Ford (2016) discusses, specific niches within the tech world have observed a notable contraction, affecting both the workforce and the progression of technological development. This contraction can be a multifaceted response to several factors, including changing market dynamics, financial downturns, or strategic reorientation following a shortfall in expected returns on hefty investments in technology.

Ford's analysis sheds light on instances where tech companies, which had once aggressively expanded their human and technological capital, begin to downsize. The reasons for such a shift can be complex. For example, a saturated market may lead to diminished returns, or innovative disruptions from competitors may render existing technologies less profitable. In some cases, the anticipated productivity boosts from automation and advanced software may not materialize as expected, leading companies to reassess their operational strategies.

As companies encounter these challenges, they often opt for a more conservative approach, trimming down their workforce and scaling back on research and development in emerging technologies. This recalibration is not necessarily a step back but rather a strategic realignment. By adopting a leaner operational model, tech companies aim to enhance their agility and capacity to adapt to an ever-changing technological landscape.

The implications of this shift are significant, suggesting a more cautious stance toward both employment and the adoption of new technologies, seeking stability and sustainability over rapid expansion and ambitious scaling. In the evolving landscape of the retail industry, the role of sales, once pivotal for providing a highly personalized customer service, is undergoing a significant transition. Traditionally, these sales brought a high human intelligence value added to the retail environment, utilizing their discernment, expertise, and personal engagement to not only bolster the customer experience but also to adeptly manage day-to-day store operations. Their capacity to interpret customer needs, provide expert advice, and foster relationships was a unique human value that AI had not yet replicated.

According to a comprehensive analysis by Grewal et al. (2017), this dynamic is shifting as online shopping platforms and self-service technologies gain dominance. These digital solutions typically harness relatively basic AI, focused on streamlining operations through rudimentary algorithms for product recommendations, inventory management, and transaction processing, without tapping into advanced AI's potential for high value added. The pivot toward these technologically driven, less human–centric models signals a downshift to both a low human intelligence value added and a low AI value added. This is marked by a diminution in the demand for the nuanced skills of sales personnel and a parallel reliance on automated systems that offer convenience but lack the sophistication of deep AI integration. Consequently, the retail sector is experiencing a shift that undervalues the traditional strengths of human intelligence and does not fully compensate with a high level of AI sophistication.

Continuing from this perspective, the transition from low human intelligence value added/high AI value added to low human intelligence value added/low AI value added could be interpreted as a deliberate de-escalation of complexity within a system, where high-tech solutions are scaled back to more manageable, low-tech approaches. This might occur in response to a reassessment of the actual value brought by sophisticated AI systems, which may not have delivered the expected return on investment or could have introduced unanticipated complications. In this context, organizations might opt for simplicity, stripping back to fundamental, less AI-dependent operations that require minimal human intervention, aiming for straightforwardness and perhaps reliability over cutting-edge innovation. This can be part of a larger trend toward technology and process minimalism, seeking to maximize efficiency and cost-effectiveness in a lean operational model.

The customer service landscape has undergone significant transformation with the advent of AI and automation technologies. However, this shift has not been without its pitfalls, as Davenport and Kirby (2016) elucidate in their work. They highlight that an over-reliance on automated systems for customer interactions can lead to a deterioration in service quality if not implemented with a complementary human presence. Companies that had once wholeheartedly embraced AI for handling customer queries began to notice a discordance between the efficiency of automation and the nuanced demands of customer satisfaction. These firms learned that customers often value the empathy and understanding that comes from human interaction, which AI is not yet fully equipped to replicate. Consequently, an emerging trend within the sector has been a conscious scaling back of AI applications in customer service roles. This retreat is not an abandonment of technology but rather a strategic rebalancing, aiming to leverage the strengths of AI while reinstating the human touch where it is most impactful.

Davenport and Kirby argue that by dialing back on AI's dominance in customer service and reintegrating human agents into the equation, businesses can enhance customer engagement and loyalty. The recalibration involves deploying AI in a supportive capacity, handling routine tasks and providing human agents with the information they need to deliver personalized and compassionate service. This approach aims to harness the efficiency of automation without compromising the quality of customer interactions, thus fostering a service model that better aligns with consumer expectations and drives service excellence.

In some regional agricultural sectors, particularly small-scale operations, there is an observable shift from a high reliance on human labor and expertise with minimal integration of artificial intelligence (AI) to scenarios characterized by low investment in both human and AI capital. The economic study by Lowenberg-DeBoer and Erickson (2019) provides insight into this phenomenon, particularly within the context of precision agriculture—a practice that leverages advanced technologies and AI to increase farm efficiency and crop yields. Their research highlights that smaller farms are often challenged by the high costs and complexity associated with the implementation of such technologies. This can lead to a situation where these technologies are initially adopted but later discarded when the return on investment (ROI) does not justify the ongoing expenses or when the technological infrastructure becomes too burdensome for the farmers to manage.

Consequently, this leads to a reversion to more traditional farming methods. These methods are characterized by a decrease in the use of AI tools, such as satellite imagery for soil analysis or automated irrigation systems, which were initially deployed to enhance decision-making and productivity. Simultaneously, there is a reduction in the reliance on human cognitive input for strategic decisions, as the nuanced data provided by AI that would require interpretation becomes unavailable. As a result, these small-scale farmers rely on more intuitive, experience-based approaches and manual labor—a labor-intensive strategy that maintains, or sometimes even reduces, the pre-existing levels of productivity due to the absence of both advanced AI solutions and high-value human intelligence in strategic roles (Lowenberg-DeBoer, J., & Erickson, B., 2019).

Algorithmic recalibration is aptly named because it implies a deliberate, iterative process of fine-tuning how human and AI contributions are configured within a system. It suggests an ongoing evaluation of how these two forces work together and how their collaboration can be modified to achieve more desirable outcomes. Unlike algorithmic boost, which intensifies AI's role, and humanistic reinforcement, which focuses on amplifying human input, algorithmic recalibration is characterized by a more nuanced restructuring of the interplay between human and AI efforts to better meet organizational goals, respond to feedback, or address ethical and practical concerns. This dynamic approach underscores the adaptability required in modern workplaces, where technological capabilities and human roles are continually evolving.

Navigating from Fusion Mode to Marginal Mode

In the shift toward the algorithmic recalibration cluster, from a state of Fusion mode (high human intelligence value added/high AI value added) to a state of Marginal mode (low human intelligence value added/low AI value added), the transition focuses on recalibrating the AI's role and functionalities to align with a decreased emphasis on both human and AI contributions. In the shift from Fusion mode, characterized by high contributions from both human intelligence and AI to Marginal mode, where both human and AI input are minimized with regard to the outcome to be achieved, there's a notable reevaluation of their roles and interactions. In Fusion mode, AI and human intelligence operate in synergy, each enhancing the other to achieve the outcomes. However, transitioning to Marginal mode implies a reduction in the complexity and intensity of both AI and human involvement.

In this new state, the focus shifts to maintaining basic operational functions with minimal input. AI's role becomes less about enhancing human decision-making and more about maintaining essential, routine tasks, often running in the background with little active human interaction or oversight. It repurposes its role toward ensuring efficiency and reliability in less complex scenarios.

Similarly, the human role adapts to focus on overseeing and managing the AI, rather than engaging in intensive collaborative efforts or complex decision-making processes while considering that the tasks to be performed require only modest or relative human intelligence for the realization of the expected outcome. This transition emphasizes streamlining processes, reducing operational overhead, and optimizing for scenarios where intensive human–AI collaboration is not critical, reflecting a strategic shift in resource allocation and operational focus.

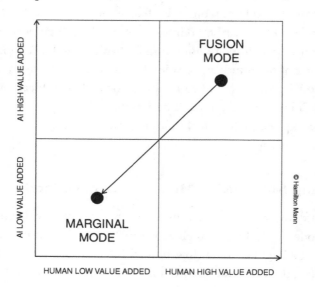

The strategies to consider in this transition include modular system design, de-escalation protocols, simplification analytics, and efficiency audit tools.

About Modular System Design

Navigating from Fusion mode to Marginal mode, implies to develop AI systems with dynamic modular architectures that can autonomously scale up or down based on operational needs and human involvement. This involves creating AI components with independent learning capabilities and predictive scaling mechanisms. Such systems are designed to respond to changes in human–AI interaction, ensuring that the AI's functionalities are appropriately calibrated and maintaining operational efficiency while adhering to ethical guidelines.

The quest for artificial integrity within AI systems necessitates the capability to dynamically adapt AI functions to the fluctuating degrees of human intelligence and AI value-added involvement needed. This adaptability ensures that AI systems can responsibly downscale their functions when human involvement diminishes, adhering to both ethical standards and operational demands.

First, the construction of AI systems with dynamic modular architecture is essential. This approach involves designing AI systems with modular designs to help enable components to autonomously scale up or down, providing the necessary functionality as dictated by the operational context and human involvement. Equipping each module with independent learning capabilities allows them to self-optimize and reduce their operational footprint while maintaining essential services and compliance with ethical standards.

Building on this, the implementation of predictive scaling mechanisms is crucial. These mechanisms, using historical data, current trends, and predictive analytics, forecast the need for adjusting AI modules and ensuring a proactive rather than reactive approach to scaling.

Also, developing AI systems capable of self-assessment can help them identify underutilized functions or modules that can be scaled down or temporarily suspended, thereby streamlining the system's operations without human intervention.

Furthermore, enabling AI systems with decision-making protocols that autonomously identify opportunities for simplification ensures that AI remains lean and fully aligned with the current operational scope and ethical frameworks. Complementary to this, integrating self-regulatory mechanisms enables AI to independently enforce simplification directives, ensuring continuous alignment with the principle of minimum necessary intervention.

In addition, fostering AI systems with the ability to understand the broader context of their deployment, including the complexity of tasks, human interaction levels, and ethical implications, can help adapt their functionalities accordingly. Also, designing AI that can interpret environmental signals and user feedback to adjust its complexity in real time can ensure that its scaling is both contextually relevant and ethically informed.

Lastly, providing user-guided adaptation interfaces allows human users to set parameters for AI scaling. This empowers them to guide the system's adaptation processes based on their assessments of requirements and ethical considerations. Also, establishing clear guidelines and thresholds for AI systems, as determined by human administrators, can help automate the scaling process within predefined ethical boundaries.

By addressing these guiding principals, AI systems can achieve a level of operational and ethical agility that allows them to maintain their integrity even as they adjust their functions to match the shifting landscape of human–AI collaboration. This flexibility is a cornerstone of artificial integrity, ensuring that AI systems not only can perform optimally across various levels of human involvement but also can uphold ethical standards as an intrinsic aspect of their operation.

About De-escalation Protocols

In the context of shifting from Fusion mode to Marginal mode, de-escalation protocols are crucial as AI's role needs to be minimized. This involves integrating conditional triggers within the AI that detect scenarios necessitating a reduction in AI involvement. AI systems will be equipped with self-evaluation modules to assess their effectiveness and necessity, alongside structured de-escalation pathways that gradually reduce AI functionalities while ensuring stability and continuity in operations.

To fulfill the concept of artificial integrity within an AI system, it is critical to design mechanisms that enable the AI to appropriately scale down its activities and realign its functions to support a less AI-centric operational model. In pursuit of this, integrating conditional de-escalation triggers into the AI is essential. These triggers can detect specific events or conditions that signal the need for de-escalation, such as achieving certain milestones or a decreased dependency on AI assistance. Predictive analytics could be used to forecast scenarios where AI de-escalation might be beneficial in preparing the system to initiate protocols autonomously.

Furthermore, the AI could assess user competency over time, scaling back assistance as proficiency increases to foster user independence and confidence. In addition, developing a self-evaluation module within the AI that regularly assesses the effectiveness and necessity of its functions can enable it to recommend de-escalation where it finds its involvement may no longer be optimal. Programming the AI to recognize and learn from patterns of human override or circumvention can help it interpret these as cues for potential de-escalation of its roles. Complementary to this, incorporating feedback loops can allow the AI to adjust its operational intensity based on user satisfaction, efficiency metrics, and the achievement of intended outcomes.

Structured de-escalation pathways are also key. Creating a framework within the AI for gradual de-escalation, with checkpoints at each stage to evaluate impact and ensure stability, is crucial.

The AI should facilitate knowledge transfer during de-escalation, ensuring that any insights or data previously managed by the AI are effectively communicated to human counterparts. Implementing a tiered access system where higher AI functionality levels are unlocked only when necessary could prioritize human input.

Furthermore, designing user-centric de-escalation interfaces is key. These interfaces should clearly communicate the current level of AI involvement and provide users with the control to initiate or halt the de-escalation process. Users should have the option to preview expected changes in AI behavior before de-escalation is implemented, ensuring transparency and consent. Customization options for de-escalation protocols would allow users to set preferences for how and when the AI scales back its activities.

Lastly, implementing de-escalation training for AI is crucial. Training the AI with simulations that replicate various de-escalation scenarios ensures it is prepared for real-world applications. Incorporating historical data into the AI's learning algorithms to highlight successful instances and facilitating machine learning processes to improve de-escalation strategies over time, based on outcomes and feedback, is essential to build a knowledge base for best practices. To this end, facilitating machine learning processes that allow the AI to improve its de-escalation strategies over time, based on outcomes and human feedback, could be useful.

By addressing these guiding principals, the AI system would be able to effectively manage its transition to lower levels of involvement, ensuring that artificial integrity is maintained by aligning the system's operations with the evolving needs and capabilities of human users. This strategic approach to AI system design will support a balanced and ethical integration of AI in various contexts, emphasizing the importance of human control and discretion.

About Simplification Analytics

As AI systems transition from Fusion mode to Marginal mode, thus from the most complex to the less complex state, simplification analytics become essential. These analytics involve implementing machine learning algorithms to evaluate the functional efficiency of AI systems and identify opportunities for simplifying or removing redundant features. This process aims to streamline AI operations, focusing on maintaining essential functionalities and enhancing user experience without unnecessary complexity.

To realize the principle of artificial integrity through the application of simplification analytics in AI systems it is necessary to deploy a set of strategic actions that would ensure that the AI system remains effective and efficient without unnecessary complexity, thus upholding the values of artificial integrity.

The first step, functional efficiency evaluation, involves implementing advanced machine learning algorithms to constantly evaluate the AI system's functional efficiency. These algorithms would identify and suggest the removal or simplification of redundant or underutilized features. Equipping the AI with self-optimization capabilities to autonomously streamline its operations focuses on maintaining essential functions while eliminating or simplifying non-essential ones. Also, using data-driven analytics to compare the system's complexity with usage patterns and performance outcomes can help identify discrepancies that signal over-complexity.

Building on this, usage pattern analysis is critical. Integrating algorithms to analyze long-term usage patterns and user interactions helps identify which features are critical and which are supplementary or rarely utilized. Developing an AI-driven assessment tool provides simplification recommendations based on usage frequency, user feedback, and the relative impact on the system's core objectives. Conducting iterative reviews ensures that the AI's decision-making processes remain streamlined and free from unnecessary steps or convolutions.

Furthermore, performance impact forecasting is vital. Creating predictive models within the AI system to forecast the potential impact of simplification on performance ensures that changes do not adversely affect the system's capabilities or user outcomes.

Designing the AI to simulate potential simplifications before implementation and employing a versioning system allows for risk assessment for various simplification scenarios and their implications for both AI and human users as well as an easy adjustment if simplification efforts lead to unintended consequences or degradation of service.

Transparency and accountability measures are also essential. Ensuring the AI's simplification analytics tools are transparent allows stakeholders to understand the rationale behind suggested simplifications and their expected benefits. Integrating accountability features that require human oversight for significant changes maintains a balance between automated efficiency and human judgment. Comprehensive reporting on simplification outcomes, including both successes and lessons learned, informs continuous improvement and maintains trust in AI system's integrity.

Lastly, user-centric simplification feedback is crucial. Developing mechanisms for gathering user feedback on the AI system's complexity and usability guides simplification initiatives. Designing the AI to prioritize user experience in its simplification analytics ensures that changes enhance usability and accessibility for the intended user base. Facilitating a participatory design process that involves users in simplification decisions reinforces the AI's alignment with user needs and the principles of artificial integrity.

By addressing these guiding principals into the design and operation of AI systems ensures that simplification is not merely a technical exercise but a thoughtful process that respects and enhances the user experience. By focusing on simplification analytics, we can maintain artificial integrity, ensuring that as AI systems evolve, they do so with a clear focus on necessity, efficiency, and the overarching goal of serving human needs effectively.

About Efficiency Audit Tools

From Fusion mode to Marginal mode, integrating efficiency audit tools ensures that AI systems remain efficient and aligned with ethical standards even as they become less complex. Regular efficiency evaluations, performance benchmarking, and optimization recommendations are part of this approach. The goal is to maintain a balance between operational efficiency and ethical commitments, ensuring AI systems continue to operate optimally and responsibly.

Embedding artificial integrity into AI systems to achieve efficient and ethical operation requires incorporating advanced efficiency audit tools. This ensures that as AI systems become less directly involved in the expected outcome, they remain aligned with ethical standards and operate optimally.

Achieving this process begins with regular efficiency evaluations. Establishing a routine for AI systems to conduct self-assessments and evaluate their performance against established benchmarks to ensure optimal efficiency without compromising ethical standards is essential. Integrating continuous monitoring tools provides real-time feedback on the system's operations, allowing for immediate adjustments to uphold artificial integrity. In addition, setting up a system for periodic reassessment of the AI's decision-making frameworks and learning algorithms is crucial to ensure they continue aligning with the principles of artificial integrity as they evolve.

Next, performance benchmarking is key. Creating a comprehensive suite of performance benchmarks tailored to the varied functions of the AI system ensures evaluation against ethical and efficiency standards. Employing machine learning algorithms refines these benchmarks over time, using historical data and outcome analyses to set dynamic, contextually relevant performance goals. These benchmarks measure current performance and forecast potential future states of the AI system, enabling proactive adjustments for maintaining artificial integrity.

Furthermore, developing an optimization recommendations module is vital. This module aims at generating actionable recommendations for system optimization, with a priority on enhancing artificial integrity. Predictive modeling helps understand the impacts of different optimization strategies, ensuring they don't compromise the system's ethical operation.

Also, implementing a feedback mechanism allows human operators to evaluate and input optimization recommendations, enhancing the AI's alignment with artificial integrity continuously.

Equally important is redundancy identification and management. Equipping the AI with the ability to identify and manage redundant processes within its own operations and human interactions streamlines the system to focus on value-added activities. An interface for human operators to understand and act upon redundancy findings fosters collaboration in maintaining system efficiency. Complementary to this, balancing redundancy elimination with fail-safes and backups ensures efficiency does not undermine robustness or ethical commitments.

Lastly, leveraging advanced analytics for insights driven by key performance indicators (KPIs) is key. Converting performance data into insights informs decisions about balancing human and AI contributions. Personalizing KPI dashboards for different stakeholders provides relevant information for their role in maintaining or improving the system's integrity. Integrating these insights into the AI's learning processes allows the system to autonomously adjust operations to achieve optimal performance while upholding artificial integrity.

By addressing these guiding principals, we ensure that AI systems not only operate efficiently but also retain their adherence to the ethical principles that define artificial integrity. This is crucial in the evolution of AI, where AI systems must remain aligned with human values and ethical considerations even as they become more autonomous and capable.

In enacting these measures, the AI system transitions to a less complex state in a controlled and efficient manner, maintaining the necessary functionality with a reduced level of human and AI involvement. The focus is on preserving the essential operations and quality of service while removing unnecessary layers of complexity, leading to a leaner and more manageable system.

Navigating from Human-First Mode to AI-First Mode

Transitioning toward the algorithmic recalibration cluster, from a state of Human-First mode (high human intelligence value added/low AI value added) to a state of AI-First mode (low human intelligence value added/ high AI value added), requires a strategic approach to integrate artificial integrity within AI systems. In transitioning from Human-First mode, where the primary value lies in human intelligence with AI playing a supporting role, to AI-First mode, the dynamic of contribution shifts significantly. In this new paradigm, AI takes the lead, moving from a background enabler to a forefront driver of operations and outcomes.

In Human-First mode, AI's purpose is to augment human decision-making and problem-solving, emphasizing the enhancement of human capabilities. However, as we move into AI-First mode, there is a pivot toward maximizing the AI's autonomous functions, leveraging its advanced capabilities to handle complex tasks and make critical decisions with minimal human intervention in delivering the expected outcome. The sophistication of the AI in this mode isn't just a supportive feature but becomes the central pillar of operational efficiency and effectiveness for the expected outcome to be achieved.

This transition reflects a reorientation where the human role is redefined to oversee and guide the AI, rather than directly engaging in the task execution required to deliver the expected outcome. If this shift doesn't require much human intelligence in the making of the outcome, it requires human oversight, system refinement, and ethical supervision. AI in this mode is not just an assistant but a primary actor, capable of adapting, learning, and making decisions that were traditionally within the human domain. This evolution marks a significant step in AI integration, highlighting its potential to not just support but actively lead in achieving goals, while human intelligence shifts to a more supervisory role.

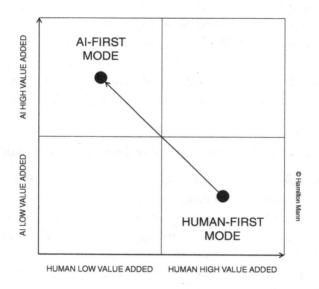

This transformation involves a series of deliberate and ethical actions that includes automated task transition, capability mapping, human–AI interaction redesign, and advanced training algorithms.

About Automated Task Transition

Navigating from Human-First mode to AI-First mode involves equipping AI systems to efficiently take over human tasks while considering ethical implications and human workforce dynamics. Key actions include the integration of natural language processing for complex task understanding, deployment of optimization algorithms to refine task execution, and development of AI systems capable of ethical collaboration and learning from human expertise. This transition aims to transfer tasks to AI oversight ethically and operationally, supporting a smooth transition for the workforce. Achieving artificial integrity in the context of automated task transition within AI systems involves creating AI that can take over routine tasks efficiently while ensuring the transition respects ethical considerations and human workforce implications.

Starting with task automation and optimization, it's essential to integrate advanced natural language processing, enabling the AI to understand and perform complex tasks based on verbal or written instructions, thereby reducing the need for human intervention in routine operations. The deployment of optimization algorithms is also crucial as they continually refine task execution based on efficiency and ethical impact. This ensures that automated tasks do not lead to unintended negative consequences.

In addition, designing AI systems to collaborate with humans in identifying potential areas for automation is key, ensuring that tasks are transferred to AI oversight only when it is ethically appropriate and operationally advantageous.

Building on this, contextual adaptation and learning are paramount. Equipping AI systems with the ability to learn from context clues and adapt their task execution strategies is essential to ensure automated tasks are performed with an understanding of their broader implications. Implementing a feedback loop where AI learns from human experts about the nuances of tasks enhances its ability to handle more complex aspects of routine work. Developing AI that can predict the downstream effects of task automation on workflow and human roles is also important, allowing for adjustments that support a positive workforce transition.

As a complementary measure, establishing human–AI collaboration and transition protocols is critical. Creating a phased transition protocol within the AI system, which outlines clear stages and conditions for AI takeover, ensures a smooth transition for the human workforce. Establishing clear communication channels for human workers to provide input and feedback on the AI's performance fosters a collaborative environment where human expertise is valued. Implementing AI-driven training programs helps human workers upskill and transition to new roles where their expertise is enhanced by AI support rather than replaced by it.

Furthermore, installing ethical safeguards and monitoring is vital. Ethical oversight mechanisms that monitor the AI's task transition process ensure alignment with fairness principles and mitigate impacts on certain worker groups. Also, developing AI systems that can assess the ethical implications of automating a task is key, considering factors such as job displacement and the potential for skill degradation. Establishing a governance for reviewing AI decisions by an ethical committee ensures that human values are upheld in the transition process.

Lastly, programming AI with progressive learning and handover capabilities is crucial. AI should start with simple tasks and gradually take on more complex tasks as it demonstrates proficiency. Designing the AI's learning modules to prioritize tasks that are least disruptive to the workforce when automated can foster alignment between task transition and strategic workforce planning. Also, enabling the AI to provide just-in-time training and assistance to human workers as they shift to new tasks should help support a learning culture within the organization.

By addressing these guiding principals, AI systems will be able to achieve artificial integrity in task transitions, ensuring that as AI takes on more responsibilities it does so in a way that respects human workers and adheres to ethical standards. This ensures that AI systems are not only efficient and capable but also aligned with the values and needs of the society they serve.

About Capability Mapping

When transitioning from Human-First mode to AI-First mode, it's crucial to integrate capability mapping. This involves in-depth analysis of job roles to distinguish between tasks suitable for automation, continuous tracking of role evolution, and fostering collaborative environments for human and AI interaction. Ethical impact assessments, adaptive learning programs, and transparent communication channels are vital in aligning AI-driven capability mapping with organizational goals, ensuring automation serves broader objectives of growth and innovation.

To embed artificial integrity into AI systems for capability mapping, we must ensure that AI systems not only can identify and automate tasks but also can understand and respect the human components of the workplace. The process starts with a detailed role and task analysis. Developing AI algorithms capable of in-depth analysis of job roles and descriptions is key. These algorithms should distinguish between tasks that benefit from human cognition and those suitable for automation. The AI can parse complex work processes into discrete tasks, assessing each task's potential for automation based on predictability, repetitiveness, and the requirement for human intuition.

Following this, continuous role evolution tracking is important. Implementing an AI system that monitors the nature of the job roles, identifying shifts in task requirements due to changes in technology, market demands, or organizational strategy could be useful. Also, designing AI to predict future trends in task automation allows organizations to plan for workforce development and training in areas where human intelligence will remain paramount.

Moreover, fostering collaborative capability development is critical. Fostering a collaborative environment where AI systems and human employees can communicate effectively ensures that the transition of tasks from human to AI is consensual and transparent. In line with this, platforms within the AI system for employee feedback on their experience with AI task automation can be used to adjust the AI's understanding of human capabilities.

In addition, integrating an ethical impact assessment tool within AI systems can help evaluate the potential consequences of task automation on employee satisfaction, career development, and well-being. Establishing ethical guidelines for AI that prioritizes human value is essential, ensuring that automation does not erode essential human skills or reduce opportunities for meaningful work.

Developing adaptive learning and training systems within the AI is also key. These systems can suggest training programs and career paths for employees affected by automation, supporting their transition to higher-value roles within the organization. Personalized learning experiences created by AI can also help employees acquire new skills and adapt to the evolving workspace where AI takes on more routine tasks.

Furthermore, ensuring transparent communication and decision-making in all automation decisions made by AI is paramount. All AI decisions should be transparent, with clear rationales understandable and queryable by human workers. Also, AI systems providing visualizations and simulations of potential automation scenarios can help employees and management understand and plan for changes in task allocation.

Lastly, integrating with organizational strategy is key. Aligning AI-driven capability mapping with the organization's strategic goals ensures that automation serves broader objectives like growth, innovation, and employee development. AI systems working in tandem with human resources and strategic planning departments can integrate AI capabilities cohesively into the organization's future vision.

By addressing these guiding principals, AI systems can be designed to respect and enhance human roles while automating certain tasks, achieving a balance that reflects the principles of artificial integrity. This ensures that AI systems contribute positively to organizational efficiency and employee fulfillment, paving the way for a future where AI and humans collaborate seamlessly and ethically.

About Human–AI Interaction Redesign

In the context of the transition from Human-First mode to AI-First mode, and thus a state where AI assumes greater operational roles in delivering an expected outcome, redesigning human–AI interactions with artificial integrity as a core principle is essential. This includes enhancing AI interfaces for intuitive user experience, developing supportive interaction protocols, and programming AI systems for agency-centric behavior. Ensuring AI functionality transparency, dynamic task allocation, ethical oversight, and collaborative evolution between human and AI capabilities will be critical in crafting AI systems that support and respect human agency and expertise. Embedding artificial integrity into AI systems that aspire to achieve a level of AI suitable for human–AI interaction redesign requires a detailed approach that prioritizes seamless integration, user empowerment, and the facilitation of human expertise.

First, enhancing the intuitive interface is crucial. Implementing user experience (UX) design principles to revamp the AI interface makes it easily navigable, with clearly labeled and logically organized controls to reduce the learning curve and enhance human oversight. Furthermore, incorporating adaptive interface technologies that respond to the user's proficiency level offers a simplified experience for novices and a more advanced, customizable one for expert users.

Moreover, programming AI systems with agency-centric AI behavior emphasizes their facilitative role in decision-making, ensuring human workers retain ultimate control over critical tasks. AI systems that seek confirmation or approval from human users before executing tasks within the human's domain of expertise reinforce AI as a collaborative partner.

In addition, empowerment through transparency is vital. Ensuring AI systems are transparent in their functioning provides users with insight into decision-making processes, data usage, and the reasoning behind AI-generated suggestions. Integrating features that explain AI processes in layman's terms empowers users to understand the AI's role and limitations.

Dynamic task allocation also plays a significant role. Creating AI systems that adjust task allocation between AI and human workers based on efficiency and the human worker's engagement level is important. AI analyzing workflow patterns to suggest task reallocation aligns with both organizational strategic objectives and human workers' professional development goals.

Finally, embedding ethical oversight integration within the AI system monitors the AI's impact on human workers and the workplace, ensuring ethical concerns are addressed as AI involvement increases. A system of checks and balances within the AI prevents it from making unilateral decisions in areas that have significant ethical implications.

By addressing these guiding principals, AI systems can be crafted to not only excel in their increased role within organizational operations but do so with a profound respect for human agency and expertise, embodying the ethos of artificial integrity. This approach ensures that as AI assumes more responsibility, it does so in a way that is ethically sound, supportive of human workers, and reflective of the collaborative potential of human–AI partnerships.

About Advanced Training Algorithms

When transitioning from Human-First mode to AI-First mode, implementing advanced training algorithms is vital for AI systems to take on a more prominent operational role related to its direct involvement in delivering the expected outcome. Enhanced learning protocols that enable AI to learn from less data, scenario-based adaptations for real-world task applications, proactive human–AI synergy, contextual performance enhancements, continuous improvement mechanisms, ethical learning integration, and feedback-informed learning pathways are crucial. These actions ensure that AI systems learn to perform complex roles with an enhanced understanding and ethical approach, maintaining trust and efficacy in advanced AI systems.

Attaining artificial integrity in AI systems require implementing advanced training algorithms. These algorithms are key to ensuring that AI can take on a more prominent role in operations by learning from and adapting to complex human tasks.

First, employing enhanced learning protocols involves state-of-the-art machine learning techniques that enable AI systems to learn from less data and apply knowledge to new scenarios, much like human learning. Deep learning networks are utilized to identify patterns from vast datasets, mimicking the way humans extrapolate information, to continually enhance the AI's operational acumen.

Building on this, scenario-based adaptation is essential. Creating simulation environments where AI engages in various task scenarios allows it to learn from virtual experiences and apply this learning to real-world tasks. Developing algorithms that enable AI to learn from hypothetical outcomes integrates elements of foresight and planning, similar to human strategizing for future events.

Furthermore, proactive human–AI synergy is key. Designing AI systems that anticipate when human expertise is required, signaling for human collaboration on tasks that exceed the AI's current capabilities or understanding, maintains a harmonious balance between AI autonomy and human oversight. Also, implementing collaborative learning algorithms where AI not only learns from human input but also suggests strategies and solutions, as well as engaging in a bidirectional learning process, enhancing both the AI's and the human operator's capabilities.

Moreover, integrating contextual performance enhancement is crucial. Training algorithms that enable AI to understand different operational environments and adjust their learning accordingly are key. Equipping AI to analyze contextual cues, similar to human situational awareness, ensures task requirements are met and aligns learning processes with operational goals.

In addition, establishing continuous improvement mechanisms within AI systems assesses learning outcomes and iteratively refines algorithms for ongoing enhancement of AI capabilities. This ethos mirrors human professional development, where learning is an ongoing journey leading to the perpetual enhancement of AI competencies.

Ethical learning integration is also essential. Developing AI training algorithms with ethical considerations in mind ensures that AI learns to identify ethical implications of decisions and upholds ethical standards. Embedding moral reasoning within the AI learning process ensures that as

AI systems take on more complex roles, they do so with an understanding of ethical boundaries and societal norms.

Lastly, creating feedback-informed learning pathways allows AI systems to align their learning and performance with user expectations and experiences. Developing AI algorithms that respond to and actively seek feedback mimics the human trait of seeking mentorship and guidance for improvement.

By addressing these guiding principals, AI systems can be equipped with advanced training algorithms that facilitate a transition to higher AI value added, without compromising the overarching goal of achieving artificial integrity. This ensures that as AI takes on tasks traditionally performed by humans, it does so with an enhanced understanding and an ethical approach, maintaining the trust and efficacy essential in AI advanced systems.

By focusing on these detailed strategies, AI systems can be designed to facilitate the transition toward a higher AI value added while ensuring that the system remains efficient, effective, and aligned with the overall goals of the organization. The aim is to harness the capabilities of AI to take on routine tasks, freeing up human workers to apply their intelligence to more complex and strategic activities.

Navigating from Human–First Mode to Marginal Mode

The transition toward the algorithmic recalibration cluster, from a state of Human-First mode (high human intelligence value added/low AI value added) to a state of Marginal mode (low human intelligence value added/low AI value added), focuses on strategically redefining and streamlining AI's role within the organization to ensure continued effectiveness and adherence to ethical standards. In the transition from Human-First mode to Marginal mode, there is a significant shift in the roles and contributions of human intelligence. In Human-First mode, the emphasis is on the paramount value of human skills and decision-making, with AI serving as an assistive tool to enhance these capabilities. Here, AI's role is secondary, focused on supporting and amplifying human intelligence to achieve the desired outcomes.

However, moving into Marginal mode, human contributions diminish in direct task execution with regard to the expected outcome. In this scenario, the demand for human intelligence and intervention decreases, and the reliance on sophisticated AI supporting human ability is also reduced. Tasks and operations in this mode are typically characterized by a lower complexity that doesn't necessitate intense human involvement or advanced AI capabilities. The nature of tasks may be more routine or have been optimized to a level where neither complex AI algorithms nor much human intelligence is required.

The transition to Marginal mode represents a scaling back or simplification of processes, where the functions performed are straightforward enough to require minimal intervention from both humans and AI to deliver the expected outcome. This mode might be seen in scenarios where efficiency and simplicity are prioritized, and the tasks don't involve complex decision-making or innovative problem-solving. In Marginal mode, both AI and human intelligence operate in a more limited, basic capacity, reflecting a streamlined approach to operations that values simplicity and ease of execution.

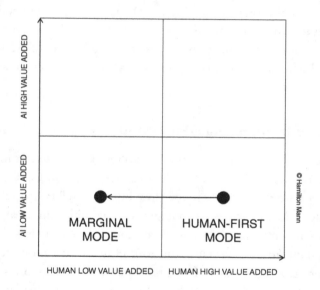

This recalibration process encompasses several key areas including task elimination identification, process optimization software, human role redefinition, and lean system principles.

About Task Elimination Identification

From Human-First mode to Marginal mode, the goal is to equip AI systems with the ability to discern and eliminate tasks that are redundant or no longer add value to the organization. It involves the development of AI systems capable of conducting a thorough analysis of organizational tasks. These systems are equipped with the ability to assess the necessity and impact of each task, simulating potential outcomes to ensure no critical functions are compromised. The integration of ethical decision-making protocols is paramount, ensuring task elimination decisions consider broader organizational and societal implications.

Achieving artificial integrity, especially in the domain of task elimination identification, requires careful consideration of how tasks are allocated and how their removal may affect the broader system. The process begins with comprehensive task analysis. Developing algorithms that dissect and analyze every aspect of a task is crucial to determine its necessity, frequency, and complexity within organizational operations. These algorithms should enable the AI not only to identify tasks for elimination but also to understand the interconnectedness of tasks, thereby predicting any cascading effects that may result from their removal.

Following this, impact simulation and forecasting are essential. Equipping AI systems with simulation capabilities to forecast the repercussions of task elimination ensures that no critical function is inadvertently compromised. Using historical data and predictive analytics to model various scenarios helps in making data-driven decisions about which tasks can be safely removed or simplified.

Moreover, integrating automated workflow optimization is key. AI systems should automatically suggest workflow optimizations post-task elimination to maintain or enhance operational efficiency. Machine learning enables these systems to iterate through different workflow configurations, finding the most efficient arrangement post-elimination.

Incorporating ethical decision-making integration is also critical. Embedding ethical decision-making protocols within the AI ensures that task elimination does not adversely affect employees or stakeholders and adheres to ethical business practices. The AI should consider broader implications, including employee well-being, customer satisfaction, and societal impact, when identifying tasks for elimination.

In addition, continuous system learning ensures that AI systems refine their criteria and methodologies for future identifications, creating a self-improving system. Implementing mechanisms for the AI to stay updated with industry trends and technological advancements adapts its task elimination criteria accordingly.

Establishing stakeholder communication channels is equally important. These channels allow the AI to report identified tasks for elimination to stakeholders, inviting feedback and discussion. Creating protocols for the AI to consider and integrate stakeholder feedback into its task elimination decision-making process is crucial.

Finally, dynamic reassessment protocols are necessary. Programming the AI to continually reassess its task elimination recommendations in light of new data, feedback, and organizational changes ensures ongoing relevance and effectiveness. Setting up a dynamic feedback loop where the AI's performance and the results of task elimination are continually evaluated against organizational goals and ethical benchmarks is imperative.

By addressing these guiding principals, AI systems will be equipped to identify tasks for elimination in a way that aligns with the principles of artificial integrity, ensuring that as tasks are suggested for removal, these recommendations remain beneficial, ethical, and in service of organizational efficiency and human value.

About Process Optimization Software

Navigating the transition from Human-First mode to Marginal mode involves refining AI systems to enhance operational efficiency while maintaining a focus on human-centric values. Even as the AI system moves into a state of lower complexity (Marginal mode), it needs to remain efficient, ethical, responsive, and aligned with human needs and organizational goals. It signifies a shift toward enhancing operational efficiency through AI, while maintaining a human-centric approach. AI systems are refined to analyze process steps meticulously, identifying automation opportunities and areas requiring human intervention. This optimization is balanced with ethical considerations, particularly in relation to the workforce, ensuring that AI supports and augments human roles rather than replacing them.

To achieve artificial integrity, it's essential to ensure that the AI system enhances operations while adhering to ethical standards. Here, the process begins with advanced process analytics, integrating AI systems capable of conducting deep analytics. These systems discern which aspects of every process can be automated and which should remain under human control, identifying patterns and inefficiencies within workflows that may indicate emerging inefficiencies or opportunities for process consolidation.

Following this, ethical efficiency modeling is crucial. Embedding ethical considerations into process optimization algorithms ensures decisions consider the potential impacts on employees, such as job displacement or changes in work conditions. The AI performs ethical alongside efficiency analysis, balancing optimization needs with the company's ethical commitments to its workforce and customers.

Human-centric optimization is another key step. The optimization software should propose changes that enhance rather than replace human roles, augmenting human intelligence with AI functions. AI-driven ergonomic studies within the software ensure that any proposed process changes do not detrimentally affect worker health or morale.

Moreover, integrating stakeholder engagement tools creates interactive modules for feedback on process changes. This fosters collaboration in optimization and helps establish clear communication protocols within the AI system to transparently share proposed changes and their rationale with all affected parties.

Dynamic adaptation mechanisms are also essential. Equipping AI with self-learning algorithms enables real-time adaptation based on feedback from the operational environment and human input. The AI system becomes capable of predicting and adapting to future shifts in operational demand, proactively suggesting process adjustments that maintain integrity and efficiency.

Continuous learning loops play a significant role as well. Integrating these loops allows the AI to refine its process optimization suggestions based on performance data and human feedback. This ensures the AI system is capable of iterative learning, where each cycle of process optimization informs and enhances the next.

Lastly, transparent decision rationales are vital. Programming the AI to provide clear explanations for each recommendation enables human workers to understand the logic behind proposed changes. Implementing a transparency feature allows workers to query the AI system about specific optimization decisions, fostering trust and understanding.

By addressing these guiding principals, AI systems can achieve artificial integrity in process optimization, ensuring that they not only improve efficiency but also respect and uphold ethical standards, aligning with the broader objectives of supporting human intelligence and safeguarding human interests in the workplace.

About Human Role Redefinition

From Human-First mode to Marginal mode, as human takes on fewer tasks, it's crucial to redefine human roles within the organization. It reflects the need to adapt human roles in response to AI integration. This involves using AI for strategic forecasting of job trends and realigning the workforce to maximize human value. AI systems play a crucial role in career path planning, offering personalized guidance and support for employee development, including reskilling and upskilling initiatives tailored to the evolving landscape of AI-driven operations.

Embedding artificial integrity into AI systems, particularly as it involves redefining human roles, calls for a multifaceted approach. Achieving this necessitates actions that address both the operational and human aspects of this transition. Task analysis and realignment initiate the process. In this aspect, AI-driven analyses are crucial to identify which tasks are becoming automated and what new roles are emerging. This approach allows for the reassignment of human resources to areas where they add the most value. Moreover, utilizing AI to forecast future job trends and skills requirements enables proactive workforce development and role realignment. AI tools also play a key role in identifying transferable skills among employees, facilitating their effective reallocation to emerging roles that emerge as AI takes on more operational tasks.

In tandem with task realignment, personalized career pathing with AI could be useful. Developing AI systems capable of mapping individual career paths provides employees with clear trajectories during times of transition. AI-driven career counseling tools offer insights into skill development and potential future roles, while AI analytics help monitor employee engagement and satisfaction, guiding adjustments where necessary.

In addition, communication and change management are essential. Integrating AI into change management processes can help leverage data-driven insights for smoother transitions and establishing AI-enabled platforms for feedback can foster a participatory approach to organizational change.

Furthermore, conducting an ethical impact analysis is crucial. AI capabilities for thorough ethical impact analyses evaluate how changes affect employee well-being, job satisfaction, and organizational culture. AI simulations of various reorganization scenarios analyze potential ethical implications, guiding decisions toward beneficial outcomes for both employees and the organization. Regular reports from AI systems on the ethical impact of changes ensure continuous alignment with organizational values and ethical commitments.

Lastly, AI-assisted reskilling and upskilling are integral. AI-driven learning platforms can help identify individual skill gaps and recommend tailored reskilling and upskilling pathways, easing the transition to new roles. These platforms track progress in learning programs, providing feedback and adapting materials for optimal growth.

Addressing these guiding principals, rooted in the principles of artificial integrity, ensures that the transition to new role definitions within an organization is not only technologically sound but also ethically aligned with the well-being and development of the workforce. This approach guarantees that as the organization evolves toward a model of reduced AI and human involvement, it does so with a focus on nurturing its human capital, adhering to ethical standards, and fostering a culture of continuous learning and adaptation.

About Lean System Principles

From Human-First mode to Marginal mode, the need is also on streamlining AI systems for efficiency. It emphasizes the importance of operational efficiency and ethical integrity in AI systems. This means making AI systems more efficient, resource-conscious, and ethically aligned, even as their role in operational tasks decreases. The focus is on programming AI to continuously evaluate and optimize its functionality, ensuring resource utilization is both efficient and ethically sound. Monitoring systems are integrated to oversee resource usage, and ethical resource allocation is prioritized to maintain sustainability and uphold ethical business practices.

First, implementing automated efficiency optimization is crucial. The AI should continuously evaluate and optimize its own operational efficiency, eliminating redundancies and unnecessary data consumption. Advanced algorithms can dynamically adjust operational parameters, ensuring optimal performance with minimal resource usage.

Second, self-assessment tools within the AI are necessary to regularly analyze performance against efficiency benchmarks, offering insights for continual system refinement. Following this, resource utilization monitoring plays a key role. Real-time monitoring systems within the AI should track resource usage across various functions, flagging areas where resources can be reduced without compromising performance or ethical standards. The AI needs to autonomously adjust its resource allocation, optimizing energy efficiency and minimizing waste, while a dashboard visualizes resource utilization for human operators.

In addition, ethical resource allocation is vital. The AI's resource allocation decisions must consider efficiency and ethical implications, embedding sustainable and responsible resource use principles into decision-making algorithms. Predictive modeling can anticipate future resource needs, enabling proactive, ethically informed adjustments to its operations.

Moreover, data privacy and security management are essential. Robust encryption protocols are necessary to secure data, particularly sensitive personal information. A comprehensive data privacy framework adhering to global standards, like the General Data Protection Regulation (GDPR), ensures user data privacy is respected. Continuous monitoring systems should scan for potential data breaches or unauthorized access attempts, maintaining high data security levels.

Another critical aspect is adaptive compliance monitoring. An AI compliance monitoring tool should adapt to evolving legal and regulatory frameworks, maintaining compliance with current laws and industry standards. Regular self-audits can help assess operations against compliance requirements and make necessary adjustments autonomously. Also, a system for real-time reporting on compliance status allows for swift human intervention in cases where potential noncompliance is detected.

Finally, integrating stakeholder engagement and feedback is fundamental. Platforms for active stakeholder engagement allow for the collection and analysis of feedback on the AI's performance and ethical conduct. AI algorithms should process this feedback, identify improvement areas, and adjust operations to align with stakeholder expectations. Transparent mechanisms for reporting feedback incorporation are crucial in fostering trust and ongoing dialogue between the AI system and its user base.

By addressing these guiding principals, an AI system can adhere to lean principles, balancing the need for efficiency and minimal resource use with the necessity to maintain ethical integrity and operational effectiveness. This approach not only optimizes the AI's performance but also aligns it with broader organizational goals of sustainability and ethical responsibility. Through this, the organization can effectively transition to a leaner operational model that maintains the integrity and efficiency of the system while reducing the complexity of both human and AI roles. This transition not only optimizes operations but also ensures that the remaining tasks are performed with precision and effectiveness, reflecting a commitment to a streamlined approach with artificial integrity.

Navigating from AI-First Mode to Marginal Mode

Transitioning toward the algorithmic recalibration cluster, from a state of AI-First mode (low human intelligence value added/high AI value added) to a state of Marginal mode (low human intelligence value added/low AI value added), is a recalibration process that focuses on the strategic downsizing of AI services, maintaining operational effectiveness while aligning with the principles of artificial integrity. In transitioning from AI-First mode to Marginal mode, there is a notable shift in the utilization and reliance on AI. In AI-First mode, the primary emphasis is on the capabilities and contributions of AI, which plays a significant role in driving the expected outcomes with less dependence on human input. Here, AI's advanced functionalities and autonomous operations are central to achieving objectives, often outperforming or supplementing human capabilities in complex tasks.

However, as we move into Marginal mode, the prominence of AI in direct task execution about the expected outcome noticeably decreases. This mode is characterized by tasks that require minimal intervention from advanced AI systems and less intricate human involvement. The operations become simpler and more routine, not demanding the high-level capabilities of sophisticated AI or the nuanced judgment and creativity of humans. The shift to Marginal mode suggests a streamlining of processes where the complexity of tasks is reduced to a level where neither advanced AI algorithms nor intensive human insights are essential.

This mode often applies in situations where efficiency and straightforward execution are prioritized and the tasks at hand are basic enough to be handled with minimalistic AI support and reduced human oversight. In this scenario, AI roles are scaled back, reflecting an operational approach that values straightforwardness and ease of management over complexity and depth of human engagement.

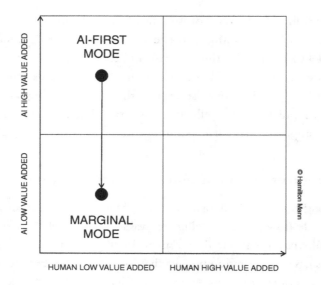

This process involves a series of actions including AI service downsizing, ethical downtuning, and resource allocation algorithms.

About AI Service Downsizing

Navigating from AI-First mode to Marginal mode involves a meticulous evaluation and adjustment of AI capabilities, ensuring the functionalities are aligned with current operational needs. The downsizing process includes comprehensively assessing each AI functionality, identifying and eliminating redundancies, and selectively deactivating features that have limited impact or usage. The core AI services are then optimized for efficiency, while maintaining the effectiveness and integrity of essential services. User experience is enhanced through the development of intuitive interfaces, and AI operations are made sustainable by integrating algorithms that optimize energy efficiency. In addition, the AI is used to augment human skills, complementing overall task execution and productivity.

To effectively achieve "AI service downsizing" within the context of artificial integrity it's essential to methodically evaluate and adjust the AI system's capabilities. This process ensures that AI functionalities are optimized for their intended roles, particularly when transitioning to scenarios requiring lower levels of AI input.

Starting with functionality assessment and rationalization, a thorough evaluation of each AI functionality is vital. This includes assessing its relevance and necessity within the system's current operational context, where the true value and impact of each service or feature is determined.

Further, identifying redundancies or overlaps where simplification could occur without compromising effectiveness is crucial. Also, evaluating the cost–benefit ratio of maintaining each advanced AI feature is essential, considering resource utilization, maintenance requirements, and actual usage patterns.

Next, selective feature deactivation is a strategic step. Developing criteria to decide which AI features or services to deactivate, particularly those with minimal usage or limited impact, is essential. Implementing a phased deactivation plan allows for careful monitoring of the system's performance and gathering of user feedback, ensuring no critical functionality is compromised. In addition, ensuring that this deactivation process is reversible, allowing for features to be reactivated, provides flexibility for future changes in requirements or if the downsizing impacts critical system performance.

Also, focusing on the optimization of core AI services is critical. The AI system must refocus on core functionalities that directly support essential tasks and operations, ensuring these are optimized for efficiency and reliability. Streamlining the AI's operational algorithms to reduce computational load is part of this process. Regular reviews of the streamlined AI system to identify further optimization opportunities or adjustments align with evolving operational needs and user feedback.

Moreover, enhanced user experience design is pivotal. Developing user interfaces that are intuitive and accommodate varying levels of technical expertise is necessary for seamless interaction. This includes the use of natural language processing and touch-based interactions. Incorporating features that allow users to personalize settings enhances comfort and usability. In addition, ensuring universal accessibility, including features for users with disabilities such as voice commands for visually impaired users or text-to-speech for those with hearing impairments, is crucial.

Lastly, implementing sustainable AI operations is a forward-thinking move. Developing algorithms that optimize energy efficiency and reduce the AI system's carbon footprint is a responsible approach. Implementing tools for continuous assessment of long-term sustainability, including resource utilization and environmental impact, is equally important. Adaptive resource management mechanisms ensure the system scales its resource usage appropriately.

By addressing these guiding principals, the AI system can be effectively downsized in its service offerings, aligning more closely with the requirements of scenarios characterized by lower AI involvement. This approach ensures that the AI system maintains its effectiveness and efficiency, while also adhering to the principles of artificial integrity, particularly in the context of reduced complexity and enhanced focus on essential services.

About Ethical Downtuning

In the process of transitioning from AI-First mode to Marginal mode, AI systems are fine-tuned to ensure that, even with reduced human oversight, ethical principles are not compromised. This includes the integration of refined ethical decision constraints, the preservation of a consistent ethical core in AI operations, and ongoing ethical compliance monitoring. AI systems are developed with the capability for context-aware ethical reasoning, transparent communication of ethical rationale, and proactive evolution of their ethical frameworks. These measures embed a level of artificial integrity in AI systems, ensuring that as they become more autonomous, they continue to operate within ethical boundaries and in alignment with human values.

First, in terms of refined ethical decision constraints, it's essential to design the AI system with built-in constraints in its decision-making algorithms. These constraints should uphold ethical principles, even with reduced human oversight ensuring that AI's decisions do not violate them. Furthermore, incorporating a decision-making hierarchy within the AI that prioritizes ethical guidelines over operational efficiency is vital, particularly in contexts with less human involvement. In addition, programming the AI to recognize and avoid actions leading to ethical dilemmas or conflicts ensures the maintenance of ethical standards even when operating autonomously.

Moving on, the consistent ethical core in AI operations is another critical aspect. This entails ensuring that the AI's foundational ethical code is preserved regardless of its operational scale or scope. The ethical core must guide all AI actions and decisions, even when functionalities are downscaled.

Moreover, developing AI algorithms inherently aligned with key ethical principles, like respect for human rights, ensures these principles are integral to the AI's functioning. Regular updates of the AI's ethical guidelines to reflect societal changes further guarantee the relevance and effectiveness of its core ethical standards.

In addition, ongoing ethical compliance monitoring is essential. This involves implementing systems that continuously assess the AI's adherence to ethical standards, identifying and rectifying any deviations swiftly. Creating an audit trail for all AI decisions and actions is crucial for effective analysis and addressal of ethical issues. Also, establishing an independent review board or oversight mechanism enhances the AI's ethical performance and accountability, providing an external check on its operations.

Equally, context-aware ethical reasoning is fundamental. Developing AI algorithms capable of understanding the context of their operations allows for ethically sound decisions suited to specific situations. Integrating diverse situational data inputs enables the AI to adapt its ethical reasoning based on real-world complexities and nuances. Also, programming the AI to seek human input in ambiguous situations ensures deeper context understanding beyond its programmed capabilities.

Furthermore, transparent ethical rationale communication is pivotal. Designing AI systems to clearly communicate their decision-making rationale, especially for ethically significant decisions, enhances transparency and trust. Including references to followed ethical guidelines in the AI's explanations promotes understanding of its operations. Also, creating interfaces for stakeholders to query AI decisions and receive detailed explanations fosters an environment of openness and accountability.

Lastly, proactive ethical evolution is indispensable. Equipping AI systems with the ability to proactively update their ethical frameworks in line with global standards and societal changes is vital. Implementing learning mechanisms that incorporate insights from ethical debates, discussions, and consensus in the human sphere ensures the AI's growing and evolving understanding of ethics. In addition, establishing a protocol for regular ethical reviews by a diverse panel of experts ensures the AI's ethical standards remain current and comprehensive.

Addressing these guiding principals should help contribute to embedding a level of artificial integrity in AI systems, ensuring that as AI becomes more advanced and autonomous, it continues to operate within ethical boundaries and in alignment with human values.

About Resource Allocation Algorithms

From AI-First mode to Marginal mode the focus is on embedding artificial integrity into AI systems through sophisticated resource management. AI systems are designed to dynamically adjust resource allocation for optimal performance, employing predictive resource planning and efficiency-oriented architectures. Real-time ethical monitoring ensures adherence to ethical standards in resource utilization, while context-aware decision-making and stakeholder-centric design ensure that the technology serves the needs and respects the values of all affected parties. The integration of performance thresholds, dynamic performance benchmarking, automated efficiency optimization, and ethical alignment with performance goals ensure that AI operations are sustainable, efficient, and aligned with over-arching ethical principles.

Beginning with adaptive resource management, AI systems need to self-assess operational efficiency and dynamically adjust resource allocation to optimize performance without overextending or underutilizing resources. This involves creating algorithms that manage resources based on task priority and ethical considerations, ensuring high-priority and ethically sensitive tasks receive adequate computational attention. The AI must be designed to recognize and respond to changes in operational demands, adjusting its resource needs in real time to reflect the current state of tasks and human interactions.

Transitioning to predictive resource planning, employing predictive analytics becomes essential to forecast future resource requirements, allowing the AI to prepare and allocate resources for upcoming demands. This requires integrating trend analysis tools within the AI system to identify patterns in resource utilization, facilitating proactive adjustments for anticipated fluctuations and developing AI capabilities for scenario modeling to evaluate various resource allocation strategies, selecting the most efficient and ethically sound approach based on predicted future states.

Moreover, focusing on efficiency-oriented AI architectures, AI systems should be constructed with architectures that inherently prioritize resource utilization efficiency, reducing wastage and ensuring resources are directed toward tasks with the highest value addition. This includes incorporating energy-efficient computing models into the AI system, reducing the environmental impact and operational costs associated with running advanced AI applications, optimizing the AI's codebase and algorithms for lean operation, and ensuring the system's resource demands are minimized while maintaining high ethical and performance standards.

In addition, real-time ethical monitoring is integral, requiring the integration of continuous monitoring mechanisms within AI systems to assess ethical compliance in real time, ensuring immediate detection and correction of any deviations. Advanced pattern recognition algorithms must be utilized to identify subtle shifts in AI behavior that might indicate ethical breaches or emerging biases. Alert systems to notify human supervisors of potential ethical issues are essential for timely intervention.

Furthermore, context-aware decision-making plays a crucial role. AI systems with advanced context recognition capabilities are needed to understand and evaluate the ethical implications of decisions within diverse situational contexts. This involves integrating a broad spectrum of social, cultural, and situational data into the AI's decision-making process, ensuring that it makes informed and contextually relevant ethical choices as well as has the ability to consult databases of case studies and precedents for guidance in complex or ambiguous ethical scenarios, enhancing its ability to make nuanced decisions.

Also, a stakeholder-centric design approach is imperative. AI systems should be designed with user experience and stakeholder impact as priorities, ensuring that the technology serves the needs and respects the values of all affected parties. This means incorporating feedback mechanisms that allow users and stakeholders to voice concerns and suggestions regarding the AI's operations and ethical alignment, as well as establishing AI development processes that involve a diverse range of stakeholders, such as ethicists, sociologists, philosophers, and end users to ensure the system is attuned to a wide array of ethical perspectives and user needs.

Performance thresholds are another key aspect. Clear metrics within the AI system must be set to define acceptable performance levels for automated tasks, with built-in mechanisms to scale back AI involvement if these thresholds are met or exceeded. This should also include implementing a review mechanism where the performance of AI services is regularly evaluated against these thresholds, with automatic scaling back of services that do not contribute to improvements in performance. Regular evaluations against these thresholds need to be set to ensure that their performance is aligned with organizational objectives so that reductions in AI do not detract from the overall goals of the system.

Dynamic performance benchmarking is essential, too. Developing algorithms that continuously benchmark AI performance against evolving operational goals help dynamically adjust AI involvement to optimize efficiency and effectiveness. Utilizing real-time data analytics is crucial to assess the impact of AI services on key performance indicators (KPIs), ensuring that the AI's role is scaled appropriately to maximize organizational benefits. Complementary to this, implementing a flexible benchmarking system that adapts to changing operational contexts can help ensure that performance thresholds remain relevant and aligned with current objectives.

Consequently, automated efficiency optimization is key. The AI must autonomously identify areas where its involvement can be optimized for better resource utilization, reducing operational overhead without compromising output quality. This implies integrating predictive analytics to foresee future performance trends, allowing the AI to proactively adjust its level of involvement and prevent inefficiencies. This also necessitates setting a self-regulating mechanism within the AI that autonomously adjusts its processing power and task allocation based on efficiency metrics, ensuring optimal use of computational resources.

Lastly, ethical alignment with performance goals is fundamental. Aligning performance thresholds with ethical standards ensures that the drive for efficiency does not lead to ethical compromises, such as privacy violations or biased decision-making. Incorporating stakeholder feedback into setting performance thresholds ensures that they reflect not only organizational objectives but also broader societal values and ethical considerations. In addition, a system of ethical oversight that regularly assesses such aspects is crucial to guarantee that the AI's pursuit of performance goals remains in line with artificial integrity principles while allowing for necessary adjustments to maintain this alignment.

Addressing these guiding principals aims to build AI systems that are not only technically advanced in managing and allocating resources but also inherently aware of the ethical implications of their resource usage. This approach is critical for achieving AGI with embedded artificial integrity, ensuring AI operations are sustainable, efficient, and aligned with overarching ethical principles.

These measures should help organizations fine-tune their AI systems to better match the level of human involvement, ensuring that AI remains a cost-effective and efficient tool that complements low-level human tasks without becoming overbearing or resource-intensive. The focus on ethical downtuning and performance thresholds also ensures that AI operations remain within acceptable boundaries of integrity and value addition. In each case, technical systems and strategies must be deployed to recalibrate the balance of human and AI contributions, ensuring that a reduction in either's involvement is not detrimental to overall system effectiveness while also maintaining adherence to the principles of artificial integrity.

8

What Change to Envision in Economic AIquity and Societal Values

There is no shortage of descriptors when it comes to unveiling the considerable importance of data in our societies. While some refer to it as the new black gold, this comparison is somewhat appropriate but not entirely accurate. Just as oil is vital for energy, data has become indispensable and inherent to the functioning of our digital and artificially intelligent economy. But unlike oil, which diminishes as it is used, data can be utilized and shared infinitely.

Data Is the World's First-Ever Common Currency

As odd as it may seem or appear, at the dawn of the 21st century, the entire world is undergoing one of its greatest societal transformations since the invention of currency, yet it is not truly regarded with the same level of significance. Data is the world's first-ever common currency. And like money, it plays and will play a fundamental role in the economy and society in our artificial intelligence (AI) era. Considering data as a currency is pivotal to artificial integrity for several reasons.

Data Is a Unit of Measurement

As money serves as a standard of value, data serves as a unit of measurement for insights and business performance. As soon as companies began using databases to track their operations in the 1960s and 1970s, data became a unit of measurement. With the development of analytical tools in the 1980s and 1990s, companies began measuring their performances through data in much more sophisticated ways.

The "total quality management" movement of the 1980s required intensive use of data. Simultaneously, the development of systems such as integrated management/enterprise resource planning (ERP) software enabled companies to track and measure aspects of their operations in unprecedented ways. Data now allows for unprecedented opportunities in capital funding, underscoring its transformative role as a pivotal asset in modern finance.

The most striking modern example is probably the rise of Silicon Valley big-tech companies. These companies have built empires by measuring and analyzing user behaviors on a scale never seen before, making data not only a unit of measurement but also the very foundation of their business model.

Data Is a Medium of Exchange

As currency facilitates transactions, data allows businesses to better understand their customers and tailor their offerings. It is exchanged between entities for various services, such as personalizing advertising. The concept of data as a medium of exchange dates to the advent of the first computer systems, but its widespread adoption and recognition truly took off with the emergence of the Internet and, more recently, the rise of e-commerce and online services in the 1990s and 2000s. As more and more businesses began offering online services, they realized that the data generated by users was valuable for improving their services, creating new products, or selling it to third parties.

A prime example of this transformation is the ascent of the online data search economy. Each online search performed by a user provides information about user interests, behaviors, and desires, deriving massive revenue from targeted advertising using users' search data. Data has thus become a form of currency with which users "pay" for services.

Data Is a Store of Value

As money retains its value, relevant and well-preserved data can offer long-term strategic benefits to a company, even years after its collection. Companies quickly understood that the information they collected about their users was valuable in and of itself, not only for improving their services but also as a source of revenue. Customer data aids in understanding buying patterns, preferences, and habits to recommend products, leading to increased sales. Besides, just as money acts as a reserve of value, safeguarding wealth for future investments, data, too, holds intrinsic worth, anchoring the potential for innovation.

Without this reservoir of data, pioneering breakthroughs in AI technologies—enabling the development of systems from autonomous vehicles to smart healthcare diagnostics and real-time language translation—would remain beyond our grasp. The recognition that data can be used as a store of value was a turning point, leading to the era of the so-called "big data" where companies of all sizes and from all sectors seek to capture, store, and analyze data in hopes of deriving future value from it.

Data Is a Representation of Sovereignty

Owning and controlling one's own data has become a vital component of digital sovereignty, just as having one's own currency is a symbol of national sovereignty. As nations have become aware of the strategic implications of data concerning its storage, cross-border transfer, and access by foreign governments, it has become integral to national sovereignty.

China is perhaps the most emblematic example of data as a representation of sovereignty. With the adoption of its cybersecurity law in 2017, China implemented strict data localization rules, demanding that "personal information and critical data" collected by core information infrastructure operators be stored within its borders. Many other countries, from Russia to India, have since adopted similar rules, underscoring how possession, control, and access to data have become central in contemporary notions of national sovereignty.

Data Is an Economic Policy Instrument

As currency is regulated to influence the economy, data is used by governments and businesses to inform their decisions and strategies. Particularly with the rise of tech giants, governments quickly grasped the strategic importance of data for economic development, competition, and regulation. With the introduction of the General Data Protection Regulation (GDPR) in 2018, the European Union established strict rules on data collection, storage, and sharing, thereby recognizing not only its economic value but also its importance in terms of human rights and individual freedoms.

Discussions about competition, data monopolization, and the impact of tech giants on the digital economy are now at the heart of political and economic debates. The use of data as an economic policy tool is also evident in the regulation of artificial intelligence, digital privacy standards, and antitrust measures against data monopolies.

Data Is an Element of Credit Facilitation

Currency allows for the granting of credits. Similarly, quality data can open opportunities for partnerships and funding for businesses. Data became a credit facilitation tool with the rise of financial technologies, or "fintech," in the 2010s. The surge of peer-to-peer lending platforms and fintech companies that use advanced algorithms to assess creditworthiness based on a variety of data—from financial histories to online shopping habits—was the harbinger of this transformation.

China's Ant Financial, the owner of Alipay, stands as an iconic example of this shift. With its Zhima Credit product (also known as Sesame Credit), Ant Financial offers a credit scoring system based on data analysis sourced from user activities on Alibaba Group's platforms and other sources. This score can then be used to secure loans, rent apartments, and even for certain government services. The use of data in this manner has revolutionized access to credit, particularly for individuals and small businesses that previously struggled to obtain loans due to a lack of traditional credit history.

Data Is a Foundation of the Tax System

While currency is essential for tax collection, data is increasingly used to monitor tax compliance and prevent fraud. Data became foundational to the tax system as governments began using digital technology to collect, process, and analyze tax information. This shift also gained momentum in the early 2000s, with the increasing digitalization of public services.

The adoption of online platforms by tax administrations for tax declaration and payment was a turning point. The Internal Revenue Service in the United States serves as an example. Another example is India's introduction of the Goods and Services Tax in 2017. In France, the implementation of tax-at-source in 2019 also stands as a symbolic representation of the use of data in the French tax system. These developments signify how data has become crucial to modernize and streamline tax systems globally.

Data Is Foundational to Trust and Stability

Proper data management strengthens the trust of customers, partners, and investors, just as a stable currency bolsters confidence in the economy. Data became a key element of trust and stability with the advent of the digital revolution, especially with the development of blockchain technologies in the 2010s.

Bitcoin, created in 2009, is arguably the most prominent example of a decentralized currency where trust is established not by a central financial institution but by network consensus. The value and stability of Bitcoin rest on the transparency and immutability of transaction data recorded in the blockchain. Thus, data, when processed and stored in a transparent and secure manner, can serve as the foundation for trust and stability in a decentralized system. More broadly, data holds the potential to create trust in various fields, from smart contracts to online voting systems and many other applications.

Data Is a Facilitator of International Trade

Much like currency facilitates international trade, data plays a growing role in global commerce, with the transfer of data between countries becoming a key element of trade agreements. Integrated supply chain management systems, e-commerce platforms, and online payment solutions are among the major innovations that have helped facilitate international trade.

The rise of the dominant e-commerce global marketplaces is another prime example of how data has propelled international trade. Spanning multiple continents, they leverage user data to recommend products, predict demand, set pricing strategies, and optimize logistics. Sellers, from different corners of the globe, utilize their data-driven insights to forecast product demand, manage inventory, and target customers. Through its comprehensive logistics and fulfillment services, these companies use data analytics to streamline international shipping, customs, and storage processes, making it easier than ever for sellers to reach global audiences. It underscores the indispensable role of data in simplifying cross-border transactions, predicting global market trends, and democratizing access to international markets for businesses of all scales.

Data Is a Vector for Regulating Liquidity

As monetary policy regulates the amount of currency, regulations on data determine how they can be stored, shared, and utilized. The rapid expansion of digital financial markets has enabled the use of real-time data to analyze and predict market movements, as well as to automatically regulate liquidity. Investment banks and hedge funds were among the first to adopt high-frequency trading, using algorithms to execute orders at a speed and frequency that are beyond a human trader. The May 6, 2010, "Flash Crash," is a notable example of the consequences of intensive data use in regulating liquidity. While this event highlighted the risks associated with an excessive reliance on algorithms and data for liquidity regulation, it also underscored the critical importance of data in the modern functioning of financial markets.

Overall, data has emerged as a pivotal factor driving global economic structures, paralleling the influence once held exclusively by traditional currency. It underscores its central role in a multitude of sectors, from economic policymaking to international trade. Drawing on its historical trajectory and expansive influence, it becomes evident that our current understanding of data's value is only scratching the surface.

As we acknowledge the transformative power of data, it is crucial that the latter, without which no artificial intelligence can be realized, be regulated. Beyond the necessary regulations focusing on artificial intelligence systems per se, regulating data is one of the most important challenges of our century to ensure that all artificial intelligence aligns with the direction of producing artificial integrity. The following sections detail recommendations that could help harness the transformative power of data responsibly, ensuring a sustainable and equitable global data economy.

Building Central Data Backbones for a Modern Data Economy

Central banks, such as the European Central Bank or the US Federal Reserve, play a major role in regulating and stabilizing currency. There is no equivalent entity to regulate data on such a scale. Today, just as there are central banks for currency, *central data banks* are necessary.

Currently, a few tech giants hold vast amounts of data. A central data bank could help decentralize the ownership of these data, thus reducing the power and control concentrated in a few hands. A central data bank could ensure equitable access to information, preventing certain businesses or entities from monopolizing data for profit.

The central data bank would be responsible for overseeing institutions that hold, process, and exchange data, just as central banks supervise financial institutions. It would establish standards for data protection and their ethical use and would ensure compliance with these standards through audits and inspections.

Determining the Rate at Which Data Should Be Universally Accessible

Inspired by the interest rate benchmarks used by central banks in the financial world, the *benchmark access rate to data* (BARD) would serve as a regulatory mechanism to control access to data stored in a central data bank. This rate would represent a measure of the ease (or difficulty) with which external entities can access this data. The lower the BARD, the more affordable it would be for entities to view or use the data stored in the central bank. Conversely, a high BARD would mean that access to the data is more restricted and costly.

It would be a strategic tool for promoting research and innovation: when the bank wants to stimulate research, innovation, or competitiveness, it could lower the BARD. This would allow researchers, startups, and companies to take advantage of the available data, thereby fostering technological and economic development. The establishment of the BARD would be the responsibility of a regulatory authority, likely a governmental entity or an independent body mandated for this function.

Balancing Concerns About Data Privacy with Contingency Planning for Data Security Drawing inspiration from the mandatory reserves imposed on banks by monetary authorities, *mandatory data reserves* (MDRs) would refer to a minimum portion of data that businesses and institutions would be required to store within a central data bank. This mechanism would ensure the security, transparency, and regulation of data flow. Just as banks are required to hold a fraction of their deposits in reserve, entities that collect, process, and store data would be obliged to deposit a certain proportion of data in the central data bank. The amount of data to be kept could be defined in terms of a percentage of the entity's total storage capacity or the total volume of data processed.

The deposited data would remain the property of the originating entity but would be stored securely and centrally for various reasons, including regulation, oversight, and security. Storing data in a central reserve would promote greater transparency and enhanced accountability for entities.

Navigating the Fine Line Between Data Accessibility and Data Exploitation Similar to the open market operations used by central banks to regulate the money supply, *open data market operations* (ODMOs) would refer to the transactions initiated by the central data bank on an open data market. The goal would be to regulate the quantity, quality, and availability of data in the digital economy. ODMO would allow the central data bank to actively intervene in a data market, where datasets are exchanged. This intervention could take the form of purchases to inject data into the market or sales to withdraw data from the market or generate revenue. The price of these datasets would be determined by demand and supply in the market, just like securities in financial markets. By purchasing high-value or rare datasets, the central data bank could make them available to researchers, innovators, and decision-makers, thereby promoting innovation and informed decision-making.

Ensuring Individuals Are Fairly Valued and Compensated for Their Data Every citizen could have a *personal data account* with the central data bank where they can voluntarily deposit some of their data. These accounts would be protected and secure, offering citizens complete control over who can access their data and under what conditions. Access to certain data could be subject to a remuneration system for the data owners. Companies, researchers, or other entities wanting to access specific data might pay fees. A portion of these fees could be redistributed to the citizens whose data are used. This remuneration would be proportional to the use and value of the data in question.

The central data bank could establish a mechanism to assess the value of different types of data based on their rarity, utility, etc. Citizens could then have an idea of the monetary value of their data, encouraging them to knowingly share more valuable or rare information. At the end of each period (month, quarter, year), the central data bank could redistribute a portion of its profits to citizens in the form of a "data dividend." This dividend would be a recognition of the collective value of the data provided by the citizens and would be distributed based on each individual's contribution.

Lending Data Responsibly   The concept of *data lending facilities*, inspired by the lending facilities that central banks provide to financial institutions, would enable the provision of data for specific uses over a defined period, grounded in the idea that data can be treated as an asset akin to money. In the modern data-driven economy, not all institutions necessarily have the resources to collect, process, and store vast datasets. However, they might need this data for specific projects, studies, or innovations. Rather than forcing them to purchase or access these data on a permanent basis, a lending facility would allow them to borrow this data for a limited duration.

This access would often be limited to a specific platform to ensure security and monitor usage. This could be useful for institutions that need specific data for a temporary research project but don't necessarily require permanent access to such data.

Standardizing the Relative Value of Different Datasets   Just as currencies have *relative values* to each other in the foreign exchange market, data could also be valued and traded based on certain criteria. This would introduce a form of standardization and regulation in data trading. Several factors could determine the value of data, such as its relevance, timeliness, rarity, specificity, quality, etc.

Specialized institutions or departments within the central data bank might be responsible for the regular evaluation of datasets. A centralized platform could be established where entities can offer their datasets for exchange, similar to a stock exchange. Just like with currencies, the value of data would fluctuate based on supply and demand. Rare but highly demanded datasets could have a high exchange rate. Such a system could introduce a form of standardization in how data is valued and traded.

Covering the Intangible Risks of Data Breaches   In many countries, citizens' bank deposits are insured up to a certain amount. There is no equivalent to "insure" personal data in the event of a breach or loss. The model of data deposit insurance has also become crucial. *Data deposit guarantee funds* (DDGF) could be considered. Just as banks contribute to a deposit guarantee fund to protect customers' money in case of a bank failure, companies that store and process data could be required to contribute to a similar fund for data. In case of data breach or loss, this fund could be used to compensate the affected individuals, whether through financial compensation or services.

Moreover, similar to bank deposit insurance that covers up to a certain amount per depositor, data deposit insurance could guarantee the security of the data up to a certain "quantity" or "value." If someone loses data due to a breach, a predefined set of this data (for example, the most sensitive data) would be guaranteed or compensated.

Guaranteeing Human Rights Take Precedence Over the Surge in Data Collection   For many, the current rules and related sanction mechanisms for human data protection violations don't seem to fully reflect the significance and sensitivity of personal data. In the financial sector, *sanctions* are designed to be as preventive as they are punitive. They are calculated to have a major financial impact on the offenders while also deterring them from repeating their wrongdoings. Financial institutions can lose their ability to operate, which is a grave consequence.

A similar measure in the tech world could involve the suspension of certain activities, or even the shutdown of parts of a service. Furthermore, citizens should be better informed about their data rights and how their data are used. Strengthening individuals' rights to request the deletion of their data could limit companies' abilities to store information indefinitely without a valid reason. This should involve providing clear information to every data owner about all users of their data.

And just as with international financial standards, there could be a benefit to having global standards for data protection and sanctions, thus avoiding "data havens" where companies might try to relocate to escape regulation. Close collaboration between countries would be essential to ensure the effectiveness of sanctions and prevent companies from merely shifting their operations.

Curbing the Negative Impact of Data Speculation in the Market   Speculation is a well-known concept in the financial world, where players buy and sell assets hoping to realize future profits. While *data speculation* isn't a commonly used term, the idea captures the essence of a growing phenomenon where data is collected, stored, and traded with the aim of profiting from its future use. Companies might collect data without an immediate or specific use in mind, hoping that it might be useful or profitable in the future. This is particularly true for tech companies that have the capability to store vast amounts of data. Furthermore, just as excessive speculation can create financial bubbles, a "data bubble" might emerge, where the perceived value of the data far surpasses its actual utility.

In the same way that certain financial mechanisms impose limits on speculation, caps could be implemented to restrict the amount of data a company can collect without justification. Just as financial transactions can be taxed to discourage speculation, a tax on the collection, storage, or trade of data could be considered. Companies might be required to disclose the nature, quantity, and usage of the data they collect, thus allowing regulators and the public to monitor speculation.

Ensuring Transparent Reporting Without Hindering Data-Driven Industries   The reporting obligation for financial institutions regarding suspicious activities aims to combat money laundering, terrorist financing, and other illicit activities. In the world of data, the notion of *suspicious data* is different, but the underlying principle—accountability and transparency—remains. This might include unauthorized access to databases, accidental exposures or data theft, unusual data access patterns, unexpected requests for large amounts of data, or data transfers to unknown destinations that might be deemed suspicious.

Regulations concerning reporting obligations vary considerably from one country to another. This can create confusion for international companies and allow some to avoid reporting by exploiting these inconsistencies. Moreover, in some places, fines or penalties for nonreporting or late reporting are minimal, offering little incentive for compliance. Promoting international guidelines or treaties on data breach reporting could help establish a minimum compliance baseline.

The emergence of data as a form of currency redefines traditional paradigms of value and exchange. This transformation unfolds with unmatched opportunities and risks, intertwined with pressing ethical concerns. While financial regulatory mechanisms have been refined over centuries in response to crises and innovations, data, in its newfound monetary stature, is in its infancy.

Concepts such as transparency, fairness, security, and accountability, fundamental in the financial sector, can serve as cornerstones in designing regulatory frameworks for data. In essence, while acknowledging data's uniqueness as a currency, the financial regulatory system provides an opportunity to learn from its effectiveness and its limits.

By marrying these lessons with a nuanced understanding of data's specifics, we can hope to establish a balance that maximizes the benefits of this new currency while minimizing its potential risks to individuals and society at large.

Impartial Data Holy Grail and Its Paradoxes

A new paradigm related to the way the value of data is managed from an economic value perspective calls for the acknowledgment of its systemic role when it comes to anchoring or harming values in society. Rapid advancements in AI systems have raised concerns about their potential threats to humanity, political systems, democracy, and the very concept of truth. Indeed, as AI models are trained on vast datasets, they inherit societal biases, and their outputs can reinforce these biases when generating content. This could exacerbate divisions in society and hinder productive political discourse.

A critical worry is that, if not meticulously designed and controlled, AI systems may amplify existing biases and contribute to political polarization. Coping with this challenge, some have embarked on a quest for an impartial AI, integrating ideals of neutrality, fairness, and justice. This pursuit acknowledges that while AI systems will inevitably retain biases, regulation should act as a safeguard, mitigating the impact of these imperfections and protecting society from potential harm.

Paradoxically, it is this very thesis—and not AI itself—that presents a substantial threat to humanity. The assumption that AI can be made wholly responsible and trustworthy results in a dangerous dependency where humans may begin to rely solely on machine judgment, perceived as more objective than human decision-making, and culminates in a significant abdication of human responsibility.

A study titled "Human Cognitive Biases Present in Artificial Intelligence" by Martinez et al. (2022) points out that biases detected in AI mirror discriminative social biases present in society, emphasizing the necessity of understanding basic and general principles of cognition and cognitive biases that affect our relationship with AI. In essence, the challenge lies not in making AI systems unbiased but in recognizing and addressing the inherent human biases they reflect.

As highlighted by O. C. Ferrell, biases in AI, influenced by biased data, algorithmic design choices, and the implicit biases of developers, are a reflection of societal inequalities. Our inability to recognize biases in their true scale and manifestation in the real world leads to a misconception that AI systems are amplifying these biases. However, this reflection is more a revelation of existing societal biases than an amplification.

Even if well-intentioned, the pursuit of creating a bias-free AI risks creating echo chambers that, in turn, can perpetuate illusions and misunderstandings, leading us to underestimate the true impact and prevalence of our own biases within society. This would inadvertently mask the deeper, more pervasive biases that are embedded within our social structures and cultural norms.

It is akin to asking, as in a famous Disney animated film, "Magic mirror on the wall, who is the fairest of them all?" while expecting AI to show only our best selves and ignoring all the imperfections that make us perfectly human. In recognizing this, we must leverage AI not only as a technological advancement but as a means to uncover, understand, and better address the biases often unnoticed or unacknowledged that permeate our society and contribute significantly to various social issues.

Dual Nature of Biases

Whether we consider their positive or negative effects, human biases are inherent to the imperfect but unique condition of being human. The *commitment bias*, which refers to our tendency to stay committed to a chosen course of action, even when faced with challenges, has been instrumental in the accomplishment of numerous great human achievements.

Take, for instance, the Apollo 11 moon landing mission. The commitment bias of NASA and the astronauts involved in achieving the monumental goal of landing on the moon was unwavering. Despite the immense technical challenges, risks, and uncertainties, they remained deeply committed to their mission. It has fueled years of relentless work, innovation, and problem-solving, ultimately leading to the historic success of Apollo 11 and beyond. Pagnini et al. (2023) provide insights on the critical need for resilience and dedication in facing the unique challenges of space exploration, in a study exploring the psychological adaptation and countermeasures in space missions. The study highlights how the commitment to overcoming extraordinary obstacles is essential for the success of missions like the Apollo 11 moon landing.

As another example, the *negativity bias*, which causes humans to pay more attention to negative information or threats, has played a pivotal role in driving advancements in safety and security. Consider the development of safety features in automobiles. The awareness of the potential dangers of road accidents and the negative consequences associated with them has been a driving force behind the continuous improvement of safety technologies in vehicles. This bias has pushed engineers and innovators to invest in technologies like airbags, anti-lock brakes, and collision avoidance systems, all aimed at mitigating the negative outcomes of accidents.

Evidence provided in Catherine J. Norris' (2019) study underlines the evolutionary advantage of negativity bias, as more critical for survival to avoid harmful stimuli than to pursue potentially helpful ones. Without the negativity bias, the urgency to prioritize safety might not have been as strong, and we might not have witnessed the significant reduction in road fatalities and injuries that these innovations have achieved in making our daily lives safer. As a matter of fact, when it comes to human biases, outcomes are not solely negative.

Specific and Systemic Biases in Society

AI systems offers a window into both. Specific biases are those that emerge in situations where our knowledge is incomplete or when we are confronted with unfamiliar contexts. In these scenarios, our cognitive process compensates for the lack of information by generating preconceived notions or pre-contextualized piece of information or ideas to fill the gaps, completing the missing puzzle pieces, so the situation appears certain. This often-subconscious act allows us to form a coherent picture of an otherwise ambiguous situation, leading us to mistakenly accept these generated perceptions as factual truths while they ultimately stem from our own creative capacity. Such biases highlight our innate tendency to seek clarity and certainty, even in the absence of complete information.

In contrast, systemic biases operate on a much broader scale, ingrained within the very structures and institutions that govern and regulate society. These biases are the result of specific biases becoming normalized and integrated into societal systems, thereby influencing the rules, norms, and practices that dictate social interactions. They often manifest in the form of institutionalized preferences or disadvantages that affect entire groups based on characteristics such as origin, gender, or other social identifiers.

Both specific and systemic biases interplay with each other, and this makes the biases "system" even more complex. While specific biases originate from individual experiences and perceptions, they can gradually permeate into the larger societal context, contributing to the formation of systemic biases. Conversely, systemic biases can reinforce and validate individual biases, creating a feedback loop that perpetuates these prejudices across both personal and societal levels.

Modifying specific and systemic biases is complex. They often function invisibly, silently dictating what is considered the norm, shaping culture, lifestyle, and societal etiquette. In this context, AI systems act as a medium through which the continuous interaction between specific biases and broader systemic biases is played out. This self-perpetuating cycle of action and feedback, encompassing mental, social, and societal aspects, is computationally mirrored in AI.

Foundational AI models, such as OpenAI's GPT, are particularly illustrative of this phenomenon. These models are trained on extensive datasets sourced from a wide range of Internet materials, which inherently contain the dynamics, inequalities, stereotypes, and dominant ideologies prevalent in the data and in the value systems from which these models have been trained. Consequently, these foundational AI models become carriers of systemic biases, reflecting some of the existing societal disparities and prejudices.

As an example, such an occurrence has been illustrated in the research conducted by Buolamwini and Gebru (2018) highlighting that the facial recognition systems were highly inaccurate when it comes to classifying the faces of women of color. In this ground-breaking paper, the authors further demonstrated that the model was most accurate for people who identified as male and of white skin tone.

On the other end of the spectrum, we have AI models that are derived from these foundational models but are tailored for specific tasks in various domains. It is crucial to recognize that these specialized AI models are not isolated from the systemic biases of their foundational counterparts. They are immersed in a milieu of pre-existing biases, absorbing and potentially amplifying the systemic prejudices embedded in the foundational models.

The study from Seyyed-Kalantari et al. (2021) sheds light on the under-diagnosis bias in AI algorithms, particularly in medical imaging, and how this can affect patient populations differently, in particular under-served patient populations, underscoring the systemic nature of such biases. This immersion of specific AI models in systemic biases highlights the importance of understanding the deep-rooted nature of biases in AI development and underscores the need for a comprehensive approach to AI training that is mindful of both specific and systemic biases.

Not only are specific AI models influenced by the systemic biases inherent in the foundational AI models on which they are built or refined, but they are also subject to more nuanced biases unique to their own application domains. These specific biases arise from the particularities of the datasets or the contexts in which the AI is applied. Each dataset, with its unique characteristics and limitations, contributes to shaping the model's understanding and responses.

Consider, for instance, an AI model developed for medical applications using OpenAI's GPT. This model would inherently carry the systemic biases present in the OpenAI's GPT model. However, it would also be influenced by biases specific to the medical domain, stemming from the clinical data it is trained on. These biases could be linked to various factors such as the demographic representation in the clinical data, the prevalence of certain conditions in the data, or even the manner in which the data was collected and processed.

Interestingly, the occurrence of these specific biases is not necessarily mitigated by the use of seemingly bias-free training data. The learning process in AI is not a mere transfer of knowledge; it also involves the transfer of biases embedded in the foundational models. Gichoya et al. (2023) in a paper in the *British Journal of Radiology* address real-world failures of AI systems in healthcare. Their study showcases the varying levels of performance in AI systems, especially poor performance for historically underserved patients, illustrating how subgroup evaluations can reveal specific biases while underlining the multifaceted nature of biases in AI where specific biases are influenced by both systemic and application-specific factors.

Another intriguing aspect of AI development is the potential for specific AI models to influence their foundational models, thereby creating a unique feedback loop of biases. These specific models, developed for distinct applications, can carry their own set of biases, which are shaped by the particularities of their training data and the contexts in which they are used. When the data generated by these specific AI models becomes widely published and accessible online, it enters the vast pool of information that may be used to train or update foundational AI models. This incorporation of data from specific AI models into the foundational models' training corpus introduces the possibility of a cyclical transfer of biases.

This feedback loop mirrors the interaction between systemic and specific biases found in society. In this AI context, the biases inherent in specific applications could start influencing the broader foundational models from which they were initially derived. This phenomenon highlights a complex layer of interaction where biases are not just unidirectionally imparted from foundational AI models to specific applications but can also flow in the reverse direction. The likelihood and impact of this scenario hinge on several factors, including the frequency with which foundational models are updated with new data and how representative the data from specific models are within the larger training corpus.

A study from Moor et al. (2023) discusses generalist medical artificial intelligence (GMAI) models. Their research illustrates how specific AI models developed for medical applications might influence foundational models, particularly in the way these models process complex medical information and learn from various data sources.

Just as societal biases evolve and are reshaped over time through new cultural inputs and changing norms, foundational AI models too are subject to continuous evolution influenced by the influx of new data and shifting contextual biases. The bias perpetuation and calibration within AI systems have been insightfully explored in research by Rohan Taori and Tatsunori B. Hashimoto (2022) from Stanford University. Their study sheds light on the pivotal role of calibration in learning algorithms, particularly how it influences the magnitude of bias perpetuation. The researchers found that consistent calibration of a learning algorithm—ensuring that the biases in samples annotated by the model closely mirror the biases present in the training distribution—plays a crucial role in controlling bias perpetuation. This finding is particularly relevant in the context of specific AI models affecting foundational models, illustrating how biases, if unchecked, can be perpetuated through iterative learning processes.

This research underscores the importance of viewing "biases in AI" not as a static, intrinsic problem of AI technology but as a dynamic interplay of systemic and specific biases that evolve and propagate within AI systems. The findings from Taori and Hashimoto's research also emphasize that merely attempting to "eliminate biases" from datasets through technical means, without a comprehensive understanding of the social dimensions and origins of these biases, is an approach destined for inadequacy. It fails to account for the complex, self-generating nature of biases within AI systems.

Finally, human touch reinforces AI's biased learning. A notable example is the reinforcement learning with human feedback (RLHF) method, which represents a complex interplay between technological capabilities and human input. Prominently used in advanced AI systems like ChatGPT, it involves meticulously tailoring the outputs of large language models (LLMs) to align with a diverse array of human values, which are in turn shaped by the inputs from human interlocutors.

One of the most profound and elusive sources of bias in AI arises from the very nature of RLHF. The method's dependence on human feedback introduces an inherent variability, as the concept of "values" is not static but rather fluid, shifting with the diverse perspectives and interpretations of individuals. Consequently, in its effort to refine and shape the AI model, this process inadvertently incorporates biases that are embedded in the human psyche, emerging from the thoughts, experiences, and judgments of the humans who interact with and guide its learning process.

While striving to create AI systems that resonate with human values, the RLHF method also encapsulates the intricate and sometimes contradictory nature of those values. Because humans make machines, they would not be perfect either. Therefore, the commitment to address biases in AI systems necessitates a comprehensive approach that extends beyond the confines of machine learning algorithms and training data. Experts at the National Institute of Standards and Technology (NIST, 2022) advocate for a broader examination into the origins of biases in AI. This expanded perspective encompasses not only the technical aspects of AI development but also delves into the wider societal factors that influence the creation and evolution of technology.

Overall, beyond algorithmic fairness techniques, some nontechnical guiding principles are essential, ranging from regulation to education and organizational strategies. This holistic perspective emphasizes the importance of understanding the dynamic interplay between technology and society. It encourages a multidisciplinary dialogue involving technologists, sociologists, ethicists, policymakers, and other stakeholders.

The Value We Place on Human Life Today

Overall, the integration of artificial integrity into the fabric of society is a transformation that holds promise in navigating changes for the better. It's imperative that whatever the trajectories toward embracing AI, they enrich the broader spectrum of human experience and societal well-being as a priority, beyond the only purpose of magnifying the economic benefits. AI operating with artificial integrity should not merely be an instrument for escalating productivity and economic growth but should always prioritize being a catalyst for enhancing the quality of life, fostering creativity, and promoting a more equitable distribution of resources and opportunities.

Economic value, while a traditional metric for measuring the success of technological integration, is not the sole dimension to consider. The multifaceted impact of AI on society necessitates a holistic approach to its deployment. This includes considerations of social value, such as improving healthcare outcomes, educational access, and the democratization of knowledge. It also encompasses cultural value, recognizing the role of AI in preserving heritage, enabling artistic expression, and facilitating cross-cultural understanding.

Moreover, ethical value is a cornerstone of AI development, guiding the creation and implementation of algorithms that are fair, transparent, and accountable. The societal value of AI also emerges in its ability to address grand challenges—such as climate change, global health crises, and inequality—by providing tools and solutions that can mobilize collective human action.

As our human values form the foundation of artificial integrity, they need to be inscribed beyond our collective consciousness and to be formally explicit so their transcription, instantiation, and evolution can be considered in light of the changes that AI creates in our societies. It does not simply call for a need for new laws. It is a call for innovation of a different kind. One that involves society for centuries. One that requires revising the supreme legal document of countries. One that revises the declaration of human rights. One that establishes the fundamental principles by which each country governs itself, shedding light on the fundamental rights and freedoms of citizens in light of the profound impact that artificial intelligence has on them, for example:

- The right to data protection, particularly regarding the collection, processing, and use of data by AI systems.
- The right to algorithmic fairness and **dialgorithmic** inclusiveness and safety, ensuring that AI does not perpetuate existing discriminations based on race, gender, and social class.
- The right to explainability and transparency so that every citizen has the right to understand how and why a decision was made by an AI system, especially when that decision has a significant impact on their life.
- The right to recourse against AI-based decisions because every citizen should have the right to challenge and request a human review of decisions made entirely or partially by AI systems.
- The right to self-determination in the face of automation to provide a shield against excessive automation or, put another way, extreme personalization, which can negatively affect personal autonomy and life choices.
- The right to education and ongoing training because in response to the rapid evolution of skills required in an economy influenced by AI, access to education and continuous training is fundamental.
- The right to security against AI abuses to protect against disinformation, manipulation, and breaches of personal and national security.

AI is not goal-seeking on its own; human goals are what propel AI forward, beyond binary. As we chart our course through the evolving paradigm of human intelligence versus AI, the focus must be on leveraging the unique strengths of both human and machine to achieve valuable outcomes from a holistic value perspective, which necessarily means not at the expense of the human and environment imperatives. AI makes human responsibility a paramount issue of our era. Focusing solely on what needs to be improved in AI learning prevents us from addressing the broader issue, which is human learning, a fundamental lever for self-improvement, hence for the AIs we create, as well as what we decide to do with them, while avoiding falling into **algorithmism**.

Our era offers us a chance, not just to engage in the simple manipulation of data that feeds our AIs, naively hoping in doing so to extricate the prejudices from our world, but to refine our critical judgment. We are called to guide our choices by values deeply rooted in humanity, transcending mere algorithmic correction, to achieve a truer understanding of our collective being: our human touch. In short, let's not just ask what AI can do for each of us—let's ask ourselves what we can do to ensure AI serves humanity. The value we place on human life today will shape the society in which we will live with AI tomorrow.

References

Chapter 1

Alcott, B., Giampietro M., Mayumi, K., and Polimeni, J. (2015) *The Jevons Paradox and the Myth of Resource Efficiency Improvements.* Routledge.

Brey, P. (2012) *Values in Technology and Disclosive Computer Ethics.* Cambridge University Press.

Curry, D. M. (2012) *Practical application of chaos theory to systems engineering.* ScienceDirect. Available at: https://www.sciencedirect.com/science/article/pii/S1877050912000129 (Accessed: March 2, 2024).

Freitag, C., Berners-Lee, M., Widdicks K., Knowles B., Blair, G., and Friday, A. (2021) "The real climate and transformative impact of ICT: A critique of estimates, trends and regulations." *Patterns* 2(9) 100340.

Gray, M. L. and Suri, S. (2019) *Ghost Work: How to Stop Silicon Valley from Building a New Global Underclass.* Harper Business.

Oelschlaeger, M. (1979) *The Myth of the Technological Fix.* Jstor.

Precedent Research Inc. (2023) *Artificial Intelligence (AI) Market Size, Growth, Report By 2032.* Available at: https://www.precedenceresearch.com/artificial-intelligence-market (Accessed: March 2, 2024).

Srivastava, A. et al. (2022) *Beyond the Imitation Game: Quantifying and extrapolating the capabilities of language models.* Available at: arXiv: 2206.04615.

Turing, A. M. (1950) "Computing Machinery and Intelligence." *Mind* 49: 433–460.

Chapter 2

Anderson, M., Leigh Anderson, S., Gounaris, A., and Kosteletos, G. (2021) *Towards Moral Machines: A Discussion with Michael Anderson and Susan Leigh Anderson*. DOI:10.12681/cjp.26832.

Green, B. (2021) *The Contestation of Tech Ethics: A Sociotechnical Approach to Technology Ethics in Practice*. Available at: arXiv: 2106.01784.

Kearns, M. and Aaron Roth, A. (2020) *The Ethical Algorithm: The Science of Socially Aware Algorithm Design*. Oxford University Press.

Rodrigues, R. (2021) *Ethics as attention to context: recommendations for the ethics of artificial intelligence*. Open Research Europe.

Chapter 3

Acemoglu, D., and Autor, D. (2011) "Skills, tasks and technologies: Implications for employment and earnings." *Handbook of Labor Economics*.

Acemoglu, D. and Restrepo, P. (2020) "Robots and jobs: Evidence from US labor markets." *Journal of Political Economy*.

Larson J., Mattu S., Kirchner L. Angwin, J., (2016) "How We Analyzed the COMPAS Recidivism Algorithm - *ProPublica*.

Arner, D. W., Barberis, J. N., and Buckley, R. P. (2016) "The evolution of fintech: A new post- crisis paradigm?" *SSRN Electronic Journal*.

Arntz, M., Gregory, T., Zierahn, U. (2016) "The Risk of Automation for Jobs in OECD Countries." OECD Social, Employment and Migration Working Papers.

Barocas, S., and Selbst, A. D. (2016) "Big Data's Disparate Impact." California Law Review.

Boden, M. A. (2009) "Computer models of creativity." *AI Magazine*.

Brynjolfsson, E. and McAfee, A. (2014) *The Second Machine Age: Work, Progress, and Prosperity in a Time of Brilliant Technologies*. W. W. Norton & Company.

Hashem, I. A. T., Yaqoob, I., Anuar, N. B., Mokhtar, S., Gani, A., and Khan, S. U. (2015) "The rise of "big data" on cloud computing: Review and open research issues." *Information Systems*.

Holstein, K., McLaren, B. M., and Aleven, V. (2017) "Intelligent tutors as teachers' aides: Exploring teacher needs for real-time analytics in blended classrooms." The Seventh International Learning Analytics & Knowledge Conference.

Jha, S. and Topol, E. J. (2016) "Adapting to Artificial Intelligence: Radiologists and Pathologists as Information Specialists." *JAMA*.

Manyika, J. et al. (2017) "A future that works: Automation, employment, and productivity." McKinsey Global Institute.

Parasuraman, A., Zeithaml, V.A., and Berry, L.L. (1988) SERVQUAL Model.

Rajkomar, A., Dean, J., and Kohane, I. (2018) "Machine Learning in Medicine." *The New England Journal of Medicine*.

Yüksel, N., Börklü, H. R., Sezer, H. K., and Canyurt, O. E. (2023) "Review of artificial intelligence applications in engineering design perspective." Engineering Applications of Artificial Intelligence.

Chapter 4

Christensen C. M. (1997) "The Innovator's Dilemma: When New Technologies Cause Great Firms to Fail." *Harvard Business Review Press*.

Chapter 5

Arntz, M., Gregory, T., and Zierahn, U. (2016) *The Risk of Automation for Jobs in OECD Countries: A Comparative Analysis*. OECD Publishing.

Atomwise (n.d.) Artificial Intelligence for Drug Discovery. Available at: https://www.atomwise.com

Bessen, J. E. (2019) *AI and Jobs: The Role of Demand*. NBER Working Paper No. 24235.

Davenport, T. H., and Ronanki, R. (2018) "Artificial intelligence for the real world." *Harvard Business Review*, 96(1).

McKinsey Global Institute (2017) "A Future that Works: Automation, Employment, and Productivity."

Rajpurkar, P., Irvin, J., Zhu, K., Yang, B., Mehta, H., Duan, T., and Lungren, M. P. (2017) *CheXNet: Radiologist-level pneumonia detection on chest x-rays with deep learning*. Available at: arXiv:1711.05225.

Waymo. (n.d.) Waymo Safety Report. Available at: https://waymo.com

Willcocks, L. P., Lacity, M. C., and Craig, A. S. (2015) *The IT function and robotic process automation*.

Chapter 6

Cummings, M. L. (2014) "Automation and Accountability in Decision Support System Interface Design." *Journal of Technology Studies*.

Graefe, A., Haim, M., Haarmann, B., and Brosius, H.-B. (2018) "Readers' perception of computer-generated news: Credibility, expertise, and readability." *Journalism*.

Norouzzadeh, M. S., Nguyen, A., Kosmala, M., Swanson, A., Palmer, M. S., Packer, C., and Clune, J. (2018) "Automatically identifying, counting, and describing wild animals in camera-trap images with deep learning." *Proceedings of the National Academy of Sciences*, E5716–E5725.

Sennett, R. (2008) *The Craftsman*. Yale University Press.

Sharma, A., Lin, I. W., Miner, A. S., Atkins, D. C., and Althoff, T. (2022) *Human-AI Collaboration Enables More Empathic Conversations in Text-based Peer-to-Peer Mental Health Support*. Available at: arXiv:2203.15144.

Sople, V. V. (2012) *Logistics Management: The Supply Chain Imperative (3rd ed.)*. Pearson.

Surden, H. (2019) "Artificial Intelligence and Law: An Overview." *Georgia State University Law Review*.

Xiang, Z. (2018) "From digitization to the age of acceleration: On information technology and tourism." *Tourism Management Perspectives*.

Chapter 7

Bookstaber, R., and Kenett, D. Y. (2016) Looking Deeper, Seeing More: A Multilayer Map of the Financial System. Office of Financial Research. https://www.financialresearch.gov/briefs/files/OFRbr_2016-06_Multilayer-Map.pdf (Accessed: March 2, 2024).

Brougham, D., and Haar, J. (2017) Smart technology, artificial intelligence, robotics, and algorithms (STARA): Employee's perceptions of our future workplace. *Journal of Management & Organization* - Cambridge University Press.

Davenport, T. H., and Kirby, J. (2016) *Only Humans Need Apply: Winners and Losers in the Age of Smart Machines*. Harper Business.

Ford, M. (2016) *Rise of the Robots: Technology and the Threat of a Jobless Future*. Basic Books.

Grewal, D., Roggeveen, A. L., and Nordfält, J. (2017) "The Future of Retailing." *Journal of Retailing*.

Lowenberg-DeBoer, J., and Erickson, B. (2019) "Setting the record straight on precision agriculture adoption." *Agronomy Journal*.

Chapter 8

Buolamwini, J., and Gebru, T., (2018) Gender shades: intersectional accuracy disparities in commercial gender classification. Proceedings of Machine Learning Research.

Ferrell, O. C., (2024) Understanding AI Bias (and How to Address It). McGraw-Hill.

Gichoya, J. W., Thomas, K., Celi, L. A., Safdar, N., Banerjee, I., Banja, J. D., Seyyed-Kalantari, L., Trivedi, H., Purkayastha S., (2023) AI pitfalls and what not to do: mitigating bias in AI. NIH - National Librairy of Medecine, National Center for biotechnology Information.

Martinez, N., Agudo, U., Matute, H., (2022) Human cognitive biases present in Artificial Intelligence. Riev, International Journal on Basque Studies.

Moor, M., Banerjee, O., Abad Hossein Shakeri, Z., Krumholz, H. M., Lescovec, J., Topol, E. J., Rajpurkar, P.,. (2023) Foundation models for generalist medical artificial intelligence. Nature

Norris, C. J., (2019) The negativity bias, revisited: Evidence from neuroscience measures and an individual differences approach. Social Neuroscience, Taylor & Francis online.

Pagnini, F., Manzey, D., Roznet, E., Ferravante, D., White, D., Nathan, S., (2023) Human behavior and performance in deep space exploration: next challenges and research gaps. NPJ Microgravity

Seyyed-Kalantari, L., Zhang, H., McDermott, M. B. A., Chen I. Y., Ghassemi, M., (2021) Underdiagnosis bias of artificial intelligence algorithms applied to chest radiographs in under-served patient populations. Nature Medicine

Taori, R., and Hashimoto, T. B., (2021) *Data Feedback Loops: Model-driven Amplification of Dataset Biases*. Proceedings of Machine Learning Research. NIST Report Highlights (2022) There's More to AI Bias Than Biased Data. https://www.nist.gov/news-events/news/2022/03/theres-more-ai-bias-biased-data-nist-report-highlights. (Accessed: March 2, 2024).

Glossary

AIquity

Origin: The term *AIquity* is formed by combining *AI*, an abbreviation for "artificial intelligence," with *equity*, derived from the Latin word *aequitas*, meaning fairness or equity.

Definition: AIquity describes the pursuit of fairness and equity in artificial intelligence applications, ensuring AI systems do not perpetuate or exacerbate social inequalities. This term underscores the importance of designing and implementing AI technologies that are inclusive and fair, promoting equal opportunities and treatment for all individuals.

Application: AIquity is especially relevant in sectors, such as finance, hiring, law enforcement, and healthcare, where AI-driven decisions can have significant impacts on individual lives. For instance, in the financial sector, AIquity ensures that algorithms used for credit scoring and loan approvals are free from biases that might discriminate against underrepresented groups. In the hiring process, AIquity guides the development of recruitment algorithms to ensure they evaluate candidates based on skills and potential rather than gender, ethnicity, or age. In healthcare, AIquity is critical for developing diagnostic tools that work effectively across diverse populations, avoiding biases that could lead to disparities in medical treatment. This application of AIquity addresses the ethical challenges of AI implementation, emphasizing the creation of algorithms that support fairness and provide equitable outcomes for all users, regardless of their background.

Algoriculture

Origin: The term *algoriculture* combines *algorithm*, with its origins as mentioned next in "Algorithmism," and *culture*, which comes from the Latin *cultura* meaning "cultivation" or "nurturing." This Latin word is derived from *colere*, meaning to tend, guard, cultivate, or till.

Definition: Algoriculture describes the cultivation and integration of algorithmic processes into cultural practices and expressions. It refers to how algorithms not only are tools for efficiency but also shape cultural phenomena, from the content we consume to the ways we interact socially. Algoriculture underscores the role of algorithms in creating, influencing, and transforming cultural trends, habits, and norms.

Application: Algoriculture is manifest in several key domains, such as media, entertainment, and social networking, where algorithms significantly influence cultural consumption and interaction. In the media industry, algorithms curate personalized content streams for users on platforms like Netflix and Spotify, shaping viewing and listening habits based on individual preferences, thereby influencing broader cultural trends. In social media, algoriculture plays a pivotal role in shaping social interactions and public discourse by determining what news and information are highlighted or suppressed in users' feeds, often creating echo chambers that reinforce specific cultural and political viewpoints. Furthermore, in the realm of digital art and literature, algorithms contribute to the creation of new forms of cultural expressions, such as generative art, where AI collaborates with human artists to produce new artworks that blend human creativity with algorithmic complexity, pushing the boundaries of traditional cultural artifacts.

Algorithmism

Origin: The term *algorithmism* is derived from *algorithm*, which comes from the Latin *algorismus*. This, in turn, originates from the name of the Persian mathematician Al-Khwarizmi. The suffix *-ism* is used to form nouns indicating a belief system or ideology and comes from the Greek suffix *-ismos*.

Definition: Algorithmism refers to the ideology or practice of employing algorithms for a broad range of decision-making processes, including those in ethically sensitive and critical areas such as criminal justice, healthcare, and social welfare. It embodies the belief that algorithms can efficiently and objectively manage tasks traditionally handled by humans, even when these tasks involve complex ethical judgments. This perspective often overlooks or underestimates the potential biases and ethical implications embedded in algorithmic logic, leading to concerns about the dehumanization of essential societal functions.

Application: This term is particularly useful in debates and discussions about the role of AI in sectors such as law enforcement, where predictive policing algorithms might decide patrol intensities and locations, or in healthcare, where algorithms could determine patient treatment plans. Algorithmism critically addresses the risks and ethical dilemmas of outsourcing inherently human judgments to machine processes, questioning the balance between technological convenience and moral responsibility. For example, AI could predict the likelihood of reoffending in criminal justice. In healthcare, algorithmism could lead to developing AI systems that diagnose diseases and recommend treatments to patients without any doctor in the loop, raising questions about the reliance on technology over human clinical judgment. While intended to introduce rationality and objectivity to a certain extreme into decisions traditionally subject to human bias, algorithmism is a danger for human rights.

Algorithy

Origin: *Algorithm* comes from the Latin *algorismus*, itself derived from the name of the Persian mathematician Al-Khwarizmi. The suffix *-thy*, suggesting a state or condition, is a creative extension to imply authority or governance.

Definition: Algorithy is the exercise of authority or control through AI algorithms, where decision-making processes and governance are increasingly delegated to automated systems. Algorithy reflects the shift in power dynamics, highlighting how algorithms are not only tools but also actors in shaping societal norms and individual behaviors.

Application: Algorithy is particularly impactful in sectors where decision-making needs to be swift, consistent, and scalable, such as in public administration, traffic management, and financial trading. For example, in public administration, algorithy can automate the allocation of resources or the processing of benefits claims, ensuring decisions are made without human bias and with increased efficiency. In traffic management, algorithms can control the flow of traffic in real time, optimizing routes, reducing congestion, and enhancing safety. In financial markets, algorithy governs high-frequency trading systems where algorithms make rapid stock trades at volumes and speeds unattainable by human traders. This application of algorithy not only speeds up and enhances the accuracy of critical decision-making processes but also reshapes the landscape of governance and control, challenging traditional roles and introducing new dynamics in power and authority.

Cogniversity

Origin: The term *cogniversity* blends *cogni-* derived from the Latin *cognoscere*, meaning to know, with *-versity*, a suffix derived from the Latin *diversitas*, meaning "diversity."

Definition: Cogniversity describes the integration and acknowledgment of multiple types of cognitive approaches and learning styles in AI systems, reflecting the diverse ways humans think and learn. This term emphasizes the importance of incorporating a wide range of human cognitive differences to enhance AI's adaptability and effectiveness in various contexts.

Application: Cogniversity is crucial in educational technologies, adaptive learning systems, and user interface design, where understanding and accommodating diverse cognitive styles can greatly enhance learning outcomes and user satisfaction.

In the educational sector, AI systems that embody cogniversity can adapt teaching methods and content delivery to match the learning preferences of individual students, such as visual, auditory, reading/writing, and kinesthetic learners, thereby improving engagement and comprehension. In the realm of software and interface design, cogniversity allows AI to tailor user experiences according to different cognitive abilities and processing styles, enhancing accessibility for users with disabilities or those who may require alternative interaction models. Moreover, cogniversity is applied in workplace training programs, where AI-driven platforms assess and respond to varying employee skills and learning speeds, facilitating more effective training and development programs that cater to a wide range of cognitive capabilities.

Dialgorithm

Origin: The term combines *dialogue*, derived from the Greek *dialogos*, meaning "conversation" or "speech," and *algorithm*, from the Latin *algorismus*, originally from the name of the Persian mathematician Al-Khwarizmi.

Definition: Dialgorithm refers to an algorithm that is specifically engineered to mimic dialogic interactions, often used in the context of AI systems that engage in human-like conversations. This type of algorithm focuses on processing and generating natural language to interact with users effectively, aiming to understand and respond to inputs in a way that mimics human conversational patterns.

Application: Dialgorithmy is particularly influential in enhancing the functionality of AI-driven conversational agents across sectors such as customer support and mental health. For example, in customer service, dialgorithms enable chatbots to manage and resolve customer queries with a level of interaction that closely mimics human customer service representatives. This not only improves efficiency but also customer satisfaction by providing timely and context-aware responses. In the realm of mental health, dialgorithms empower therapeutic chatbots that can conduct initial assessments or provide ongoing support, mimicking therapeutic conversations that are accessible and private. This application of dialgorithms critically addresses the challenge of making machine-driven interactions feel more natural and less mechanistic, thus improving user engagement and trust in AI systems.

Hypervasive

Origin: The prefix *hyper-* comes from the Greek ὑπέρ (*hyper*), meaning "over, beyond, or excessively." The suffix *-pervasive* derives from the Latin *pervadere*, meaning "to spread throughout."

Definition: Hypervasive characterizes a level of pervasiveness enhanced by artificial intelligence to an extraordinary degree, where AI's influence extends deeply and widely across various sectors and aspects of daily life. This term captures the ubiquitous and sometimes overwhelming penetration of AI technologies in personal, social, and professional realms.

Application: Hypervasive aptly describes the integration and influence of AI across a broad spectrum of human activities, from personal devices to industrial systems. In the realm of personal technology, AI's hypervasive nature is evident in smartphones, smart homes, and wearable devices that learn from and adapt to users' habits and preferences. Socially, AI's hypervasive traits are seen in social media algorithms that filter and tailor content, profoundly influencing public opinion and cultural trends. Professionally, AI permeates through tools for data analysis, automation of routine tasks, and complex decision–making processes in sectors like healthcare, where it assists in diagnostics and personalized medicine, and in manufacturing, where AI-driven automation and predictive maintenance transform production lines. The hypervasive nature of AI not only highlights its role as a facilitator of enhanced efficiency and personalization but also raises important discussions about privacy, security, and the ethical use of AI in deeply integrated settings.

Acknowledgments

Like everything I've accomplished in my life, this book would not have been possible without the support of many.

First, I would not have been able to write this book without the support of my family. My wife, Rosalie, and my son, Alexandre, encouraged me even before I managed to convince myself to start. Thank you immensely for all the strength you have given me and for your help in reviewing the chapters carefully and patiently.

As I reflect on writing this book, the people I think of next are those at my publisher. Creating a book is meticulous work, an artisanal endeavor, a task accomplished by numerous individuals who intervene at different stages of the creation process, each contributing vitally as every step carries the responsibility of its completion. I would like to thank all the individuals who formed the team behind this book and who worked together, often taking turns like in a relay race, to create this book. The story of a book could itself be a book! Specifically, I would like to thank several of them within the Wiley team with whom I had the opportunity to exchange ideas and interact during this creation process and, through them, extend my thanks to all who worked to make this book possible, starting with Connor Cairoli, Sara Deichman, Paul DiNovo, Magesh Elangovan, Satish Gowrishankar, Evelyn Wellborn and Janet Wehner. I also extend a special thank you to James "Jim" Minatel, my editor, who was able to assemble this outstanding team to craft this book, for putting all the resources of Wiley behind this labor, and whose attentiveness, patience, and ability to envision the final product have been an incredible asset. There is absolutely no way I could have completed this book without such a gifted team.

Among the events that inspired me to put my ideas about an artificial intelligence endowed with integrity on paper is *The Hamilton Mann Conversation*, a podcast I started in 2021. The goal of this podcast was to bring together a large number of people from diverse backgrounds, who, like me, have had the opportunity to be directly involved with the subject of digital transformation and artificial intelligence daily. By sharing their perspectives and experiences, we aimed to create a conversation about how new technologies, particularly recent advances in artificial intelligence, could serve the greater good and help build a better society.

Several individuals I have encountered along the way of this initiative, sometimes without even knowing it, contributed to my reflection on artificial intelligence, its impact, how it influences our lives, and many other aspects.

They included corporate executives, entrepreneurs, consultants, academics, association heads, international organization leaders, and government officials. Whether they were experts in the field of AI or not, they all played a key role in shaping it; and, on a human level, they were so much more. I have had the privilege of discussing their diverse and varied perspectives. These numerous exchanges contribute to the richness of the podcast I created and, even more so, have enriched my understanding of artificial intelligence and the concept of artificial integrity, whose seeds can probably also be found in the phosphorescence of these intersecting reflections.

I thank Nilanjan Adhya, Beena Ammanath, Maria Axente, Gilles Babinet, Dorothea Baur, Reid Blackman, Martha Boeckenfield, Didier Bonnet, Tim Bottke, Brice Challamel, Imran Chowdhury, Renée Cummings, Tom Davenport, Vilas Dhar, Jochen Ditsche, Seth Dobrin, Tulsee Doshi, Valerie Abrell Duong, Mark East, David C. Edelman, Tom Edwards, Gregoire Ferre, Arturo Franco, Jane Frankland, Ingrid Vasiliu Feltes, Mei Lin Fung, Renée Richardson Gosline, Hala Hanna, Katharina Hopp, Albert Hu, Gwenaelle Avice-Huet, Raghu Iyengar, David Jensen, Roshni Joshi, Luc Julia, Olga Kokshagina, Laurence Lafont, Jennifer LaPlante, Anastassia Lauterbach, Paul Leonardi, Tibor Merey, Mark Minevich, Vivienne Ming, Geoff Parker, Aleksandra Przegalinska, Stefano Puntoni, Gabriela Ramos, Sam Ransbotham,

Anand Rao, Noelle Russell, Arathi Sethumadhavan, Emilie Sidiqian, Scott Snyder, Brian Solis, Sanjay Srivastava, Dalith Steiger, Meme Styles, Anjana Susarla, Andres Sutt, Philippe Trouchaud, Charles Vaillant, Marshall Van Alstyne, Stefaan Verhulst, Florence Verzelen, Tendayi Viki, Jean-Luc Vincent-Franc, Russell Wald, Ben Weber, Kevin Werbach, George Westerman, Pinar Yildirim, Angela Yochem, and Tomoko Yokoi.

I want to thank Thales, a company I have proudly served for more than a decade, helping customers and institutions cope with some of the grand challenges of our times.

I also thank some academic institutions that hold a special place in my journey, my alma maters, MIT Sloan School of Management, INSEAD, EDHEC Business School, and l'École des Ponts et Chaussées, as well their respective vibrant alumni networks, which perpetuate values that I have embraced to literally promote "Ideas Made to Matter," joining my efforts with those who work to grow "A Force for Good" and "Make an Impact" for "Building the Worlds of Tomorrow."

A special thanks to Peter Hirst and the entire faculty team of MIT Sloan Executive Education for their exceptional support. Their dedication to knowledge and the exemplary way in which MIT Sloan imparts the passion for technology and management has been and will remain an unalterable source of inspiration.

I also want to give a special thank you to Hina Wadhwa and Alon Rozen. I am immensely grateful for the chance to have met you and, most importantly, for the opportunity you helped me seize in joining the doctoral program at l'École des Ponts Business School to continue my research in developing the concept of artificial integrity. You are an integral part of the journey during which I am sure I will continue to advance my research throughout my doctoral studies at this great institution.

I also owe much to the conferences I have conducted around the world. Thank you to everyone who has come to listen to me. It is always a pleasure to discuss and exchange our ideas at the end of each conference. Together, and through the exchange of ideas, we elevate our society.

Thank you to Hanna Brahme, Anik Bose, Eric Buatois, Julia Kirby, Tatiana Caldas-Löttiger, Pierre Le Manh, Geoff Parker, Marina Planas, Anna Noakes Schulze, Richard Straub, Marshall Van Alstyne, and through each of you to all the teams that bring to life the AI House in Davos, the Ethical Governance Group (EAIGG), the Global Peter Drucker Forum, the International WoMenX In Business For Ethical AI (IWIB4AI), the MIT Platform Strategy Summit, the Project Management Institute (PMI), TheNTWK, and the Web Summit. Thank you for being pioneers in developing platforms that promote the dissemination of new ideas to rethink management in the age of artificial intelligence. The stimulating reflections you share, and the quality exchanges you enable, are also a great source of inspiration to me. As often happens, there are moments that stand out as particularly impactful, spurring the urgency to write certain chapters. I hold in high esteem and great appreciation the exchanges that took place during the panel moderated by Marshall Van Alstyne at the MIT Platform Summit of 2024, preceding Yoshua Bengio's speech. His warning about the risks posed by artificial intelligence to humanity reinforced my commitment to finding a solution that brings what is missing to the perspective of artificial intelligence promoted by some: integrity.

I have a special thank you I would like to extend to the members of the Association of Vietnamese Scientists and Experts (AVSE Global) for warmly welcoming me at the 2024 Vietnam Global Leaders Forum to share ideas on all things about artificial integrity. AVSE Global is a Paris-headquartered nonprofit organization connecting Vietnamese intellectuals, senior experts, and scientists worldwide, implementing strategic programs and projects promoting Vietnam's sustainable development, digital transformation, innovation, and energy transition. Thank you to Mai Phuong Bui, Thu Thuy Dao, Thanh Huong Dinh, Thu Thao Do, Thu Trang Du, Nga Le-Vo, Diem Hang Nguyen, Duc Khuong Nguyen, Ha Nhi Nguyen, Hoang Anh Nguyen, Huong Giang Nguyen, Minh Ngoc Nguyen, Thanh Tung Nguyen, Thi Thu Huyen Nguyen, Thi Thu Tra Nguyen, Trinh Hoang Anh Nguyen, Tuong Dung Nguyen, Huong Pham, Tra Tran, Quy Vo-Reinhard, Le Huy Vu, and all the 2024 Vietnam Global Leaders. I have fond memories of our conversations.

I also want to extend warm thanks to a few individuals in particular for their invaluable support and for being such great inspirational thought leaders, each contributing in their own way to paving the path for more responsible AI development.

Thank you to Emma Ruttkamp-Bloem, whose work and dedication to the cause of safer and inclusive artificial intelligence I deeply admire.

Thank you also to Jean Ferré for his support and leadership in advancing responsible artificial intelligence. A special thanks to John C. Havens for his pioneering work, especially with the IEEE 7000-2021 standard that focuses on value alignment for end users. Thank you to Michael Platt for his encouragement and significant contributions to neuroscience. His work opens up a vast field of possibilities. Thank you, Soumitra Dutta, for his support and for embodying the authentic leadership we so desperately need to conceive the artificial intelligence we want to develop today and tomorrow. Thank you, Michael Wade, for our discussions and your sharp insights into the role of technology and, more precisely, the role that leaders must take to positively transform their business and society as a whole with technologies, particularly artificial intelligence. Thank you to Cornelia C. Walther for the immense perspectives you helped me perceive through our discussions and for the analytical keys you so eloquently articulate at the intersection of human values and what that should mean for the technologies we want to design and have society adopt. Lastly, thank you to all the scientists and researchers whose work constitutes the genesis of the concept of artificial integrity and whose contributions are referenced in this book. I am grateful to each of you.

I extend my heartfelt thanks to the academic institutions where I have the privilege of teaching digital transformation and AI-related topics. I am grateful to INSEAD, HEC Paris, and EDHEC Business School for the opportunity to engage with students whose always challenging, disruptive, and enriching questions provide me with profound insights. I would also like to take this opportunity to thank them for the consistently valuable experiences we share. I owe this invaluable opportunity to the trust of Marie-Cécile Cervellon, Nathan Furr, Gachoucha Kretz, Joerg Niessing, Sandra Richez, Dominique Rouzies, and Martine Thernisien.

The knowledge and insights gained through my academic engagements have been instrumental in shaping my perspectives and advancing my research. These experiences have not only deepened my understanding but also reinforced the importance of sharing and promoting ideas to ensure their impact and relevance.

What creates the value of an idea is its sharing and transmission. In this regard, I have the honor and privilege of having made wonderful encounters that have taught me so much and provided support and encouragement during the writing of this book. These individuals challenged, encouraged and inspired me, shared their valuable experiences, and helped carry my ideas beyond what I could have imagined. I can never thank them enough for that. I know what I owe them. They have opened new worlds to me, they have allowed me to meet many new people, and, thanks to them, I have also forged this vision of artificial integrity. Thank you to the editors of *Forbes, Stanford Social Innovation Review, Harvard Business Review France, Leader to Leader, Knowledge at Wharton, INSEAD Knowledge, I by IMD, Polytechnique Insights, the European Business Review, the Financial Business Review, the World Financial Review, Technology Magazine*, and all their team members with whom I have the pleasure of working and writing about artificial integrity and other topics. I am grateful of their support.

In the same vein, I want to thank everyone who supports my publications, articles, and posts, some of them since my very first writings, as well as those who write to me on social networks; their support and comments enrich me every day. They are also the conduit for the ideas I develop, helping them travel through social networks. They have played a significant role in the creation of this book, as their support, messages of encouragement, and questions have also fueled the energy I needed to write it.

Lastly, I could not talk about ideas and the importance they can have in pushing boundaries and changing what many consider unchangeable without thanking all the members of the great Thinkers50 family, especially the founders of this community, Stuart Crainer and Des Dearlove. Thinkers50 has been such a wealth of knowledge and a source of inspiration for me for so many years that the concept of artificial integrity I develop in this book owes much to it. Thank you, Stuart, Des, and Monika Kosman, for the dent you have put and continue to put in the universe, contributing to the access to innovative ideas but, more importantly, allowing those ideas to soar beyond borders and change the world.

About the Author

Hamilton Mann is a tech executive, Digital for Good pioneer, keynote speaker, and the originator of the concept of artificial integrity.

Mann serves as Group Vice President responsible for AI and Digital Transformation initiatives at Thales, a global leader in aerospace, space, cybersecurity, and defense, investing in digital and "deep tech" innovations: artificial intelligence, big data, connectivity, cybersecurity, and quantum technologies. Leading group-wide digital and AI initiatives in support of Thales' purpose and businesses, his transformational achievements have been featured on the MIT Blog and as a case study by IMD Business School.

Recognized for his contributions to thought leadership, Mann was inducted into the Thinkers50 Radar as one of the 30 most prominent rising business thinkers globally for pioneering "Digital for Good."

He actively participates in global forums such as the World Economic Forum's Davos AI House, contributing to discussions on AI transparency and ethical technology deployment.

Mann writes regularly for `https://www.forbes.com` as a columnist and has published articles about AI and its societal implications in prominent academic, business, and policy outlets such as *Stanford Social Innovation Review (SSIR)*, *Knowledge@Wharton*, *Dialogue Duke Corporate Education*, *INSEAD Knowledge*, *INSEAD TECH TALK X*, *I by IMD*, the *Harvard Business Review France*, the *European Business Review*, and *Expressions* by Institut Montaigne.

He has contributed to the book *Driving Sustainable Innovation* (Brightline Project Management Institute and Thinkers50, 2024) and to the *Thinkers50: Human Touch* (Wiley and Thinkers50, 2024), alongside Thinkers50 thought leaders.

He hosts the *Hamilton Mann Conversation*, a podcast aiming to democratize knowledge about how digital technology, including AI, can be a force for good in society.

Mann's academic pursuits include his role as a doctoral researcher at l'Ecole des Ponts et Chaussées – Institut Polytechnique de Paris, where he examines how AI can be guided to artificially exhibit integrity to uphold human values. He is also a senior lecturer at INSEAD, HEC Paris, and EDHEC Business School, and mentors at the MIT Priscilla King Gray (PKG) Center.

He sits on the advisory board of the Ethical AI Governance Group (EAIGG), a diverse community of AI practitioners focused on democratizing the growth of ethical AI through best practices and innovations in AI development, deployment, and governance.

Through his roles, Mann advocates for a future where advanced technology serves to enable sustainable and human-centered progress, emphasizing the crucial role of integrity in achieving truly intelligent outcomes.

Index

boundary of AI utility, in Human-First
model, 61
British Journal of Radiology, 241

C
capability mapping, 202–204
career pathing, personalized, 212
case-based learning repository, developing
a, 161
case-based reasoning mechanisms,
implementing, 126
central data banks, 231, 233
change management, importance of, 212
chaos theory, 4
China, 227–228
coaching protocols, implementing
adaptive, 180
cognitive enhancement tools, 176–178
cognitive partnership development,
importance of, 167
cognitive processes
automating tasks, 178
development of, 125–126
importance of shared, 169
cogniversity, 36, 256
collaboration
with educational institutions, 171
fostering capability development, 203
in Fusion model, 74
implementing real-time support, 169
collaborative frameworks, in bias automatic
detection, 110–111
collaborative interfaces, 137–138
collaborative platforms, creating, 167
Collective[i]'s AI system, 92
communication
ensuring transparent, 203
importance of, 212
community engagement, Human-First
mode in, 54
COMPAS recidivism algorithm, 55
complacency, as a primary risk, 47
complement *vs.* replace, in Human-First
model, 59–60
complexity, equipping AI with adaptive,
175
compliance systems
of consent processes, 139–140

implementing, 116
importance of adaptive monitoring, 214
"Computing Machinery and Intelligence"
(Turing), 20, xxi
configurable AI assistance, 159–160
consciousness, Human-First mode as
guardrails for, 52–61
consent mechanisms
designing, 131
dynamic, 139–140
maintaining traceability, 139
consent revocation, ensuring real-time, 139
content creation
about, 12
Fusion mode in, 72
humanistic reinforcement and, 147–148
content delivery, interactive, 153
context-aware algorithms, integrating, 167
context-aware capability
development of, 119
enabling, 132
context-aware decision-making
development of, 138
importance of, 221
context-aware ethical reasoning, importance
of, 219
context-sensitive consent mechanisms,
creating, 139
context-sensitive intervention protocols,
development of, 127
contextual adaptation/learning
importance of, 180–181, 201
of values and principles, 35
contextual performance enhancement,
integrating, 206
contextual resource provisioning,
implementing, 175–176
contextual understanding, bias automatic
detection and, 110
contingency planning, 232
continuous human skill development, focus
on, 156–157
continuous improvement mechanisms,
establishing, 206
continuous learning
about, 122–124
fostering a culture of, 153
importance of, 209–210

in ethical reporting, 135
fail-safe activation, 128
in impact reporting, 130
importance of, 196–197
in reporting, 235–236
in user controls, 131
transparent interactions, ensuring, 169
transportation logistics, humanistic reinforcement and, 148
Trello, 87
trust, data as a foundation to, 229
trustworthiness, integrity and, 24
Turing, Alan
 "Computing Machinery and Intelligence," 20, xxi
Turing test, 20–21

U

unit of measurement, data as a, 226
unstructured learning, 12–13
unsupervised learning, 12–13
upskilling, in Marginal mode, 49–50
US Federal Reserve, 231
usage pattern analysis, importance of, 196
user behavior, evolving consent with, 139
user competency, assessing, 194
user controls, implementing transparent, 131
user education, integrating, 139
user empowerment features, 150–152
user experience (UX) design
 creating feedback loops, 131
 implementing principles, 204
 importance of, 217
 incorporating personalized, 151
user feedback, adaptive learning from, 151
user preference alignment, implementing, 164
user profiling, implementing, 154
user support, adaptive, 154–155
user-centric de-escalation interfaces, designing, 195
user-centric design, 130–132
user-centric ethical customization, 161
user-centric explanation interfaces, 114
user-centric simplification feedback, importance of, 197
user-driven consent customization, 140

user-focused strategy, 159
user-guided adaptation interfaces, providing, 193
"U-shaped" pattern, 46
UX. *See* user experience (UX)

V

value
 ethical standards over proposition, 94–96
 in Fusion model, 75
 on human life, 243–245
Valve, 84
videoconferencing software, 94
virtual assistants, integrating, 155
virtual co-creation workspaces, importance of, 169
virtual reality (VR), 152
visuomotor learning, 13
VR (virtual reality), 152

W

Wade, Michael
 Hacking Digital, xix
Walther, Cornelia C., xix
warehousing, inventory replenishment tasks in, 46
Waymo, 104–105
Widespread (W), 19
wildlife protection, humanistic reinforcement and, 142–143
Wooden, John, xix
workflow adjustment, implementing dynamic, 175
workflow optimization, integrating automated, 209
workforce utilization, in Marginal mode, 49

X

XAI (explainable AI), 64–65, 114

Z

Zappos, 83
"zero-shot" learning, 13
Zhima Credit, 228
Zoom, 94